declined by ...

Sir

I have in my ...
comprised in three Vol...
Evelina. As I am well ...
work of this sort should ...
:table name I apply to you. Shall be much obliged therefore if
you will inform me whether you chuse to be concerned in it;
what will be the expence of publishing at the Author's risk;
& what you will venture to advance for the Property of it,
if on a perusal it is approved of.

Should your answer give me encouragement I will
send you the Work.

I am, Sir, y.ʳ ob.ᵗ h.ble Serv.ᵗ

Geo Austen.

Steventon near Overton
Hants
1.ˢᵗ Nov.ʳ 1797.

Frontispiece George Austen's letter of 1 November 1797, offering to send the manuscript of his daughter Jane Austen's novel *First Impressions* to the London publisher Thomas Cadell. The manuscript was 'declined by Return of Post', but Jane Austen later revised it as *Pride and Prejudice*.

Jane Austen's
Pride and Prejudice

Jane Austen's *Pride and Prejudice* (1813) is the best-known and most celebrated of her novels. It combines enormous charm with deceptively deep anxieties to chart the fortunes of Elizabeth Bennet, Austen's sparkling and defiant central character and, in Austen's own opinion, 'as delightful a creature as ever appeared in print'.

Taking the form of a sourcebook, this guide to Austen's classic novel offers:

- extensive introductory comment on the contexts and many interpretations of the text, from publication to the present
- annotated extracts from key contextual documents, reviews, critical works and the text itself
- cross-references between documents and sections of the guide, in order to suggest links between texts, contexts and criticism
- suggestions for further reading.

Part of the *Routledge Guides to Literature* series, this volume is essential reading for all those beginning detailed study of *Pride and Prejudice* and seeking not only a guide to the novel, but a way through the wealth of contextual and critical material that surrounds Austen's text.

Robert Morrison is Professor of English literature at Queen's University, Kingston, Ontario.

Routledge Guides to Literature*

Editorial Advisory Board: Richard Bradford (University of Ulster at Coleraine), Jan Jedrzejewski (University of Ulster at Coleraine), Duncan Wu (St. Catherine's College, University of Oxford)

Routledge Guides to Literature offer clear introductions to the most widely studied authors and literary texts.

Each book engages with texts, contexts and criticism, highlighting the range of critical views and contextual factors that need to be taken into consideration in advanced studies of literary works. The series encourages informed but independent readings of texts by ranging as widely as possible across the contextual and critical issues relevant to the works examined and highlighting areas of debate as well as those of critical consensus. Alongside general guides to texts and authors, the series includes 'sourcebooks', which allow access to reprinted contextual and critical materials as well as annotated extracts of primary text.

Available in this series

D. H. Lawrence by Fiona Becket
The Poems of W. B. Yeats: A Sourcebook edited by Michael O'Neill
E. M. Forster's A Passage to India: A Sourcebook edited by Peter Childs
Samuel Beckett by David Pattie

* Some books in this series were originally published in the Routledge Literary Sourcebooks series, edited by Duncan Wu, or the Complete Critical Guide to English Literature series, edited by Richard Bradford and Jan Jedrzejewski.

Jane Austen's
Pride and Prejudice
A Sourcebook

Edited by Robert Morrison

Routledge
Taylor & Francis Group

NEW YORK AND LONDON

First published 2005
by Routledge
270 Madison Ave, New York, NY 10016

Simultaneously published in the UK
by Routledge
2 Park Square, Milton Park, Abingdon, Oxon, OX14 4RN

Routledge is an imprint of the Taylor & Francis Group

Typeset in Sabon and Gill Sans by RefineCatch Ltd, Bungay, Suffolk
Printed and bound in Great Britain by
TJ International Ltd, Padstow, Cornwall

Library of Congress Cataloging in Publication Data
Jane Austen's pride and prejudice : a sourcebook / edited by Robert Morrison.
    p. cm.–(Routledge guides to literature)
Includes bibliographical references and index.
    1. Austen, Jane 1775–1817. Pride and prejudice–Sources.   1. Morrison, Robert.   II. Series.
    PR4034.P72J368 2005
    823'.7–dc22   2004017563

British Library Cataloguing in Publication Data
A catalogue record for this book is available from the British Library

ISBN 0–415–26849–4 (hbk)
ISBN 0–415–26850–8 (pbk)

For Carole

Contents

The Novel in Performance

3: Key Passages

Introduction

Key Passages

4: Further Reading   161

ILLUSTRATIONS

Annotation, Footnotes and Referencing

Annotation is a key feature of this series. Both the original notes from the reprinted text and new annotations by the editor appear at the bottom of the relevant page. The reprinted notes are prefaced by the author's name in square brackets, e.g. '[Robinson's note]'.

Most references to *Pride and Prejudice* are cross-referenced to the Key Passages section in this sourcebook. In cases where the reference does not appear in the Key Passages section, it is given in the standard edition of the novel: R. W. Chapman (ed.), *Pride and Prejudice* (Oxford: Clarendon Press, 1923). However, in all such instances, 'Volume' and 'Chapter' numbers also appear as part of the reference so that the quotation is easily traced even if a different edition of the text is being used.

Acknowledgements

I would like to thank Duncan Wu, who suggested that I write this sourcebook, and who has been generous and supportive throughout its production. It has been a pleasure to work with Fiona Cairns, Kate Parker and Liz Thompson at Routledge. I am grateful to the staffs of the Joseph S. Stauffer Library and the Douglas Library, W. D. Jordan Special Collections, Queen's University. For assistance and advice of all kinds, I would like to thank Brandon Alakas, Peter Bell, Geoffrey Carnall, Christopher Fanning, Robert Irvine, Mark Jones, Shelley King, Fred Lock, Mary Millar, Martha and Nick Paul, Michael Phillips, Christopher Ricks, John Strachan, Tammi Smith, Laura White, Paul Wiens and Romira Worvill. Special thanks to Paul James, who long ago shared with me his enthusiasm for *Pride and Prejudice*, and to Richard Hamilton, who discussed this book with me at length. This edition is for Carole, who has been my partner in the entire production of it, and who has taught me the most about Austen's complicated and exhilarating novel.

I would like to thank the following for permission to reprint copyright material:

Volume ii, pp. 10 from 'The Letters of Charlotte Brontë, 1848–1851' edited by Smith, Margaret © Oxford University Press (2000) by permission of Oxford University Press.

D. W. Harding, 'Regulated Hatred: An Aspect of the Work of Jane Austen' in *Scrutiny*, 8 (1939–1940), by permission of the Leavis literary estate.

M. Poovey, 'Ideological contradictions and the consolations of form' in *The Proper Lady and the Woman Writer* © University of Chicago Press (1984) by permission of The University of Chicago and the author.

John Wiltshire, '*Pride and Prejudice*, love and recognition' from *Recreating Jane Austen* © Cambridge University Press (2001) by permission of Cambridge University Press and the author.

Lisa Hopkins, 'Mr. Darcy's Body: Privileging the Female Gaze' from *Jane Austen in Hollywood* © The University Press of Kentucky (1998) by permission of The University Press of Kentucky.

Sue Birtwistle and Susie Conklin, 'A Conversation with Colin Firth' (pp. 97–105) from *The Making of Pride and Prejudice* (Penguin Books/BBC Books, 1995). Copyright © Sue Birtwistle and Susie Conklin, 1995. Reproduced by permission of Penguin Books Ltd.

Colin Firth/Jennifer Ehle photograph by permission of the BBC.

Illustration by Charles Brock from Jane Austen, *Pride and Prejudice*, introduction by Austin Dobson, illustrated by Charles E. Brock (London: Macmillan, 1922), p. 174 by permission of Queen's University Library, Kingston, Canada.

Frontispiece from Jane Austen, *Pride and Prejudice: a Novel* from the Bentley Standard Novels series (London: Bentley, 1833) by permission of The Vaughan Memorial Library, Acadia University, Canada.

Letter from George Austen by permission of The President and scholars of Saint John Baptist College in the University of Oxford.

'When the Party entered', Hugh Thomson, Illustrations for Jane Austen's *Pride and Prejudice* (London: G. Allen, 1984) by permission of The Department of Printing and Graphic Arts, Houghton Library, Harvard College Library.

'Fin Tragique de Louis XVI', by permission of Cornell University Division of Rare Manuscript Collections.

Miniature of Tom Lefroy (Ref. No. 23M93/83/1/1) by permission of Hampshire Record Office.

Drawing of Jane Austen by Cassandra Austen by permission of the National Portrait Gallery, London.

Greer Garson/Laurence Olivier photograph by permission of the British Film Institute.

Every effort has been made to trace and contact copyright holders. The publishers would be pleased to hear from any copyright holders not acknowledged here so that this section may be amended at the earliest opportunity.

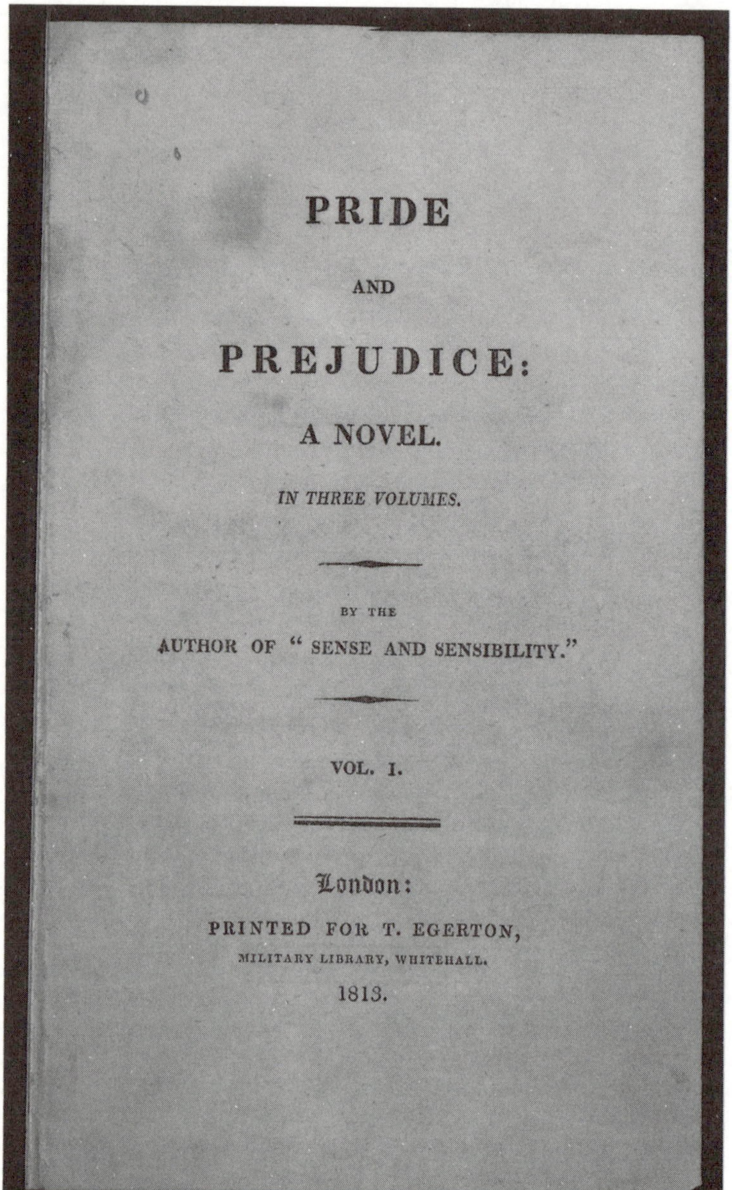

PRIDE

AND

PREJUDICE:

A NOVEL.

IN THREE VOLUMES.

BY THE

AUTHOR OF " SENSE AND SENSIBILITY."

VOL. I.

𝔏𝔬𝔫𝔡𝔬𝔫:

PRINTED FOR T. EGERTON,
MILITARY LIBRARY, WHITEHALL.

1813.

Figure 1 Title page of the first edition of *Pride and Prejudice* (1813).

Introduction

Pride and Prejudice has always been Jane Austen's most popular novel. Famously, she fretted that it was 'rather too light & bright & sparkling', and certainly readers have been captivated by its comedy, wit, romance, and splendid heroine Elizabeth Bennet, whom Austen herself thought 'as delightful a creature as ever appeared in print' (see Contemporary Documents, **p. 41**). Yet *Pride and Prejudice* is also a novel of ironic shadows and dark anxieties. Austen was 'mistress of much deeper emotion than appears upon the surface',[1] observes Virginia Woolf, and beneath the glittering veneer of *Pride and Prejudice* lie pressing questions concerning money, matrimony, class, subjugation, and the fate of women. Austen, writes Carol Shields, uses 'an arch, incontrovertible amiability' to conceal 'a ferocious and persistent moral anger'.[2]

Austen first drafted *Pride and Prejudice* when she was twenty, the same age as Elizabeth Bennet. The novel was originally called *First Impressions*, and Austen wrote it in a ten-month period beginning in October 1796 and finishing in August 1797. The Austen family enjoyed the novel a great deal, and Austen's father George thought so highly of it that, on 1 November 1797, he wrote to the well-known London publisher Thomas Cadell asking him if he would be interested in publishing 'a Manuscript Novel, comprised in three volumes'. George Austen did not name the author, nor did he discuss the pleasure the novel had brought him, but he did ask what would be the expense of publishing it 'at the Author's risk', indicating his willingness to invest his own money if necessary (see Frontispiece, **p. i**).[3] His proposal, however, was speedily 'declined by Return of Post'. In January 1799 Austen wrote teasingly to her sister Cassandra: 'I do not wonder at your wanting to read *first impressions* again, so seldom as you have gone through it, & that so long ago'. Later that same year she told Cassandra that she would not let a friend 'read First Impressions again upon any account & am very glad that I did not leave it in your power. – She is very cunning, but I see through her design; – she means to publish it from Memory, & one more perusal must enable her to do it'.[4]

---

1 *The Essays of Virginia Woolf*, ed. Andrew McNeillie, 4 vols (London: Hogarth Press, 1986– continuing), vol. iv, p. 149.
2 Carol Shields, *Jane Austen* (New York: Viking, 2001), p. 57.
3 MS 279, St. John's College, Oxford.
4 *Jane Austen's Letters*, ed. Deirdre Le Faye (Oxford: Oxford University Press, 1995), pp. 35, 44.

Austen may have sporadically revisited and revised *First Impressions* over the next dozen years, but she was certainly working hard on revisions in 1812, following the appearance a year earlier of *Sense and Sensibility*, another novel she had written in the 1790s and then revised for publication. Austen changed the title from *First Impressions* to *Pride and Prejudice*, and 'lopt & cropt so successfully [. . .] that I imagine it must be rather shorter than S. & S. altogether' (see Contemporary Documents, **p. 41**). She asked £150 for the completed manuscript, but accepted £110 from **Thomas Egerton** of the Military Library. Figure 1 (see p. xx) is the title page of the first edition of *Pride and Prejudice*, which appeared in three volumes in late January 1813, nearly sixteen years after Austen had completed her initial draft. It was priced at eighteen shillings, and identified only as 'by the author of "Sense and Sensibility"'. The first printing sold out, and a second edition appeared later that same year. A third edition was published in 1817. Figure 2 (see **p. 3**) is the title page of the first American edition, published in 1832 and called *Elizabeth Bennet; or, Pride and Prejudice*, a change in title which reflects Elizabeth's early and widespread appeal. *Pride and Prejudice* has been the most frequently translated of Austen's novels. In 1975 Andrew Wright documented how it had 'made its appearance – or reappearance – in Austria, Belgium, Brazil, China, Czechoslovakia, Egypt, Finland, France, Germany, Holland, Iceland, Italy, Japan, Mexico, Portugal, Romania, Spain, Sweden, Switzerland, Turkey, the USSR, and Yugoslavia'.[5] 'Of all of Jane Austen's novels', notes Sue Parrill, '*Pride and Prejudice* [. . .] has been [. . .] the most often adapted for television and film'[6] (see The Novel in Performance, **pp. 99–107**.) In a British poll conducted in 2003, *Pride and Prejudice* was 'voted the "best-loved" novel by a woman author'.[7]

Critics have long debated whether *Pride and Prejudice* is set in the 1790s when it was first written, or in the 1810s when it was first published. Ralph Nash outlines the case for composition and revision by the calendars of 1799 and 1802, and P. B. S. Andrews argues that Austen 'had always imagined' *Pride and Prejudice* as a novel of the 1790s.[8] Chapman, however, finds that the novel follows the calendar of 1811–12.[9] Critics have also commented at length on the title. The two terms are conjoined in several eighteenth-century texts, and most notably toward the end of **Frances Burney**'s second novel *Cecilia* (see Contemporary Documents, **pp. 32–3**). 'Pride and prejudice are both flaws of character which preclude the recognition of several different points of view', writes Cynthia Griffin.

> Pride is inordinate self-esteem (and indicates a lack of regard for the values or opinions of others); prejudice is preconceived opinion or judgment (and indicates the unwillingness or inability to be influenced by

5   Andrew Wright, 'Jane Austen Abroad' in *Jane Austen: Bicentenary Essays*, ed. John Halperin (Cambridge: Cambridge University Press, 1975), p. 298.
6   Sue Parrill, *Jane Austen on Film and Television* (Jefferson, NC: McFarland, 2002), p. 48.
7   Nigel Reynolds, 'Books Lovers put Austen in Pride of Place' in the *Daily Telegraph*, 12 May 2003, p. 5.
8   Ralph Nash, 'The Time Scheme for *Pride and Prejudice*' in *English Language Notes*, 4 (March 1967), pp.194–8; and P. B. S. Andrews, 'The Date of *Pride and Prejudice*' in *Notes and Queries*, 213 (September 1968), p. 342.
9   R. W. Chapman, 'Chronology of *Pride and Prejudice*' in *Pride and Prejudice*, ed. R. W. Chapman (Oxford: Clarendon Press, 1923), pp. 400–8.

ELIZABETH BENNET;

OR,

PRIDE AND PREJUDICE:

A NOVEL.

IN TWO VOLUMES.

BY THE
AUTHOR OF "SENSE AND SENSIBILITY," &c.

VOL. I.

FIRST AMERICAN FROM THE THIRD LONDON EDITION.

Philadelphia:
CAREY & LEA.
1832.

Figure 2 **Title page of the first American edition of *Pride and Prejudice* (1832), now entitled *Elizabeth Bennet; or, Pride and Prejudice*.**

others). Furthermore, the juvenile work upon which *Pride and Prejudice* was built was called *First Impressions* – a title again indicative of Austen's concern with point of view.[10]

In the mid-nineteenth-century, Julia Kavanagh asserted that in the novel 'Pride assumes the shape of the handsome, haughty Mr. Darcy; and Elizabeth Bennet, the lively, spirited girl, is Prejudice'.[11] But most commentators have long since accepted that both Darcy and Elizabeth suffer from both pride and prejudice.

Park Honan remarks that the 'deepest subject' of the novel 'is happiness',[12] yet *Pride and Prejudice* is perhaps more centrally concerned with how difficult happiness is to attain. Its irony is light and omnipresent, but it illuminates much that is disturbing and unkind. It contains some of the silliest characters in English fiction, but it is also intimately concerned with humiliation, fear, male privilege, and the threat of spinsterhood. It has often been condemned as politically irresponsible, yet it clearly combines bourgeois aspirations with conservative mythmaking. It carefully avoids any explicit mention of sex, yet it contains a predatory rake who seduces two underage girls. It is a love story, yet cold economics are at the root of much of the action and behaviour. Elizabeth and Jane come through victoriously, but the same cannot be said for Charlotte Lucas, Lydia Bennet, or indeed Mrs. Bennet, all of whom live in loveless marriages. Class barriers are overcome, but they can hardly be said to be overturned. An urgent feminism pervades the novel, yet it ends with fantasy weddings to rich and privileged men. In *Pride and Prejudice*, happiness triumphs but it comes at a cost, when it comes at all.

The aim of this sourcebook is to bring together a wide range of writings and readings that elucidate *Pride and Prejudice*, and to explore both its sparkling surface and its deepening shadows. There are, of course, no simple answers to the critical questions and paradoxes in the novel, and readers will continue to debate its central issues without ever resolving all of their disagreements. It is my hope, though, that anyone who reads this sourcebook will feel more knowledgeable about the key debates, and in a stronger position to advance whatever case s/he wishes to make.

The sourcebook is organized into four main sections and a series of subsections. Cross-references appear throughout the book, and are designed to help readers navigate their way around the different sections, and to make connections between Austen's novel and the various kinds of material included in the sourcebook. Such an approach, however, is also designed to promote independent thought by giving readers the opportunity to compare different materials, and to develop, extend, and reevaluate their own ideas and conclusions.

The first section of the sourcebook is entitled Contexts, and is in four subsections. A Contextual Overview outlines the social and intellectual milieux in which Austen wrote and revised *Pride and Prejudice*. A Chronology situates the signifi-

---

10 Cynthia Griffin, 'The Development of Realism in Jane Austen's Early Novels' in *ELH*, 30.1 (March 1963), p. 49. See also, Everett Zimmerman, 'Pride and Prejudice in *Pride and Prejudice*' in *Nineteenth-Century Fiction*, 23.1 (1968), pp. 64–73.
11 Julia Kavanagh, *English Women of Letters*, 2 vols (London: Hurst and Blackett, 1863), vol. ii, p. 213.
12 Park Honan, *Jane Austen: Her Life* (New York: St. Martin's Press, 1987), p. 320.

cant events in Austen's life within the larger literary and political world, and includes the key incidents that bear directly on *Pride and Prejudice*. A collection of Contemporary Documents features selections from epistolary and domestic novels, educational and economic tracts, female conduct books, feminist treatises, and political tales of terror. These documents are intended to expose readers to the material Austen read or might have read as she wrote *Pride and Prejudice*, and to explicate the conventions and opinions that would have been known to her, even if she rejected them herself. This subsection also contains a series of Austen's own letters, in which she details the heady experience of her first romance, the exhilaration of receiving published copies of *Pride and Prejudice*, and her thoughts on the defining features of her own novel writing. The fourth subsection is a Biographical Directory, which features people who are mentioned often in the sourcebook, in connection with either Austen's immediate personal circle, or as part of the larger cultural context that she inhabits and illuminates. All the people mentioned in the Biographical Directory are marked in bold text on their first appearance in the sourcebook.

The second section, Interpretations, is in five subsections. A Critical History surveys the dominant trends and departures in criticism of *Pride and Prejudice*. Early Critical Reception features two reviews, and other contemporary material. Novelists on *Pride and Prejudice* contains responses to *Pride and Prejudice* by a series of famous nineteenth- and twentieth-century novelists. Modern Criticism brings together a wide range of twentieth and twenty-first century commentary, and from a variety of theoretical perspectives, including feminist, formalist, New Historicist, Marxist, and psychoanalytic. The Novel in Performance comprises extracts from commentators who focus on the celebrated 1995 BBC film of *Pride and Prejudice*, featuring Jennifer Ehle as Elizabeth Bennet and Colin Firth as Mr. Darcy.

The third section, Key Passages, selects a series of fourteen extracts from the novel itself. There is no substitute for reading the novel in full, but the extracts are designed to suggest the power and range of Austen's text, and have been chosen based on both their centrality to the narrative, and for the ways in which they help to shed light on the ironies and arguments explored elsewhere in the sourcebook.

The fourth section, Further Reading, is in six subsections: Recommended Editions, Companions and Encyclopedias, Books and Edited Collections, Chapters and Essays, Biographies, and Bibliographies. It is designed to highlight studies not extracted in previous sections of the sourcebook, and to suggest directions for future study and research.

Throughout the sourcebook the intention has been to reveal *Pride and Prejudice* as a novel of rich lineage, remarkable complexity, enormous charm, and deceptively deep anxiety.

1

Contexts

Contextual Overview

Jane Austen lived in a revolutionary age that both missed and marked her. Her writings evince a strong allegiance to the literary and cultural traditions of the eighteenth century, but they also betray a debt to the conflicts and vast upheavals of the early nineteenth century. In *Pride and Prejudice*, Austen both embraces the old order and advocates the new.

Revolution defined Austen's age. Beginning in the 1760s, the Industrial Revolution transformed Britain from an agrarian economy to one dominated by industry and machine manufacture. Technological innovations included the use of new basic materials such as steel and iron, the exploitation of new energy sources like coal and the steam engine, and the invention of new machines such as the power loom and the spinning jenny. Labour was reorganized and purpose-built factories sprang up, while a massive shift in population from the country to the city produced a host of serious problems, including overcrowded housing, inadequate sanitation, and widespread urban crime. The age was also dominated by political revolution. In 1775, the American War of Independence broke out, when thirteen British colonies in North America took up arms against their parent country, Great Britain. 'Red rose the clouds from the Atlantic in vast wheels of blood', wrote the poet **William Blake**.[1] 'And in the red clouds rose a Wonder o'er the Atlantic sea; / [. . .] The King of England looking westward trembles at the vision'.[2] The thirteen colonies were eventually joined by France, Spain, and Holland, and the war came to an end when the British surrendered at Yorktown, southeastern Virginia, in 1781. Britain officially recognized American independence two years later. The conflict was seen as a victory for liberty over British tyranny, and inaugurated government based on democratic principles. Advocates hoped fervently that the ideals of the American Revolution would spread to Europe, and help to overturn the corrupt monarchical systems that had been in place for centuries. Their wishes seemed to be realized when, on 14 July 1789, an armed Parisian mob stormed the Bastille prison, a symbol of royal despotism, and set in motion the momentous events of the French Revolution. In Britain, reaction

---

1 As noted in the Introduction, figures whose names appear in bold are included in the Biographical Directory, **pp. 44–8**.
2 *The Complete Poetry and Prose of William Blake*, ed. David V. Erdman, commentary by Harold Bloom (New York: Anchor Books, 1982), p. 53.

to the downfall of the French monarchy was divided. **Edmund Burke** spoke for many conservatives when in his *Reflections on the Revolution in France* (1790) he denounced democracy and the revolutionaries, and celebrated traditional wisdom, inherited values, the virtues of the English constitution, and the responsible leadership of the aristocracy (see Contemporary Documents, **pp. 34–6**). Burke was vigorously opposed by a series of radical writers, including **Mary Wollstonecraft** in *A Vindication of the Rights of Men* (1790) and *A Vindication of the Rights of Woman* (1792), Thomas Paine in *The Rights of Man* (1791), and **William Godwin** in *Political Justice* (1793) and his terror novel *Caleb Williams* (1794) (see Contemporary Documents, **pp. 37–8**). Major poets such as Blake, **William Wordsworth**, and **Samuel Taylor Coleridge** were also for a time caught up in the political ferment, and championed the ideals of the French Revolution. A twenty-year-old Wordsworth visited France in 1790, just one year after the fall of the Bastille, and in his autobiographical poem *The Prelude* recollected the heady nature of those days: 'Bliss was it in that dawn to be alive', he enthused, 'But to be young was very heaven'.[3]

Meanwhile, in France and across Europe, the initial euphoria of the Revolution began steadily to give way to factionalism, confusion, and violence. In September 1792 more than a thousand prisoners were massacred by a Paris mob. Louis XVI was guillotined in January 1793, and his queen Marie Antoinette in October (see Figure 3, **p. 14**). That same year a group of radicals known as the Jacobins overthrew the Girondists, a group of more moderate republicans. The Jacobins were led by Maximilien Robespierre, and they soon instituted the systematic brutality of the Reign of Terror, in which thousands of ostensible opponents of the Revolution were guillotined, including Robespierre himself in July 1794. The Revolution had started to swallow its own children. Chaos and violence spread across Europe. Britain went to war with France in 1793 and, with the exception of a brief hiatus (the Peace of Amiens in 1802–3), the two countries were at the centre of a fierce international battle that lasted for nearly a quarter of a century, France under the leadership of Napoleon Bonaparte and England and its allies increasingly under the direction of the Duke of Wellington. Lasting peace did not come until British forces helped defeat Bonaparte at the Battle of Waterloo in 1815. 'The French Revolution', Percy Shelley told Lord Byron a year later, is 'the master theme of the epoch in which we live.'[4]

Austen lived through this turbulent and transformative age, yet in many respects she was remarkably untouched by it. She was born in 1775 in the quiet Hampshire village of Steventon, the seventh child in a family of eight. Her father, the Reverend **George Austen**, was rector of the village, and a gentle, intelligent man who encouraged a love of reading in his children. Her mother Cassandra was a countrywoman and a ready wit, the niece of a famous master of Balliol College, Oxford. Her beloved older sister **Cassandra Austen** was her closest companion. Acting was a family passion, and together they staged everything from Christmas plays to contemporary comedies, including *The Rivals*, a brilliant comedy of

---

3   William Wordsworth, *The Thirteen-Book Prelude*, ed. Mark L. Reed, 2 vols (Ithaca: Cornell University Press, 1991), vol. i, p. 285.

4   *The Letters of Percy Bysshe Shelley*, ed. Frederick L. Jones, 2 vols (Oxford: Clarendon Press, 1964), vol. i, p. 504.

manners by **Richard Brinsley Sheridan**. Austen thrived in this affectionate and dynamic family circle, and as she grew older she began to mix with the country clergy and minor gentry, in the neighbourhood and occasionally in Bath and London. Her first known romantic attachment was a brief flirtation with a handsome young Irishman named **Tom Lefroy** (see Figure 4, **p. 39**). They met in December 1795, and over the next two months danced together at four balls. His family, however, seems to have feared a formal proposal, and he was sent off to London to continue his legal studies. The two seem not to have met again. In 1801 Austen's father retired and the family moved to Bath. A year later Austen agreed to marry a man named **Harris Bigg-Wither**, the twenty-one-year-old heir of a Hampshire estate, but she changed her mind and withdrew her acceptance the next day. Other men seem to have expressed an interest in her during these years, but details are slight and she seems to have received no other formal offer of marriage. Austen's father died in 1805, and the family left Bath, eventually settling in Southampton, where they spent most of the next three years. Austen must at this time have had to come to terms with the reality of spinsterhood. Fortunately, in 1809, her brother Edward was able to provide her, Cassandra, and their mother with a large cottage in the village of Chawton, within his Hampshire estate, not far from Steventon. During these years Austen was a housekeeper, an attendant on her mother, and a favourite maiden aunt to her brother's children. In 1816, however, her health began to fail, and by March 1817 she was too ill to work. She died in Winchester on 18 July 1817, and was buried in Winchester Cathedral. She was only forty-two-years-old at her death. 'What a pity such a gifted creature died so early!', remarked her famous contemporary **Walter Scott** (see Novelists on *Pride and Prejudice*, **p. 60**).

Austen started to write in the late 1780s, and like Blake, Wordsworth, and Coleridge, was highly productive throughout the 1790s. Her juvenilia includes pieces such as *Love and Freindship* [*sic*] (1790) and *Catharine, or The Bower* (1792), while *Lady Susan* (*c.* 1794) is a more ambitious novel in letters. In 1795, Austen completed *Elinor and Marianne*, the lost epistolary original of *Sense and Sensibility*. A year later she began *First Impressions*, which was subsequently revised as *Pride and Prejudice* (see Frontispiece, **p. i**). In 1798, the same year as Wordsworth and Coleridge published their celebrated *Lyrical Ballads*, Austen likely began work on *Susan*, later rewritten as *Northanger Abbey*. Her productivity declined dramatically in the first decade of the nineteenth century, but in 1809 she was attempting to secure publication of *Susan*, and a renewal of enthusiasm for writing and revision soon culminated in the publication of her first novel, *Sense and Sensibility* (1811). Thereafter five other novels followed in quick succession: *Pride and Prejudice* (1813), *Mansfield Park* (1814), *Emma* (1815) and, posthumously, *Persuasion* and *Northanger Abbey* (both 1818). All six novels are poised and tightly constructed comedies of manners. They concern a young woman's errant but ultimately successful voyage to self-discovery, and feature small groups of largely middle-class and provincial characters in a circumscribed (some say confined) environment. The action centres on ordinary, apparently trivial events. Courtship is the foremost interest, and marriage the highest ambition. War and revolution dominated her age, yet Austen revealingly observed of her own novelistic technique that '3 or 4 Families in a Country Village is the very thing to work on'. Later, she described herself as creating on a 'little bit (two Inches wide) of Ivory [. . .] with so fine a Brush, as produces little effect after much labour' (see Contemporary Documents, **p. 43**). Commentators have frequently discussed this aspect of her work, and not always sympathetically. 'She is capital as far as she goes', remarked Edward Fitzgerald: 'but she never goes out of the Parlour.'[5] Frederic Harrison was a good deal more severe, notoriously condemning Austen as 'a rather heartless little cynic . . . penning satirettes about her neighbours while the Dynasts were tearing the world to pieces and consigning millions to their graves'.[6] More recently, Mary Poovey finds that in *Pride and Prejudice* Austen offers an 'aesthetic solution, which pushes aside social realism'.[7] In short, for critics such as these, Austen lived in a revolutionary era, but shirked the responsibility or lacked the courage to confront its manifold implications, and so simply wished the problems away with comedic characters, quaint satire, or fairytale endings.

Adding to the impression of Austen as out of step or touch with the social conflicts and radical energies of her own day is her backward-looking commitment to the literary conventions and attitudes of the eighteenth century. **Alexander Pope** was one of the most admired and influential poets of his age, and Austen was indebted to him 'for her general ideas about self-love, reason, the passions, the predominant passions, instinct, happiness, the characters of men and women, the use of riches, and the various kinds of stupidity to be found in society', as Frank Bradbrook aptly summarizes it.[8] George Saintsbury argues that Austen's humour is most clearly akin to that of the great eighteenth-century essayist **Joseph Addison**, for in addition to 'demureness, extreme minuteness of touch, avoidance of loud tones and glaring effects', there is in both a 'restrained and well-mannered' but 'insatiable and ruthless delight in roasting and cutting up a fool'.[9] Harold Bloom observes that Austen 'truly is the daughter' of **Samuel Richardson**, one of the preeminent novelists of the eighteenth century, and especially admired by Austen for his *Sir Charles Grandison*.[10] **Samuel Johnson** (see Contemporary Documents, **pp. 23–4**) was 'the greatest man of letters in the literary scene in the mid-eighteenth century'; and **William Cowper** was 'the most eminent poet in the last quarter of it', writes Christopher Gillie. 'They dominated Austen's youthful horizon.'[11] Though Austen published all of her novels in the second decade of the nineteenth century, her writings are steeped in the works of the eighteenth. David Cecil concludes: 'Jane Austen – it is one of the most important facts about her – was born in the eighteenth century; and, spiritually speaking, she stayed there. A contemporary of Coleridge and

5   *The Letters of Edward Fitzgerald*, eds Alfred McKinley Terhune and Annabelle Burdick Terhune, 4 vols (Princeton: Princeton University Press, 1980), vol. iii, p. 260.
6   F. B. Pinion, 'Background' in *A Jane Austen Companion* (London: Macmillan, 1973), p. 24.
7   Mary Poovey, *The Proper Lady and the Woman Writer* (Chicago: University of Chicago Press, 1984), p. 206.
8   Frank Bradbrook, *Jane Austen and her Predecessors* (Cambridge: Cambridge University Press, 1966), p. 76.
9   George Saintsbury, 'On *Pride and Prejudice*' in Jane Austen, *Pride and Prejudice*, ed. George Saintsbury (London: George Allen, 1894), p. xiii.
10 Harold Bloom, 'Introduction' in *Jane Austen*, ed. Harold Bloom (New York: Chelsea House, 1986), p. 2. A selection from Richardson's *Sir Charles Grandison* appears in Contemporary Documents (**pp. 24–6**).
11 Christopher Gillie, *A Preface to Jane Austen* (London: Longman, 1974), p. 37.

Wordsworth, her view of things had much more in common with that of Dr. Johnson'.[12]

Yet despite her restricted subject matter and dedication to the eighteenth century, Austen is an author of remarkable range and force who did confront some of the central conflicts of her age, and who in *Pride and Prejudice* combines provincial preoccupations and the intricacies of courtship with an incisive and thoroughgoing response to a series of revolutionary anxieties and pressure points. Walter Scott, whose own Waverley novels explore great historical events and the processes of social and political change, was among the first to identify Austen's ability to reveal the exceptional within the mundane, and the compelling within the familiar. 'The Big Bow wow strain I can do myself like any now going', he declared, 'but the exquisite touch which renders ordinary common-place things and characters interesting from the truth of the description and the sentiment is denied to me.' Later, G. K. Chesterton observed that 'Austen may have been protected from truth: but it was precious little of truth that was protected from her' (see Novelists on *Pride and Prejudice*, **p. 60** for Scott, **p. 66** for Chesterton). In *Pride and Prejudice*, Austen recognizes how our largest hopes sometimes rest on the most ephemeral events, and how tragedy can be played out, not just on the national stage, but in a drawing-room conversation or on a country walk. There are enormous depths within her narrow domestic settings, and intense passions within characters who are governed by polite restraint (see Highmore, Contemporary Documents, **pp. 27–8**). A polished and formal veneer exposes emotions that are deep-seated and broadly felt. 'More than any other novelist', writes **Virginia Woolf**, '[Austen] fills every inch of her canvas with observation, fashions every sentence into meaning, stuffs up every chink and cranny of the fabric until each novel is a little living world, from which you cannot break off a scene or even a sentence without bleeding it of some of its life.'[13] Austen's canvas is small, but its meanings resonant, diverse, and wide-ranging.

What is more, though she lived in rural isolation and genteel spinsterhood, she was closely connected to the contemporary world. Three of her brothers were in the military, and they all provided her with much detailed information on the war effort. Frank and Charles had already joined the Navy when war broke out between England and France, and both men went on to have long and distinguished military careers. Frank fought mainly in the Mediterranean and the Baltic, and was intimately involved with British naval operations throughout the Napoleonic Wars. Charles served in the Mediterranean and on the North American Station, and was again in the Mediterranean after Napoleon's escape from Elba in 1815. **Henry Austen** became a Lieutenant in the Oxfordshire Militia in 1793, and spent a year in Dublin when it seemed probable that the French might use Ireland to invade England. Other members of Austen's immediate family were also profoundly affected by the war. When the French threatened English interests in the West Indies, Cassandra's fiancé, the Reverend Thomas Fowle, went out as a private chaplain to his patron Lord Craven. Fowle lasted only a year and then, like thousands of British soldiers, he contracted yellow fever and died,

12 David Cecil, *A Portrait of Jane Austen* (London: Book Club Associates, 1978), pp. 12–13.
13 *The Essays of Virginia Woolf*, ed. Andrew McNeillie, 4 vols (London: Hogarth Press, 1986–continuing), vol. ii, p. 14.

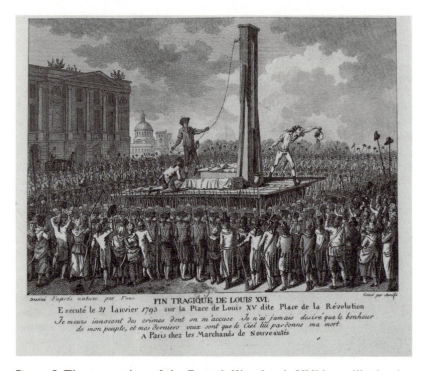

Figure 3 **The execution of the French King Louis XVI by guillotine in January 1793. Austen's cousin Eliza de Feuillide was to lose her husband to the guillotine just over a year later.**

bringing Cassandra's sole engagement to a tragic termination. Austen's cousin **Eliza de Feuillide** had an even more lurid story to tell. She and her French husband, Jean François Capot de Feuillide, were in Paris in early 1794 during the height of Robespierre's Reign of Terror. They were perhaps planning an escape to England, but mischance intervened and only Eliza made it across the channel. Within weeks her husband was arrested in Paris, tried on fraudulent charges, and then guillotined on 22 February 1794. Figure 3 illustrates the execution of Louis XVI by guillotine on 21 January 1793, and graphically depicts the ways in which these executions turned state violence into both spectacle and threat. Eliza seems almost certain to have stayed with the Austen family only weeks after her husband's execution, 'bringing first-hand news of the horrors then being enacted in France directly into the peaceful English parsonage', as Deirdre Le Faye observes.[14] Later Eliza married Austen's brother Henry, and when during the 1802–3 Peace of Amiens the couple rashly visited France in the hope of recovering Feuillide's property, they narrowly escaped internment on the way home. Austen did not make war or political violence the explicit subject of her novels, but she had first-hand knowledge of military conflict and the damage wrought by

14 Deirdre Le Faye, *Jane Austen* (London: The British Library, 1998), p. 50.

warfare, and her novels betray a keen awareness of the contemporary political situation, particularly as regards the fate of women. Politics burden the apparently private, familial decisions made by Austen's women, and their aesthetic inclinations are repeatedly shaped and distorted by economic realities. 'Money is the vital substance in her world', asserts **Martin Amis**; 'the moment you enter it, you feel the candid horror of moneylessness, as intense as the tacit horror of spinsterhood.'[15] *Pride and Prejudice* seems committed to the private and domestic sphere, but it constantly illuminates the larger pressures and restrictions of the age. 'I think of [Austen] as a war-novelist', states V. S. Pritchett, 'formed very much by the Napoleonic wars, knowing directly of prize money, the shortage of men, the economic crisis and change in the value of capital' (see Novelists on *Pride and Prejudice*, **p. 68**). Nina Auerbach agrees: 'In presenting these drawing rooms full of women watching the door and watching each other, Jane Austen tells us what an observant, genteel woman has to tell about the Napoleonic Wars: she writes novels about waiting' (see Modern Criticism, **p. 82**).

Further, though she looks often to the past, Austen's novels are also profoundly reflective of some of the central anxieties of her own day. In *Pride and Prejudice*, she embraces many of the conservative doctrines passionately explicated by Burke in *Reflections on the Revolution in France* and a year later in *An Appeal from the New to the Old Whigs*, including the importance of aristocratic duty, privilege, tradition, and property, while her conclusion rewards Elizabeth with a spectacularly successful marriage that elevates her into the highest ranks of English society and affirms the claims of a hierarchical system. Yet at the same time, Elizabeth enacts many of the democratic and feminist values championed by Wollstonecraft in *A Vindication of the Rights of Woman*. She is strong, independent, candid, and physically active, with a quick and incisive mind that rejects the simpering and affectation endorsed by female conduct books, and challenges Darcy as his intellectual equal (see Contemporary Documents, Burke **pp. 34–6**, Wollstonecraft **pp. 36–7**, Fordyce **p. 29**, Gregory **pp. 30–1**). She refuses to cower to gender convention or aristocratic rank, and her rebellious and leveling muse is clearly in evidence when she informs Lady Catherine that Darcy 'is a gentleman; I am a gentleman's daughter; so far we are equal' (see Key Passages, **p. 154**). According to the twentieth-century novelist and essayist Rebecca West, Austen 'put the institutions of society regarding women through the most grueling criticism they have ever received'.[16] And if, in the end, she legitimates the aristocratic order by showing it to be capable of assimilating the new, the impression remains of her central belief in the importance of individual desire and merit. 'Austen's fictions', Clara Tuite states, 'are [. . .] part of that conflicted and vicarious bourgeois or middle-class project of seeking to appropriate the trappings of aristocratic authority, whilst making the aristocratic class over in the image of bourgeois virtue.'[17]

Austen's era was one of massive technological advance and violent social and political revolution. Her novels are tightly structured, narrowly focused, and profoundly indebted to the previous age, yet they also reveal a penetrating knowledge

---

15 Martin Amis, 'Miss Jane's Prime' in *The Atlantic*, 265.2 (February 1990), p. 101.
16 Rebecca West, 'Preface' in Jane Austen, *Northanger Abbey* (London: Jonathan Cape, 1932), p. vii.
17 Clara Tuite, *Romantic Austen: Sexual Politics and the Literary Canon* (Cambridge: Cambridge University Press, 2002), p. 143.

of wartime circumstance, and a close relationship with some of the key contro-versies of her age. Though a glittering comedy, *Pride and Prejudice* carries a powerful political charge in reference especially to rank, class and gender, though Austen's manner is exploratory and ironic, rather than didactic and exhortatory. In its concentration on the tension between romance and realism, private and public, money and love, aristocrat and bourgeois, and individual and society, *Pride and Prejudice* both draws on the literary achievements of the eighteenth century, and shapes key concerns that will dominate literature in the nineteenth century, and well beyond.

Chronology

Bullet points denote events in Austen's life; asterisks denote historical and literary events.

1775
- Jane Austen (JA) born 16 December at Steventon
* Outbreak of the American Revolution; James Watt perfects the steam engine; Samuel Johnson, *A Journey to the Western Islands of Scotland*; Richard Brinsley Sheridan, *The Rivals*

1776
* American Declaration of Independence; Adam Smith, *The Wealth of Nations*

1777
* Richard Brinsley Sheridan, *The School for Scandal*

1778
* Frances Burney, *Evelina, or The History of a Young Lady's Entrance Into the World*; Jean-Jacques Rousseau dies

1779
- JA's brother James Austen matriculates at St. John's College, Oxford
* William Cowper, *The Olney Hymns*; Richard Brinsley Sheridan, *The Critic*

1781
* Samuel Johnson, *The Lives of the Poets*

1782
- First amateur theatrical production at Steventon
* Frances Burney, *Cecilia, or Memoirs of an Heiress*

1783
- JA and her sister Cassandra go to Mrs. Cawley's boarding school, first in

Oxford and then in Southampton, where Jane is critically ill with 'putrid fever'

* George Crabbe, *The Village*; William Blake, *Poetical Sketches*

1784

• Richard Brinsley Sheridan's *The Rivals* performed at Steventon

* Samuel Johnson dies

1785

• JA and Cassandra go to the Abbey School, Reading

* James Watt and Matthew Boulton install a steam engine in a Nottinghamshire cotton factory; William Cowper, *The Task*

1786

• JA and Cassandra leave the Abbey School; JA's brother Francis Austen enters Royal Naval Academy, Portsmouth

1787

• JA starts writing her *Juvenilia*

* Mary Wollstonecraft, *Thoughts on the Education of Daughters*; Mary Russell Mitford born

1788

• Mr. and Mrs. Austen take JA and Cassandra to Kent and London; JA's brother Francis Austen sails to the East Indies

* George Gordon, the future Lord Byron, born

1789

* French mob storms the Bastille prison in Paris, marking the outbreak of the French Revolution; French National Assembly proclaims Declaration of the Rights of Man

1790

• JA writes *Love and Freindship* [*sic*], a burlesque on tales of passion and romance; James Austen takes up residence as curate of Overton

* Edmund Burke, *Reflections on the Revolution in France*

1791

• JA writes her *History of England*, a work by a 'partial, prejudiced, & ignorant Historian'; JA's brother Charles Austen enters Royal Naval Academy, Portsmouth

* King Louis XVI flees, but is captured and returned to Paris; Edmund Burke, *An Appeal from the New to the Old Whigs*; Thomas Paine, *The Rights of Man*; James Boswell, *The Life of Samuel Johnson*

1792

• JA completes *Catharine, or The Bower*; James Austen marries Anne Mathew; Cassandra engaged to the Reverend Thomas Fowle

* France declares war on Austria; guillotine introduced into France; the September Massacres in Paris; France declares itself a Republic; Mary Wollstonecraft, *A Vindication of the Rights of Woman*; Percy Shelley born

1793
* JA's brother Henry Austen becomes Lieutenant in Oxfordshire Militia
* Execution of Louis XVI and Marie Antoinette; Britain goes to war with Republican France; radical Jacobin leader Maximilien Robespierre assumes control of the Committee of Public Safety, and France descends into the Reign of Terror; in Scotland, suspected 'Jacobins' are tried for treason; William Godwin, *An Enquiry Concerning Political Justice*; William Blake, *America: A Prophecy*

1794
* JA possibly writes *Lady Susan*; Jean François Capot de Feuillide, the husband of JA's cousin, is guillotined in Paris
* Imprisonment without trial in Britain; leaders of the radical London Corresponding Society are tried by the state for sedition and acquitted; Robespierre is guillotined in Paris, ending the Reign of Terror; William Godwin, *Things as They Are; or, The Adventures of Caleb Williams*; William Blake, *Europe: A Prophecy*

1795
* JA probably writes *Elinor and Marianne* (later *Sense and Sensibility*); she begins her brief flirtation with Tom Lefroy
* British government passes the repressive Two Acts, which increase state censorship and ban most meetings of over fifty people; Napoleon puts down royalist revolt in Paris; William Blake, *The Book of Los*; John Keats born

1796
* JA starts writing *First Impressions* (later *Pride and Prejudice*)
* France threatens to invade England; Napoleon rises to prominence after a series of brilliant military victories in Italy; Edmund Burke, *Letters on a Regicide Peace*; Frances Burney, *Camilla*; Samuel Taylor Coleridge, *Poems on Various Subjects*

1797
* JA finishes writing *First Impressions* in August; her father offers the manuscript to the publisher Thomas Cadell, and it is rejected sight unseen; JA begins transforming *Elinor and Marianne* into *Sense and Sensibility*; Cassandra's fiancé dies
* Mutinies in the British Navy; Edmund Burke dies; Mary Wollstonecraft dies; Mary Wollstonecraft Godwin, later Mary Shelley, born

1798
* JA perhaps starts writing *Susan* (later *Northanger Abbey*)
* Napoleon invades Egypt; Horatio Nelson leads the British Navy in the Mediterranean; rebellion breaks out in Ireland; William Godwin, *Memoirs of*

Mary Wollstonecraft; William Wordsworth and Samuel Taylor Coleridge, *Lyrical Ballads*

1799
- JA probably finishes writing *Susan* (later *Northanger Abbey*)
* Napoleon becomes First Consul under new constitution

1800
- JA's father decides to retire and move to Bath
* William Cowper dies

1801
- JA apparently becomes romantically involved with a man met while vacationing at Sidmouth, but he dies shortly thereafter. Henry Austen resigns his commission in the Oxfordshire Militia
* Union of Great Britain and Ireland

1802
- Harris Bigg-Wither proposes to JA on 2 December; she accepts, but changes her mind overnight and rejects his proposal the following morning
* Peace of Amiens brings a pause in the war between Britain and France; Walter Scott, *Minstrelsy of the Scottish Border*; Harriet Martineau born

1803
- JA sells *Susan* (*Northanger Abbey*) to the publisher Crosby of London, but the novel does not appear
* War breaks out again between Britain and France; Henry Austen nearly trapped in France; Francis Austen stationed at Ramsgate

1804
- JA begins *The Watsons*
* Napoleon proclaimed Emperor of France

1805
- JA's father dies; she is possibly courted in the summer by Edward Bridges
* British Admiral Horatio Nelson defeats Napoleon at the Battle of Trafalgar; William Godwin, *Fleetwood*; Walter Scott, *The Lay of the Last Minstrel*; Amelia Opie, *Adeline Mowbray*; William Wordsworth finishes his thirteen-book *Prelude*

1806
* The first steam-driven textile mill opens in Manchester

1807
- JA and her family move to Southampton
* Britain abolishes the Slave Trade; France invades Portugal and Spain; Lord Byron, *Hours of Idleness*; William Wordsworth, *Poems, in Two Volumes*

1809
- JA attempts to secure publication of *Susan* (*Northanger Abbey*)
* The Duke of Wellington takes control of British troops in Spain; William Wordsworth, *The Convention of Cintra*; Lord Byron, *English Bards and Scotch Reviewers*

1810
- JA's *Sense and Sensibility* accepted for publication
* Napoleon at the peak of his power

1811
- JA publishes *Sense and Sensibility* as 'A Novel . . . by a Lady'
* George III declared insane and the Prince of Wales becomes Regent; Luddite anti-factory riots break out in England

1812
- JA sells copyright of *Pride and Prejudice* to Thomas Egerton for £110
* United States declares war on Britain; Napoleon's disastrous Russian campaign; British Prime Minister Spencer Perceval is assassinated in the House of Commons, and is succeeded by Lord Liverpool; Amelia Opie, *Temper*; Lord Byron, *Childe Harold's Pilgrimage* (Cantos I and II)

1813
- JA publishes *Pride and Prejudice* as 'by the author of "Sense and Sensibility"'; JA finishes *Mansfield Park*
* Napoleon in full retreat across northern Europe; Wellington liberates the Iberian peninsula from Napoleonic rule; Lord Byron, *The Giaour*

1814
- JA publishes *Mansfield Park*
* Allied armies invade France and Paris falls; Napoleon abdicates and is exiled to the Italian island of Elba; restoration of the French monarchy; Lord Byron, *The Corsair*; Walter Scott, *Waverley*; William Wordsworth, *The Excursion*

1815
- JA publishes *Emma*, and dedicates it to the Prince Regent
* Napoleon breaks from Elba and returns to France; Britain and its allies soundly defeat Napoleon at the Battle of Waterloo; Lord Byron, *Hebrew Melodies*; Walter Scott, *Guy Mannering*

1816
- JA begins to feel unwell; Henry Austen buys back the manuscript of *Susan* (*Northanger Abbey*), which JA revises
* Labour unrest grows throughout Britain; Samuel Taylor Coleridge, *Christabel*; Walter Scott, *Old Mortality*; Percy Shelley, *Alastor and Other Poems*; Charlotte Brontë born

1817
- JA begins *Sanditon* in January but ceases work in March; she dies 18 July
- *   Continuing unrest and depression in Britain; William Godwin, *Mandeville*; Lord Byron, *Manfred*; Samuel Taylor Coleridge, *Biographia Literaria*; John Keats, *Poems*; George Henry Lewes born

1818
- *Northanger Abbey* and *Persuasion* published posthumously
- *   Withdrawal of foreign armies from France; Lord Byron, *Beppo*; John Keats, *Endymion*; Walter Scott, *The Heart of Midlothian*; Mary Shelley, *Frankenstein*; Percy Shelley, *The Revolt of Islam*; Karl Marx born; Emily Brontë born

Contemporary Documents

Introduction

This section contains a wealth of source material Austen drew upon in writing *Pride and Prejudice*, as well as a fascinating series of letters by Austen herself. *Pride and Prejudice* is rooted in the writings of eighteenth-century authors like Samuel Johnson, Samuel Richardson, and Frances Burney. The law of entail is central to the novel, and is given concise expression by **Adam Smith**, while the ideal of politeness pervades the text, and is suggestively summarized by **Joseph Highmore**. *Pride and Prejudice* can be read as a feminist text because it both challenges the essentialist conceptions of woman promulgated by writers such as **Jean-Jacques Rousseau, James Fordyce** and **John Gregory**, and because it enacts many of the doctrines set forth by Mary Wollstonecraft in *A Vindication of the Rights of Woman*. But *Pride and Prejudice* can also be read as a deeply conservative work because of its ties to the political philosophy of Edmund Burke, and its suppression of the bloody events and profound anxieties of the French Revolution that so preoccupied radical writers like Wollstonecraft and William Godwin. Austen's allegiances to both Wollstonecraftian feminism and Burkean conservatism complicate and energize her novel. An opening scene in *Temper* by **Amelia Opie** demonstrates that, while *Pride and Prejudice* is often celebrated for its freshness and insight, it draws on characters and scenarios that would have been very familiar to contemporary readers. Austen's own letters also throw a great deal of light on *Pride and Prejudice*. They reveal her giddy enjoyment of a world of balls, gossip, and handsome men highly reminiscent of the one she creates in *Pride and Prejudice*, and contain intriguing comments on Elizabeth Bennet, Mr. Darcy, and the distinguishing features of her novelistic art.

From **Samuel Johnson, 'Number 56' in *The Rambler*,** eds W. J. Bate and Albrecht B. Strauss, 3 vols (New Haven: Yale University Press, 1969), vol. i, p. 302

Austen was a great admirer of Samuel Johnson, and responded both to his wit and his moral seriousness. 'Austen trained herself in Johnson's school', writes

Mary Lascelles, and 'that was not [. . .] the limit of her debt to him [. . .] some tones of his voice seem to be echoed in her style'.[1] In a twice-weekly column for a twopenny periodical called *The Rambler* (1750–2), Johnson presented himself as a moralist intent on instructing his readers in piety and wisdom. His discussion of 'an exuberance of pride' clearly illuminates Darcy's behaviour when he first encounters Elizabeth at the Meryton ball, and informs Elizabeth's subsequent rejection of his marriage proposal because of what she cuttingly describes as his 'selfish disdain of the feelings of others' (see Key Passages, **pp. 114–17, p. 137**). 'Darcy's central fault, after all, is to have been careless about pleasing other people', Claudia Johnson asserts, '[. . .] and Lady Catherine and he both are judged wanting precisely because their own pride renders them incapable of regarding the happiness of their inferiors'.[2]

Some, indeed, there are, for whom the excuse of ignorance or negligence cannot be alleged, because it is apparent that they are not only careless of pleasing, but studious to offend; that they contrive to make all approaches to them difficult and vexatious, and imagine that they aggrandize themselves by wasting the time of others in useless attendance, by mortifying them with slights, and teazing them with affronts.

Men of this kind, are generally found to be among those that have not mingled much in general conversation, but spent their lives amidst the obsequiousness of dependants, and the flattery of parasites; and by long consulting only their own inclination, have forgotten that others have a claim to the same deference.

Tyranny thus avowed, is indeed an exuberance of pride.

From **Samuel Richardson, *Sir Charles Grandison,*** ed. Jocelyn Harris (Oxford: Oxford University Press, 1972), vol. i, pp. 83–4

Samuel Richardson's *Sir Charles Grandison* (1753–4) is an epistolary novel that blends serious moral concern with keen psychological insight and a comic ending, and that features a virtuous hero divided between his love for two different women. According to her nephew James Edward Austen-Leigh, 'every circumstance narrated in Sir Charles Grandison [. . .] was familiar to her',[1] and in *Pride and Prejudice* Austen transforms and assimilates several of the novel's key themes and situations. Early in the novel the wealthy and dishonourable Sir Hargrave Pollexfen pursues the attractive and accomplished Harriet Byron, but she repeatedly rebuffs his insolent proposals of marriage. Jocelyn Harris argues

1 Mary Lascelles, *Jane Austen and her Art* (Oxford: Clarendon Press, 1939), p. 109.
2 Claudia Johnson, *Jane Austen: Women, Politics, and the Novel* (Chicago: University of Chicago Press, 1988), p. 81.

1 James Edward Austen-Leigh, *A Memoir of Jane Austen and Other Family Recollections*, ed. Kathryn Sutherland (Oxford: Oxford University Press, 2002), p. 71.

that Pollexfen's proposal to Harriet Byron 'follows exactly the same sequence' as Mr. Collins's proposal to Elizabeth.[2] But Jan Fergus asserts that the same scene from Richardson more closely mirrors Darcy's first proposal to Elizabeth. 'When Sir Hargrave proposes marriage to Harriet', writes Fergus, 'we encounter a spirited woman and a suitor who is incredulous at being rejected and whose pride is outraged by it'.[3]

I would have played a little female trifling upon him, and affected to take his professions only for polite raillery, which men call *making love* to young women, who perhaps are frequently but too willing to take in earnest what the wretches mean but in jest; but the fervour with which he *renewed* (as he called it) his declaration, admitted not of fooling; and yet his *volubility* might have made questionable the sincerity of his declarations. As therefore I could not think of encouraging his addresses, I thought it best to answer him with openness and unreserve.

To seem to question the sincerity of such professions as you make, Sir Hargrave, might appear to you as if I wanted to be assured. But be pleased to know that you are directing your discourse to one of the plainest-hearted women in England; and you may therefore expect from me nothing but the simplest truth. I thank you, Sir, for your good opinion of me; but I cannot encourage your addresses.

You *cannot*, madam, *encourage my addresses*! And express yourself so seriously! Good heaven! [He stood silent a minute or two, looking upon me, and upon himself; as if he had said, foolish girl! knows she whom she refuses?] I have been assured, madam, recovering a little from his surprize, that your affections are not engaged. But surely it must be a mistake: Some happy man –

Is it, interrupted I, a necessary consequence, that the woman who cannot receive the addresses of Sir Hargrave Pollexfen, must be engaged?

Why, madam – As to that – I know not what to say – But a man of my fortune, and I hope, not *absolutely* disagreeable either in person or temper; of some rank in life – He paused; then resuming – What, madam, if you are as much in earnest as you seem, can be your objection? Be so good as to name it, that I may know, whether I cannot be so happy as to get over it?

We do not, we *cannot*, all like the same person. Women, I have heard say, are very capricious. Perhaps I am so. But there is a *something* (we cannot always say what) that attracts or disgusts us.

Disgusts! madam – *Disgusts*! Miss Byron.

I spoke in general, Sir; I dare say, nineteen women out of twenty would think themselves favoured in the addresses of Sir Hargrave Pollexfen.

But *you*, madam, are the twentieth that I must love: And be so good as to let me know –

Pray, Sir, ask me not a reason for a *peculiarity*. Do you not yourself shew a peculiarity in making me the twentieth?

2   Jocelyn Harris, *Jane Austen's Art of Memory* (Cambridge: Cambridge University Press, 1989), p. 112.
3   Jan Fergus, *Jane Austen and the Didactic Novel* (Totowa, New Jersey: Barnes & Noble, 1983), p. 74.

Your merit, madam –

It would be vanity in me, Sir, interrupted I, to allow a force to that plea. You, Sir, may have more merit, than perhaps the man I may happen to approve of better; but – *shall* I say? (Pardon me, Sir) You do not – You do not, hesitated I – hit my fancy – Pardon me, Sir.

If pardon depends upon *my* breath, let me die if I *do*! – *Not hit your fancy*, madam! [And then he look'd upon himself all round] *Not hit your fancy*, madam!

I told you, Sir, that you must not expect any-thing from me but the simplest truth. You do me an honour in your good opinion; and if my own heart were not, in this case, a very determined one, I would answer you with more politeness. But, Sir, on such an occasion as this, I think it would not be honourable, it would not be just, to keep a man in an hour's suspense, when I am in none myself.

From **Jean-Jacques Rousseau, *Émile, ou de l'Education,*** ed. Allan Bloom (New York: Basic Books, 1979), pp. 358, 365

In his enormously influential educational treatise *Émile* (1762), Jean-Jacques Rousseau establishes the fundamental tenets of a natural (that is, virtuous and simple) education, as opposed to the artificial and formal education provided by society. In the final book he describes the education of Sophie, the girl Émile marries. For Rousseau, men and women are fundamentally different. Women are the weak, passive, inferior counterparts of men. They pursue power through their charms, accomplishments, sexuality, sensibility, and physical beauty, but their proper role is to study and promote the happiness and pleasure of men. Margaret Anne Doody observes that *Émile* concerns 'the taming of a girl as she dwindles into a wife – the story of a girl learning her place'.[1] In the novel itself, Mary Bennet emphasizes the importance of a woman's reputation, which is 'no less brittle than it is beautiful',[2] and Rousseau would applaud Caroline Bingley's account of what makes an accomplished woman: 'a thorough knowledge of music, singing, drawing, dancing, and the modern languages', as well as 'a certain something in her air and manner of walking, the tone of her voice, her address and expressions'.[3] Yet throughout *Pride and Prejudice* Austen mocks these kinds of attitudes and aligns herself with radical feminists like Mary Wollstonecraft (see Contemporary Documents, **pp. 33, 36–7**). Elizabeth attracts Darcy with wit, intelligence, and assertiveness, rather than frivolity, docility, or delicate feminine charm. Margaret Kirkham observes that 'it is because the Austen heroines [. . .] are shown as representatives of "human" rather than "feminine" nature [. . .] that we may speak of her as a feminist moralist, connected with Wollstonecraft in opposing the antifeminism most powerfully expressed in *Émile*'.[4]

1   Margaret Anne Doody, 'The Short Fiction' in *The Cambridge Companion to Jane Austen*, eds Edward Copeland and Juliet McMaster (Cambridge: Cambridge University Press, 1997), p. 95.
2   Jane Austen, *Pride and Prejudice*, ed. R. W. Chapman (Oxford: Clarendon Press, 1923), Volume III, Chapter 5, p. 289.
3   Ibid., Volume I, Chapter 8, p. 39.
4   Margaret Kirkham, 'Jane Austen and Contemporary Feminism' in *The Jane Austen Handbook*, ed. J. David Grey (London: The Athlone Press, 1986), p. 158.

In the union of the sexes each contributes equally to the common aim, but not in the same way. From this diversity arises the first assignable difference in the moral relations of the two sexes. One ought to be active and strong, the other passive and weak. One must necessarily will and be able; it suffices that the other put up little resistance.

Once this principle is established, it follows that woman is made specially to please man. If man ought to please her in turn, it is due to a less direct necessity. His merit is in his power; he pleases by the sole fact of his strength. This is not the law of love, I agree. But it is that of nature, prior to love itself.

If woman is made to please and to be subjugated, she ought to make herself agreeable to man instead of arousing him. Her own violence is in her charms. It is by these that she ought to constrain him to find his strength and make use of it. The surest art for animating that strength is to make it necessary by resistance. Then *amour-propre*[5] unites with desire, and the one triumphs in the victory that the other has made him win. From this there arises attack and defense, the audacity of one sex and the timidity of the other, and finally the modesty and the shame with which nature armed the weak in order to enslave the strong. [. . .]

The good constitution of children initially depends on that of their mothers. The first education of men depends on the care of women. Men's morals, their passions, their tastes, their pleasures, their very happiness also depend on women. Thus the whole education of women ought to relate to men. To please men, to be useful to them, to make herself loved and honoured by them, to raise them when young, to care for them when grown, to counsel them, to console them, to make their lives agreeable and sweet – these are the duties of women at all times, and they ought to be taught from childhood. So long as one does not return to this principle, one will deviate from the goal, and all the percepts taught to women will be of no use for their happiness or for ours.

From **Joseph Highmore, *Essays, Moral, Religious, and Miscellaneous,*** 2 vols (London: White, 1766), vol. ii, pp. 47–8, 52

Martin Amis notes that the restraints and formalities of *Pride and Prejudice* are revealed 'most clearly, perhaps, in its language. Mr. Darcy's first name is Fitzwilliam, which is a nice name – but Elizabeth will never use it. She will call him "Mr. Darcy" or, occasionally, "My dear Mr. Darcy". You call your mother "Madam" and your dad "Sir" (see Novelists on *Pride and Prejudice*, **p. 70**).[1] Decorum, gentility, and deference are at the heart of *Pride and Prejudice*, and the novel both endorses and resists the eighteenth-century 'ideal of politeness', an ideal which 'permeated every aspect of cultural life' in the eighteenth century, and which 'was at once a philosophy, a way of life to which one committed oneself, and the means to understand oneself and one's place in the world', as John Brewer

---

5 'Self-esteem'.

1 For further discussion, see R. W. Chapman, 'Modes of Address' in Jane Austen, *Pride and Prejudice*, ed. R. W. Chapman (Oxford: Clarendon Press, 1923), pp. 410–13.

observes.[2] Politeness sought to combat religious intolerance and political partisanship, and anything that was brash, mean, clumsy, dull, inelegant, self-centred. It was social, ameliorative, and interactive, a code of conduct that prized amicability, educability, and respectability, as well as good manners, good taste, and good breeding. Its great ambassador was *The Spectator* (1711–12), a daily news-sheet written by Joseph Addison and Richard Steele that had as its aim to 'Cultivate and Polish Human Life, by promoting Virtue and Knowledge, and by recommending whatsoever may be either Useful or Ornamental to Society'.[3] Joseph Highmore defines the term as 'a habit of saying and doing obliging things', of being conscious of giving pleasure to others, of being socially judicious, and of cultivating liberty, intercourse, and ease. In *Pride and Prejudice*, Austen embraces the principles and language of politeness, perhaps most memorably when Elizabeth rejects Darcy's first proposal of marriage. According to Highmore, politeness involves 'an apparent endeavour to give pleasure, and to avoid giving pain'. In Austen's text, Darcy wonders why with 'so little *endeavour* at civility' he is rejected, and Elizabeth is 'sorry to have occasioned pain' (see Key Passages, **pp. 135–6**; Austen's italics). For Highmore and Austen 'the manner is as significant as the matter'. Yet while Austen believed profoundly in the values of politeness, she is clearly aware in *Pride and Prejudice* that these codes inflict all kinds of social embarrassment, and thwart in particular the needs and aspirations of women. 'Writing from inside the ideology of propriety', Mary Poovey asserts, '[. . .] Austen eventually achieved the freedom necessary not only to identify this ideology but – always tactfully and with ladylike restraint – to criticize the way it shaped and deformed women's desires.'[4]

In general, politeness may be considered as a habit of saying and doing obliging things, or an apparent endeavour to give pleasure, and to avoid giving pain; with a particular attention to the taste and inclination of others, in which the manner is as significant as the matter, and will be as visible in little circumstances as in greater; but does not necessarily include in it an indiscriminate subjection to the caprice of all, who may without reasonable ground expect it, or an unlimited deference even to such who may have just pretensions to a proper regard; for in this, as in all other cases, there must be bounds, otherwise one virtue would exclude all the rest [. . .] Politeness, in the sense here exhibited, is to be industriously cultivated, as conducive to the liberty, ease, pleasure, and mutual satisfaction of society.

2   John Brewer, *The Pleasures of the Imagination: English Culture in the Eighteenth Century* (London: HarperCollins Publishers, 1997), p. 100.

3   Joseph Addison and Richard Steele, *The Spectator*, ed. Donald F. Bond, 5 vols (Oxford: Clarendon Press, 1965), vol. v, p. 174.

4   Mary Poovey, *The Proper Lady and the Woman Writer* (Chicago: University of Chicago Press, 1984), p. 47.

From **James Fordyce, *Sermons to Young Women*,** fourth edition, 2 vols
(London: Millar and Cadell, 1767), vol. i, pp. 192–4

James Fordyce's popular conduct book for young females and married ladies
followed Rousseau in *Émile*, and emphasized how it was 'natural' for women to
be dependent, modest, gentle, meek, grateful, and profoundly ignorant of anything important. In *Pride and Prejudice*, Mr. Collins reads 'with very monotonous
solemnity' from Fordyce's *Sermons*.[1] Fordyce's insistence that a wise man does
not want a 'witty female' collides with Austen's representation (and Darcy's
love) of Elizabeth. 'I dearly love a laugh', Elizabeth remarks, and later her clever
and forthright badinage prompts Darcy 'smilingly' to respond, 'I am not afraid of
you' (see Key Passages, **p. 123, p. 132**). What Fordyce deplores Darcy finds
both formidable and profoundly attractive.

When I speak on this subject, need I tell you, that men of the best sense have
been usually averse to the thought of marrying a witty female?

You will probably tell me, they were afraid of being outshone; and some of
them perhaps might be so. But I am apt to believe, that many of them acted on
different motives. Men who understand the science of domestic happiness, know
that its very first principle is ease. Of that indeed we grow fonder, in whatever
condition, as we advance in life, and as the heat of youth abates. But we cannot
be easy, where we are not safe. We are never safe in the company of a critic; and
almost every wit is a critic by profession. In such company we are not at liberty to
unbend ourselves. All must be the straining of study, or the anxiety of apprehension: how painful! Where the heart may not expand and open itself with freedom, farewel to real friendship, farewel to convivial delight! But to suffer this
restraint at home, what misery! From the brandishings of wit in the hand of ill
nature, of imperious passion, or of unbounded vanity, who would not flee? But
when that weapon is pointed at a husband, is it to be wondered if from his own
house he takes shelter in the tavern? He sought a soft friend; he expected to be
happy in a reasonable companion. He has found a perpetual satirist, or a self-
sufficient prattler. How have I pitied such a man, when I have seen him in con-
tinual fear on his own account, and that of his friends, and for the poor lady
herself; lest, in the run of her discourse, she should be guilty of some petulance, or
some indiscretion, that would expose her and hurt them all! But take the matter
at the best; there is still all the difference in the world between the entertainer of
an evening, and a partner for life. Of the latter a sober mind, steady attachment,
and gentle manners, joined to a good understanding, will ever be the chief
recommendations; whereas the qualities that sparkle will be often sufficient for
the former.

---

1   Jane Austen, *Pride and Prejudice*, ed. R. W. Chapman (Oxford: Clarendon Press, 1923), Volume I,
     Chapter 14, p. 68.

From **John Gregory, *A Father's Legacy to His Daughters*,** new edition (London: Millar, Law, and Cater, 1789), pp. 91–5

Like Rousseau and Fordyce, John Gregory espoused an essentialist view of men and women. He believed that women had very little chance of marrying for love, and that an abiding love had gratitude as a key element. Tellingly, when Darcy first proposes to Elizabeth, she responds, 'It is natural that obligation should be felt, and if I could *feel* gratitude, I would now thank you. But I cannot' (see Key Passages, **p. 135**). When, however, Darcy proposes a second time, Elizabeth 'gave him to understand, that her sentiments had undergone so material a change [. . .] as to make her receive with gratitude and pleasure, his present assurances'.[1] Austen would have rejected a good deal of Gregory's advice, but as Debra Teachman observes, both Austen and Gregory 'recognize many of the same motivating factors for marriages'.[2]

People whose sentiments, and particularly whose tastes, correspond, naturally like to associate together, although neither of them have the most distant view of any farther connexion. But as this similarity of minds often gives rise to a more tender attachment than friendship, it will be prudent to keep a watchful eye over yourselves, lest your hearts become too far engaged before you are aware of it. At the same time, I do not think that your sex, at least in this part of the world, have much of that sensibility which disposes to such attachments. What is commonly called love among you, is rather gratitude, and a partiality to the man who prefers you to the rest of your sex; and such a man you often marry, with little of either personal esteem or affection. Indeed, without an unusual share of natural sensibility, and very peculiar good fortune, a woman in this country has very little probability of marrying for love.

It is a maxim laid down among you, and a very prudent one it is, that love is not to begin on your part, but is entirely to be the consequence of our attachment to you. Now, supposing a woman to have sense and taste, she will not find many men to whom she can possibly be supposed to bear any considerable share of esteem. Among these few, it is a very great chance if any of them distinguishes her particularly. Love, at least with us, is exceedingly capricious, and will not always fix where Reason says it should. But supposing one of them should become particularly attached to her, it is still extremely improbable that he should be the man in the world her heart most approved of.

As, therefore, Nature has not given you that unlimited range in your choice which we enjoy, she has wisely and benevolently assigned to you a greater flexibility of taste on this subject. Some agreeable qualities recommend a gentleman to your common good liking and friendship. In the course of his acquaintance, he contracts an attachment to you. When you perceive it, it excites your gratitude;

1   Jane Austen, *Pride and Prejudice*, ed. R. W. Chapman (Oxford: Clarendon Press, 1923), Volume III, Chapter 16, p. 366.
2   Debra Teachman, *Understanding Pride and Prejudice* (Westport, Conn.: Greenwood Press, 1997), p. 61.

this gratitude rises into a preference, and this preference perhaps at last advances to some degree of attachment, especially if it meets with crosses and difficulties; for these, and a state of suspense, are very great incitements to attachment, and are the food of love in both sexes. If attachment was not excited in your sex in this manner, there is not one of a million of you that could ever marry with any degree of love.

From **Adam Smith, *The Wealth of Nations*,** eds R. H. Campbell and A. S. Skinner, 2 vols (Oxford: Clarendon Press, 1976), vol. i, pp. 383–4

In his seminal treatise on *The Wealth of Nations* (1776), Adam Smith championed a *laissez-faire* economic system in which government interference was kept to a minimum, and individuals were free to pursue their financial interests. Not surprisingly, Smith was firmly against the laws of primogeniture and entail, for they gave exclusive right of inheritance to the eldest son and beggared 'all the rest of the children'. The law of entail is at the heart of *Pride and Prejudice*, and casts a long shadow over the Bennet women. When Mr. and Mrs. Bennet were first married, 'economy was held to be perfectly useless; for, of course, they were to have a son', and this son 'was to join in cutting off the entail, as soon as he should be of age, and the widow and younger children would by that means be provided for'.[1] But Mr. Bennet produced no son and his property is thus 'entailed in default'[2] on a distant male relation, Mr. Collins, for in the law of entail 'the male sex is universally preferred to the female', and five daughters count only as a burden. Smith condemned the law as absurd but it weighs heavily on the Bennet sisters, emphasizing both their acute legal and economic vulnerability, and their urgent need for marriage as the best means of avoiding the destitution that most probably awaits them at the death of their father. 'I do think it is the hardest thing in the world', Mrs. Bennet rightly tells her husband, 'that your estate should be entailed away from your own children'.[3]

The law of primogeniture [. . .] came to take place, not immediately, indeed, but in process of time, in the succession of landed estates, for the same reason that it has generally taken place in that of monarchies, though not always at their first institution. That the power, and consequently the security of the monarchy, may not be weakened by division, it must descend entire to one of the children. To which of them so important a preference shall be given, must be determined by some general rule, founded not upon the doubtful distinctions of personal merit, but upon some plain and evident difference which can admit of no dispute. Among the children of the same family, there can be no indisputable difference but that of sex, and that of age. The male sex is universally preferred to the female; and when all other things are equal, the elder everywhere takes place of

---

1   Jane Austen, *Pride and Prejudice*, ed. R. W. Chapman (Oxford: Clarendon Press, 1923), Volume III, Chapter 8, p. 308.
2   Ibid., Volume I, Chapter 7, p. 28.
3   Ibid., Volume I, Chapter 13, p. 61.

the younger. Hence the origin of the right of primogeniture, and of what is called lineal succession.

Laws frequently continue in force long after the circumstances, which first gave occasion to them, and which could alone render them reasonable, are no more. In the present state of Europe, the proprietor of a single acre of land is as perfectly secure of his possession as the proprietor of a hundred thousand. The right of primogeniture, however, still continues to be respected, and as of all institutions it is the fittest to support the pride of family distinctions, it is still likely to endure for many centuries. In every other respect, nothing can be more contrary to the real interest of a numerous family, than a right which, in order to enrich one, beggars all the rest of the children.

Entails are the natural consequences of the law of primogeniture. They were introduced to preserve a certain lineal succession, of which the law of primogeniture first gave the idea, and to hinder any part of the original estate from being carried out of the proposed line either by gift, or devise, or alienation; either by the folly, or by the misfortune of any of its successive owners [. . .] They are founded upon the most absurd of all suppositions, the supposition that every successive generation of men have not an equal right to the earth, and to all that it possesses; but that the property of the present generation should be restrained and regulated according to the fancy of those who died perhaps five hundred years ago. Entails, however, are still respected through the greater part of Europe.

From **Frances Burney, *Cecilia: or Memoirs of an Heiress*,** eds Peter Sabor and Margaret Anne Doody (Oxford: Oxford University Press, 1988), p. 930

Austen was a great admirer of Frances Burney, whose famous first novel, *Evelina* (1778) was followed by *Cecilia* (1782), which in plot and theme resembles *Pride and Prejudice* 'more nearly than any other single work', as Kenneth Moler details.[1] What is more, though the conjunction of the terms 'pride' and 'prejudice' appears in a number of eighteenth-century texts, including Samuel Richardson's *Sir Charles Grandison*, the most famous precursory instance of the phrase occurs toward the close of *Cecilia*, and draws the moral of the tale.[2]

'The whole of this unfortunate business,' said Dr. Lyster, 'has been the result of PRIDE and PREJUDICE. Your uncle, the Dean, began it, by his arbitrary will, as if an ordinance of his own could arrest the course of nature! and as if *he* had power to keep alive, by the loan of a name, a family in the male branch already extinct. Your father, Mr. Mortimer, continued it with the same self-partiality, preferring the wretched gratification of tickling his ear with a favourite sound, to the solid happiness of his son with a rich and deserving wife. Yet this, however,

1   Kenneth Moler, *Jane Austen's Art of Allusion* (Lincoln: University of Nebraska Press, 1968), p. 81.
2   R. W. Chapman, '*Pride and Prejudice* and *Cecilia*' in *Pride and Prejudice*, ed. R. W. Chapman (Oxford: Clarendon Press, 1923), pp. 408–9.

remember; if to PRIDE and PREJUDICE you owe your miseries, so wonderfully is good and evil balanced, that to PRIDE and PREJUDICE you will also owe their termination'.

From **Mary Wollstonecraft, *Thoughts on the Education of Daughters*** in *The Works of Mary Wollstonecraft*, eds Marilyn Butler and Janet Todd, 7 vols (London: Pickering and Chatto, 1989), vol. iv, pp. 25–6

In *Thoughts on the Education of Daughters* (1787), Mary Wollstonecraft described how the social training young women received enslaved them to men, and vividly outlined the fate that awaited women (like Charlotte Lucas or the five Bennet sisters) if they were 'fashionably educated' but 'left without a fortune'. For all the joy, wit, and fun of *Pride and Prejudice*, there is a pressing social reality which runs just below the surface: for women there must be marriage. If there is not, they face the misery of occupations such as 'companion', 'teacher', or 'governess'. Mrs. Bennet is extravagant and irritating, but she is also under pressure to get all five daughters advantageously matched before spinsterhood sets in. Even sensible Charlotte Lucas is happy to marry a fool like Mr. Collins to avoid such a fate.

I have hitherto only spoken of those females, who will have a provision made for them by their parents. But many who have been well, or at least fashionably educated, are left without a fortune, and if they are not entirely devoid of delicacy, they must frequently remain single.

Few are the modes of earning a subsistence, and those very humiliating. Perhaps to be an humble companion to some rich old cousin, or what is still worse, to live with strangers, who are so intolerably tyrannical, that none of their own relations can bear to live with them, though they should even expect a fortune in reversion. It is impossible to enumerate the many hours of anguish such a person must spend. Above the servants, yet considered by them as a spy, and ever reminded of her inferiority when in conversation with the superiors. If she cannot condescend to mean flattery, she has not a chance of being a favorite; and should any of the visitors take notice of her, and she for a moment forget her subordinate state, she is sure to be reminded of it.

Painfully sensible of unkindness, she is alive to every thing, and many sarcasms reach her, which were perhaps directed another way. She is alone, shut out from equality and confidence, and the concealed anxiety impairs her constitution; for she must wear a cheerful face, or be dismissed. The being dependent on the caprice of a fellow-creature, though certainly very necessary in this state of discipline, is yet a very bitter corrective, which we would fain shrink from.

A teacher at a school is only a kind of upper servant, who has more work than the menial ones.

A governess to young ladies is equally disagreeable. [. . .] The few trades which are left, are now gradually falling into the hands of the men, and certainly they are not very respectable.

From **Edmund Burke, *Reflections on the Revolution in France,*** ed.
J. C. D. Clark (Stanford: Stanford University Press, 2001), pp. 154–5, 237–8

In *Reflections on the Revolution in France* (1790), Edmund Burke damned the French Revolution as unnatural and ruinously wrongheaded, drawing the ire of radicals like Mary Wollstonecraft and William Godwin, but brilliantly articulating a vision of a naturalized social hierarchy in which tradition, rank, culture, and property were revered, and the King and Queen venerated as beloved objects of loyalty and benevolence. Burke regarded the French Revolution as monstrous, for it attacked the aristocracy and the time-honoured institutions of church and state, undermining the deeply-felt if irrational prejudices that bound all of society together. The young Marie Antoinette is for Burke the embodiment of the virtues and civility of the state, and he deplores her degradation at the hands of the revolutionaries. In *Pride and Prejudice*, the conservative element in Austen's thought is often well to the fore as she displays the property and wealth of the British upper classes, and rewards Elizabeth with a rise to aristocratic privilege, and the order, grace, and splendour of Pemberley.

All circumstances taken together, the French revolution is the most astonishing that has hitherto happened in the world. The most wonderful things are brought about in many instances by means the most absurd and ridiculous; in the most ridiculous modes; and apparently, by the most contemptible instruments. Every thing seems out of nature in this strange chaos of levity and ferocity, and of all sorts of crimes jumbled together with all sorts of follies. In viewing this monstrous tragi-comic scene, the most opposite passions necessarily succeed, and sometimes mix with each other in the mind; alternate contempt and indignation; alternate laughter and tears; alternate scorn and horror. [. . .]

It is now sixteen or seventeen years since I saw the queen of France, then the dauphiness, at Versailles;[1] and surely never lighted on this orb, which she hardly seemed to touch, a more delightful vision. I saw her just above the horizon, decorating and cheering the elevated sphere she just began to move in, – glittering like the morning-star, full of life, and splendor, and joy. Oh! what a revolution! and what an heart must I have, to contemplate without emotion that elevation and that fall. Little did I dream when she added titles of veneration to those of enthusiastic, distant, respectful love, that she should ever be obliged to carry the sharp antidote against disgrace concealed in that bosom; little did I dream that I should have lived to see such disasters fallen upon her in a nation of gallant men, in a nation of men of honour and of cavaliers. I thought ten thousand swords must have leaped from their scabbards to avenge even a look that threatened her with insult. – But the age of chivalry is gone. – That of sophisters, oeconomists, and calculators, has succeeded; and the glory of Europe is extinguished for ever. Never, never more, shall we behold that generous loyalty to rank and sex, that

1   Marie Antoinette (1755–93), Queen consort of King Louis XVI of France from 1774 until her death. Burke saw her during his visit to France in early 1773. She died by the guillotine three years after Burke's *Reflections* appeared.

proud submission, that dignified obedience, that subordination of the heart, which kept alive, even in servitude itself, the spirit of an exalted freedom. The unbought grace of life, the cheap defence of nations, the nurse of manly sentiment and heroic enterprize is gone! It is gone, that sensibility of principle, that chastity of honour, which felt a stain like a wound, which inspired courage whilst it mitigated ferocity, which ennobled whatever it touched, and under which vice itself lost half its evil, by losing all its grossness.

From **Edmund Burke, *An Appeal from the New to the Old Whigs*** in *The Works of the Right Honourable Edmund Burke*, 8 vols (London: Bohn, 1854–89), vol. iii, p. 85–6

In his *Appeal from the New to the Old Whigs* (1791), Burke continued to condemn the new revolutionary government in France and celebrate the traditions and hierarchies of the old monarchical government in Britain. The British aristocracy enshrined the virtue, wisdom, custom, and achievement of the nation, and acted 'as a reconciler between God and man'. Darcy is 'bred in a place of estimation'. He is 'taught to respect' himself. He has the 'leisure to read'. His conduct is 'guarded and regulated'. He stands 'upon such elevated ground as to be enabled to take a large view of the wide-spread and infinitely diversified combinations of men and affairs in a large society'. He is acutely aware that 'the slightest mistakes draw on the most ruinous consequences'. For Burke, a man like Darcy is legitimately, justly, and necessarily proud, for he is a member of what 'I should call a *natural* aristocracy, without which there is no nation'. Scarce wonder then that Darcy is initially dismissive of pert and provincial Elizabeth Bennet. 'I was spoilt by my parents', he tells her toward the close of the novel, 'who [. . .] allowed, encouraged, almost taught me to be selfish and overbearing [. . .] to think meanly of all the rest of the world, to *wish* at least to think meanly of their sense and worth compared with my own'.[1] In contemporary Britain, as in the novel itself, such aristocratic hauteur comes under keen and constant pressure, and though Burke would have strongly objected, Darcy is 'properly humbled' by Elizabeth, and his conception of the role of an aristocrat is both discredited and transformed.

A true natural aristocracy is not a separate interest in the state, or separable from it. It is an essential integrant part of any large body rightly constituted. It is formed out of a class of legitimate presumptions, which, taken as generalities, must be admitted for actual truths. To be bred in a place of estimation; to see nothing low and sordid from one's infancy; to be taught to respect one's self; to be habituated to the censorial inspection of the public eye; to look early to public opinion; to stand upon such elevated ground as to be enabled to take a large view of the wide-spread and infinitely diversified combinations of men and affairs in a large society; to have leisure to read, to reflect, to converse; to be enabled to draw

---

1   Jane Austen, *Pride and Prejudice*, ed. R. W. Chapman (Oxford: Clarendon Press, 1923), Volume III, Chapter 16, p. 369.

the court and attention of the wise and learned wherever they are to be found; – to be habituated in armies to command and to obey; to be taught to despise danger in the pursuit of honour and duty; to be formed to the greatest degree of vigilance, foresight, and circumspection, in a state of things in which no fault is committed with impunity, and the slightest mistakes draw on the most ruinous consequences – to be led to a guarded and regulated conduct, from a sense that you are considered as an instructor of your fellow-citizens in their highest concerns, and that you act as a reconciler between God and man – to be employed as an administrator of law and justice, and to be thereby amongst the first benefactors to mankind – to be a professor of high science, or of liberal and ingenuous art – to be amongst rich traders, who from their success are presumed to have sharp and vigorous understandings, and to possess the virtues of diligence, order, constancy, and regularity, and to have cultivated an habitual regard to commutative justice – these are the circumstances of men, that form what I should call a *natural* aristocracy, without which there is no nation.

From **Mary Wollstonecraft,** *A Vindication of the Rights of Woman* in *The Works of Mary Wollstonecraft,* eds Marilyn Butler and Janet Todd, 7 vols (London: Pickering and Chatto, 1989), vol. v, pp. 75, 91, 92–3

In *A Vindication of the Rights of Woman* (1792), Wollstonecraft urges women to aspire to independence, virtue, and dignity, and she condemns the insidious educational doctrines of Rousseau and John Gregory, which 'render women more artificial, weak characters, than they would otherwise have been' (see Contemporary Documents, Rousseau **pp. 26–7**, Gregory **pp. 30–1**). Wollstonecraft also discusses the dangerous lure of 'standing armies', with officers who are 'particularly attentive to their persons' and 'fond of dancing' and 'adventures'. Such advice on soldiers might have benefited both Elizabeth and Lydia. As it is, Elizabeth learns of Wickham in time, but Lydia is more fatally tempted.

My own sex, I hope, will excuse me, if I treat them like rational creatures, instead of flattering their *fascinating* graces, and viewing them as if they were in a state of perpetual childhood, unable to stand alone. I earnestly wish to point out in what true dignity and human happiness consists – I wish to persuade women to endeavour to acquire strength, both of mind and body, and to convince them that the soft phrases, susceptibility of heart, delicacy of sentiment, and refinement of taste, are almost synonymous with epithets of weakness, and that those beings who are only the objects of pity and that kind of love, which has been termed its sister, will soon become objects of contempt.

Dismissing then those pretty feminine phrases, which the men condescendingly use to soften our slavish dependence, and despising that weak elegancy of mind, exquisite sensibility, and sweet docility of manners, supposed to be the sexual characteristics of the weaker vessel, I wish to shew that elegance is inferior to virtue, that the first object of laudable ambition is to obtain a character as a human being, regardless of the distinction of sex; and that secondary views should be brought to this simple touchstone. [. . .]

I may be accused of arrogance; still I must declare what I firmly believe, that all the writers who have written on the subject of female education and manners from Rousseau to Dr. Gregory, have contributed to render women more artificial, weak characters, than they would otherwise have been; and, consequently, more useless members of society. I might have expressed this conviction in a lower key; but I am afraid it would have been the whine of affectation, and not the faithful expression of my feelings, of the clear result, which experience and reflection have led me to draw. [. . .]

Standing armies can never consist of resolute, robust men; they may be well disciplined machines, but they will seldom contain men under the influence of strong passions, or with very vigorous faculties. And as for any depth of understanding, I will venture to affirm, that it is as rarely to be found in the army as amongst women; and the cause, I maintain, is the same. It may be further observed, that officers are also particularly attentive to their persons, fond of dancing, crowded rooms, adventures, and ridicule. Like the *fair* sex, the business of their lives is gallantry. – They were taught to please, and they only live to please. Yet they do not lose their rank in the distinction of sexes, for they are still reckoned superior to women, though in what their superiority consists, beyond what I have just mentioned, it is difficult to discover.

From **William Godwin, *Things as They Are; or, The Adventures of Caleb Williams*** in *Collected Novels and Memoirs of William Godwin*, ed. Pamela Clemit (London: William Pickering, 1992), vol. iii, pp. 161–2

William Godwin's *Caleb Williams* (1794) is a tale of terror and political persecution. Caleb is unjustly imprisoned by a murderous British aristocrat, and in his anger invokes the Bastille, a French state prison stormed by an armed mob of Parisians on 14 July 1789. The dramatic event came to symbolize the beginning of the French Revolution. The British conservative backlash was led by Burke and climaxed with the outbreak of war between England and France in February 1793. A year later, at the very moment Godwin was writing *Caleb Williams*, Austen herself had the deepening political crisis in Europe brought directly home to her when she received the grievous news that Jean Capot de Feuillide, the husband of her cousin, had been guillotined in Paris. In *Caleb Williams*, Godwin gives voice to the kinds of outrage and anxiety that critics complain Austen knew but too easily suppressed in *Pride and Prejudice* in order to represent England as a green and pleasant place of gossiping ladies, beautiful dresses, stunning houses, harmless snobs, and handsome aristocrats.

Thank God, exclaims the Englishman, we have no Bastille! Thank God, with us no man can be punished without a crime! Unthinking wretch! Is that a country of liberty where thousands languish in dungeons and fetters? Go, go, ignorant fool! and visit the scenes of our prisons! witness their unwholesomeness, their filth, the tyranny of their governors, the misery of their inmates! After that show me the man shameless enough to triumph, and say, England has no Bastille! Is there any charge so frivolous upon which men are not consigned to these detested abodes? Is there any villainy that is not practised by justices and prosecutors? But against all this, perhaps you have been told, there is redress. Yes, a redress, that it is the consummation of insult so much as to name! Where shall the poor wretch, reduced to the last despair, and to whom acquittal perhaps comes just time enough to save him from perishing – where shall this man find leisure, and much less money, to see counsel and officers, and purchase the tedious, dear-bought remedy of the law? No, he is too happy to leave his dungeon and the memory of his dungeon behind him; and the same tyranny and wanton oppression become the inheritance of his successor.

For myself I looked round upon my walls, and forward upon the premature death I had too much reason to expect; I consulted my own heart that whispered nothing but innocence; and I said, This is society. This is the object, the distribution of justice, which is the end of human reason. For this sages have been toiled, and the midnight oil has been wasted. This!

From **Jane Austen, 'Letter to Cassandra Austen: 9–10 January 1796, Steventon' in** *Jane Austen's Letters,* ed. Deirdre Le Faye (Oxford: Oxford University Press, 1995), p. 1

This is Austen's first-known letter, and was written in the same year that she began *First Impressions,* the novel she later transformed into *Pride and Prejudice.* Like the novel, it concerns tittle-tattle, dancing, attractive women, and marriageable men. Austen discusses her first love, her 'Irish friend' Tom Lefroy (see Figure 4, **p. 39**), and sounds very much like Lydia Bennet when she recounts how she and Tom indulged in 'everything most profligate and shocking in the way of dancing and sitting down together'. Austen's relationship with Lefroy ended only a few months later, and though she 'tried to show that Tom had meant nothing to her', notes Park Honan, 'her self-esteem and pride soon became driving forces in her own creative work. Ten months after Tom left she began with zeal her Elizabeth Bennet and Darcy story'.[1] In 1798 Austen spoke directly to Lefroy's aunt, but 'she did not once mention the name of [her nephew] to *me,* and I was too proud to make any enquiries'.[2] Details on most of the people mentioned in Austen's letters can be found in the 'Biographical Index' of *Jane Austen's Letters.*[3]

In the first place I hope you will live twenty-three years longer. Mr. Tom Lefroy's birthday was yesterday, so that you are very near of an age.[4] After this necessary preamble I shall proceed to inform you that we had an exceeding good ball last night, and that I was very much disappointed at not seeing Charles Fowle of the

1   Park Honan, *Jane Austen: Her Life* (New York: St. Martin's Press, 1987), pp. 112–3.
2   *Jane Austen's Letters,* ed. Deirdre Le Faye (Oxford: Oxford University Press, 1995), p. 19.
3   'Biographical Index' in ibid., pp. 483–589.
4   Tom Lefroy was born on 8 January 1776 and Cassandra on 9 January 1773.

Figure 4 **Miniature of Tom Lefroy (c. 1800). Austen flirted with him during the winter of 1795–6, just before she began to write** *First Impressions,* **the lost original of** *Pride and Prejudice.*

party, as I had previously heard of his being invited. In addition to our set at the Harwoods' ball, we had the Grants, St. Johns, Lady Rivers, her three daughters and a son, Mr. and Miss Heathcote, Mrs. Lefevre, two Mr. Watkins, Mr. J. Portal, Miss Deanes, two Miss Ledgers, and a tall clergyman who came with them, whose name Mary would never have guessed. We were so terrible good as to take James in our carriage, though there were three of us before; but indeed he deserves encouragement for the very great improvement which has lately taken place in his dancing. Miss Heathcote is pretty, but not near so handsome as I expected. Mr. H. began with Elizabeth, and afterwards danced with her again; but *they* do not know how *to be particular*. I flatter myself, however, that they will profit by the three successive lessons which I have given them. You scold me so much in the nice long letter which I have this moment received from you, that I am almost afraid to tell you how my Irish friend and I behaved. Imagine to yourself everything most profligate and shocking in the way of dancing and sitting down together. I *can* expose myself, however, only *once more*, because he leaves the country soon after next Friday, on which day we *are* to have a dance at Ashe after all. He is a very gentlemanlike, good-looking, pleasant young man, I assure you.

From **Amelia Opie, *Temper, or Domestic Scenes*,** 3 vols (London: Longman, Hurst, Rees, Orme, and Brown, 1812), vol. i, pp. 20–2

The superb opening chapters of *Pride and Prejudice* make it easy to forget that they present a set of themes and situations which were entirely commonplace in the period. Amelia Opie was Austen's contemporary, and like Austen she wrote novels of 'domestic heroism, the moral drama of the home, of conjugal and family life', and she too 'often sets these scenes and motifs against the artificialities and intrigues, the hypocrisy, self-interest, and vice of the public and social world', as Gary Kelly puts it.[1] In *Temper*, Opie clearly anticipates Austen when she introduces in her opening pages a ball which is attended by a young and pretty woman named Agatha Torrington, who 'begins with a partner such as her mother would have most cordially approved', but who is soon interested in a young, handsome, 'proud and fastidious' man named Danvers. He is apparently 'very agreeable [. . .] when he pleases', but on this occasion he leans against the wall and 'dances with no one' because he 'does not think any lady in this part of the world worth the trouble of pleasing'. Elizabeth Bennet meets Mr. Darcy at the Meryton ball only one year later, and in remarkably similar circumstances (see Key Passages, **pp. 114–17**).

Agatha had not been long in the ballroom before her hand for the first two dances was solicited by the eldest son of a viscount, and she began the ball with a partner such as her mother would have most cordially approved. But as her partner was neither young nor handsome, Agatha resolved that, having done homage to pride and propriety in her first choice, she would either dance no more that evening, or dance with one more calculated to please than the right honourable partner whom she had just quitted.

At this minute her attention was directed to a very handsome young man, who, apparently uninterested in any thing that was going forward, was leaning against the wall and seemingly looking on vacancy.

'Look, Miss Torrington, look! that is the handsome Danvers,' said the young

---

1   Gary Kelly, *English Fiction of the Romantic Period, 1789–1830* (London: Longman, 1989), p. 84.

lady on whose arm Agatha was leaning: 'There he is! in a reverie as usual! and though almost all the women in the room are dying to dance with him, the insensible creature looks at no one and dances with no one; but, after exhibiting his fine person for an hour, he will lounge home to bed.'

'Perhaps,' said Agatha, 'the poor man is in love with an absent lady, and thence his indifference to those who are present. He is very handsome.'

'Yes, and very agreeable too, I am told, when he pleases; but he is so proud and fastidious, (for he is not in love, they say,) that he does not think any lady in this part of the world worth the trouble of pleasing.'

'Who is he?' asked Agatha; 'and whence does he come?'

From **Jane Austen, 'Letter to Cassandra Austen: 29 January 1813, Chawton' in** *Jane Austen's Letters,* ed. Deirdre Le Faye (Oxford: Oxford University Press, 1995), pp. 201–2

In the following three letters, Austen describes the publication of *Pride and Prejudice* ('my own darling Child'), the reception it received from her family and friends, and the ways in which her characters lived in her imagination as she searched for their faces in the exhibitions of London portrait painters such as **Sir Joshua Reynolds**. Austen's search lends vivid support to Virginia Woolf's assertion that Austen's characters were 'so rounded and substantial that they have the power to move out of the scenes in which she placed them into other moods and circumstances'.[1] Similarly, Somerset Maugham declared that *Pride and Prejudice* was so readable because Austen 'was so immensely interested in her characters and in what happened to them and because she profoundly believed in them' (see *Novelists on Pride and Prejudice*, **p. 68**).

I want to tell you that I have got my own darling Child from London [. . .] Miss Benn[2] dined with us on the very day of the Books coming, & in the even^g we set fairly at it & read half the 1st vol. to her — prefacing that having intelligence from Henry that such a work w^d soon appear we had desired him to send it whenever it came out — & I beleive it passed with her unsuspected. — She [. . .] really does seem to admire Elizabeth. I must confess that *I* think her as delightful a creature as ever appeared in print, & how I shall be able to tolerate those who do not like *her* at least, I do not know [. . .] The 2^d vol. is shorter than I c^d wish — but the difference is not so much in reality as in look, there being a larger proportion of Narrative in that part. I have lopt & cropt so successfully however that I imagine it must be rather shorter than S. & S.[3] altogether.

1 *The Essays of Virginia Woolf*, ed. Andrew McNeillie, 4 vols (London: Hogarth Press, 1986 – continuing), vol. ii, p. 12.
2 Mary Benn (d. 1816) was a neighbour of the Austens, and living in straitened circumstances in Chawton.
3 Austen's first novel, *Sense and Sensibility* (1811).

From **Jane Austen, 'Letter to Cassandra Austen: 4 February 1813, Chawton' in *Jane Austen's Letters*,** ed. Deirdre Le Faye (Oxford: Oxford University Press, 1995), p. 203

Your letter was truely welcome & I am much obliged to you all for your praise; it came at a right time, for I had had some fits of disgust; — our 2^d evening's reading to Miss Benn had not pleased me so well, but I beleive something must be attributed to my Mother's too rapid way of getting on — & tho' she perfectly understands the Characters herself, she cannot speak as they ought. — Upon the whole however I am quite vain enough & well satisfied enough. — The work is rather too light & bright & sparkling; — it wants shade; — it wants to be stretched out here & there with a long Chapter — of sense if it could be had, if not of solemn specious nonsense — about something unconnected with the story; an Essay on Writing, a critique on Walter Scott, or the history of Buonaparte — or anything that would form a contrast & bring the reader with increased delight to the playfulness & Epigrammatism of the general stile. — I doubt your quite agreeing with me here — I know your starched Notions.

From **Jane Austen, 'Letter to Cassandra Austen: 24 May 1813, London' in *Jane Austen's Letters*,** ed. Deirdre Le Faye (Oxford: Oxford University Press, 1995), pp. 212–3

Henry[1] & I went to the Exhibition in Spring Gardens. It is not thought a good collection, but I was very well pleased — particularly (pray tell Fanny) with a small portrait of Mrs Bingley, excessively like her. I went in hopes of seeing one of her Sister, but there was no Mrs Darcy [. . .] Mrs Bingley's is exactly herself, size, shaped face, features & sweetness; there never was a greater likeness. She is dressed in a white gown, with green ornaments, which convinces me of what I had always supposed, that green was a favourite colour with her. I dare say Mrs D. will be in Yellow [. . .] *Monday even*^{g} — We have been both to the Exhibition & Sir J[oshua]. Reynolds', — and I am disappointed, for there was nothing like Mrs D. at either. — I can only imagine that Mr D. prizes any Picture of her too much to like it should be exposed to the public eye. — I can imagine he w^d have that sort [of *omitted*] feeling – that mixture of Love, Pride & Delicacy.

From **Jane Austen, 'Letter to Anna Austen: 9–18 September 1814, Chawton' in *Jane Austen's Letters*,** ed. Deirdre Le Faye (Oxford: Oxford University Press, 1995), p. 275

In the following two letters, Austen responds to her niece Anna and her nephew James Edward, both of whom are trying their hand at novel writing. Austen's advice clearly suggests her own practices in *Pride and Prejudice*.

---

1   Jane Austen's brother Henry (see Biographical Directory, **p. 44**).

You are now collecting your People delightfully, getting them exactly into such a spot as is the delight of my life; — 3 or 4 Families in a Country Village is the very thing to work on — & I hope you will write a great deal more, & make full use of them while they are so very favourably arranged. You are but *now* coming to the heart & beauty of your book; till the heroine grows up, the fun must be imperfect.

From Jane Austen, 'Letter to James Edward Austen: 16–17 December 1816, Chawton' in *Jane Austen's Letters,* ed. Deirdre Le Faye (Oxford: Oxford University Press, 1995), p. 323

By the bye, my dear Edward, I am quite concerned for the loss your Mother mentions in her Letter; two Chapters & a half to be missing is monstrous! It is well that *I* have not been at Steventon lately, & therefore cannot be suspected of purloining them; — two strong twigs & a half towards a Nest of my own, would have been something. — I do not think however that any theft of that sort would be really very useful to me. What should I do with your strong, manly, spirited Sketches, full of Variety & Glow? — How could I possibly join them on to the little bit (two Inches wide) of Ivory on which I work with so fine a Brush, as produces little effect after much labour?

Biographical Directory

For reasons of space, some names have been omitted; please consult the Contextual Overview for further details of the period. The names in this section appear in bold on their first occurrence in the sourcebook.

Addison, Joseph (1672–1719), English essayist and poet, was a leading contributor to the periodicals *The Tatler* (1709–11) and *The Spectator* (1711–12, 1714).

Amis, Martin (1949–), English novelist, is best known for *The Rachel Papers* (1973), *Dead Babies* (1975), *Success* (1978), and *Time's Arrow* (1991).

Austen, Cassandra (1773–1845) was Austen's devoted sister, heiress, and executrix. In 1792 she was engaged to Reverend Thomas Fowle (1765–97), but he died in the West Indies and she remained single.

Austen, George (1731–1805) was Austen's father, and rector of Steventon from 1761 to 1801.

Austen, Henry (1771–1850), Austen's fourth brother, was Captain of the Oxfordshire Militia and later perpetual curate of Bentley in Hampshire. He was the first to provide biographical information about his sister in his introduction to the posthumously published *Northanger Abbey* and *Persuasion* (1818).

Bigg-Wither, Harris (1781–1833) proposed to Austen on 2 December 1802. She accepted him, only to withdraw her consent the next day.

Blake, William (1757–1827) was a poet, painter, and engraver. His major works include *America: A Prophecy* (1793), *Europe: A Prophecy* (1794), *The Book of Los* (1795), and *The Four Zoas* (c. 1796–1807).

Bridges, Edward (1779–1825) seems to have proposed to Austen in the summer of 1805. He was perpetual curate of Goodnestone (1802–9) and Wingham (1817–25), both in Kent.

Brontë, Charlotte (1816–55), English novelist, is best known for *Jane Eyre* (1847). She is one of Austen's most famously unsympathetic readers.

Burke, Edmund (1729–97), Irish-born statesman, orator, and political philosopher, is most celebrated for his *Reflections on the Revolution in France* (1790), which champions conservatism and denounces the radical doctrines of the French revolutionaries.

Burney, Frances (1752–1840), English letter writer and novelist, is best remembered for *Evelina* (1778), *Cecilia* (1782), and *Camilla* (1796).

Chesterton, G. K. (1874–1936) was a poet, essayist, and critic, but is best known for novels such as *The Napoleon of Notting Hill* (1904) and *The Man Who Was Thursday* (1908), as well as the popular series of detective stories that began with *The Innocence of Father Brown* (1911).

Coleridge, Samuel Taylor (1771–1834), English poet, literary critic, and philosopher, co-wrote *Lyrical Ballads* with William Wordsworth in 1798, and published *Biographia Literaria* in 1817.

Cowper, William (1731–1800), English poet, was much admired by Austen. He wrote the *Olney Hymns* (1779) and *The Task* (1785).

Davy, Jane (1780–1855) was a wealthy widow well known in English social and literary circles. In 1812 she married the famous chemist Sir Humphrey Davy.

Egerton, Thomas was Austen's first publisher, and brought out *Sense and Sensibility*, *Pride and Prejudice*, and the first edition of *Mansfield Park*.

de Feuillide, Eliza (née Hancock; 1761–1813) was Austen's cousin. In 1781 she married Jean François Capot de Feuillide, who was guillotined in Paris in 1794. Three years later she married Austen's brother Henry (see above).

Fordyce, James (1720–96), Scottish minister and writer, was a devout follower of Rousseau's unenlightened opinions on women. He authored the popular conduct book, *Sermons to Young Women* (1766).

Godwin, William (1757–1836) was a radical political philosopher who in *An Enquiry Concerning Political Justice* (1793) attacked the conservative ideologies of Edmund Burke. He continued his hostile critique of the British aristocracy in his terror novel *Things as they are; or The Adventures of Caleb Williams* (1794).

Gregory, John (1724–73), Scottish physician and author, followed the doctrines of Rousseau in his popular conduct book, *A Father's Legacy to His Daughters* (1774).

Highmore, Joseph (1692–1780) was an English painter who in 1744 designed a series of twelve illustrations for Samuel Richardson's novel *Pamela* (1740). He was also a prolific author.

Howells, William Dean (1837–1920), American novelist, editor and critic, was a champion of literary realism. He wrote dozens of novels, including *A Modern Instance* (1882), *The Rise of Silas Lapham* (1885), and *A Hazard of New Fortunes* (1890).

Johnson, Samuel (1709–84), essayist, poet, lexicographer, critic, and biographer, was one of the foremost literary figures of the eighteenth century.

Lefroy, Tom (1776–1869) was Austen's first serious flirtation in 1795–6. He married Mary Paul in 1799. He became Lord Chief Justice of Ireland in 1852.

Lewes, George Henry (1817–78) is best known as the consort of the novelist George Eliot (née Mary Anne Evans), but he was a distinguished critic, editor, scientist, and philosopher. He published two novels, *Ranthorpe* (1847) and *Rose, Blanche and Violet* (1848).

Lodge, David (1935–) has produced important works of literary criticism such as *Working with Structuralism* (1981) and *After Bakhtin* (1990), as well as a series of novels, including *Ginger, You're Barmy* (1962), *Changing Places* (1975), *Small World* (1984), and *Nice Work* (1988).

Martineau, Harriet (1802–76) first found publishing success with *Illustrations of Political Economy* (1832–34), a monthly series of didactic fables. Later she wrote on all the major social and political issues of the day.

Maugham, W. Somerset (1874–1965) produced novels such as the semi-autobiographical *Of Human Bondage* (1915), as well as a series of fine short stories, collected in volumes such as *The Trembling of a Leaf* (1921) and *Ashenden* (1928). As a playwright, he wrote a string of highly successful social comedies.

Milbanke, Annabella (1792–1860) was a clever but spoiled child who liked mathematics and read widely. She entered London society in the spring of 1812. Her disastrous marriage to Lord Byron in 1815 lasted less than a year.

Mitford, Mary Russell (1787–1855), dramatist, novelist, poet, and essayist, wrote charming sketches of English village life that were collected as *Our Village* (1824–32). Her other fiction includes *Belford Regis: Sketches of a Country Town* (1835) and a novel, *Atherton, and Other Tales* (1854).

Oliphant, Margaret (1828–97) was a prolific Scottish novelist whose greatest success came with the seven-volume *Chronicles of Carlingford*, which featured *Salem Chapel* (1863), *The Perpetual Curate* (1864) and, most enduringly, *Miss Marjoribanks* (1866), a comic novel whose heroine is clearly reminiscent of Austen's Emma Woodhouse.

Opie, Amelia Alderson (1769–1853), English novelist and poet, inherited the radicalism of her parents, and was in her youth a friend of Mary Wollstonecraft and William Godwin. In 1798 she married the portrait painter John Opie. Her novels include *Father and Daughter* (1801), *Adeline Mowbray* (1805), and *Temper* (1812).

Pope, Alexander (1688–1744), English poet and satirist, celebrated for *The Rape of the Lock* (1712–14), *The Dunciad* (1728), and *An Essay on Man* (1733–4).

Pritchett, V. S. (1900–97) wrote collections of short stories such as *You Make Your Own Life* (1938) and *When My Girl Comes Home* (1961), as well as a series of novels, including *Dead Man Leading* (1937) and *Mr. Beluncle* (1951).

Reynolds, Sir Joshua (1723–92), portrait painter and aesthetician, exerted an enormous influence on English artistic life in the middle and late eighteenth century. In 1768 he was elected the first president of the Royal Academy.

Richardson, Samuel (1689–1761), English novelist, is celebrated for the detailed intensity and psychological subtlety of *Pamela* (1740), *Clarissa* (1747–8), and *Sir Charles Grandison* (1753–4).

Robinson, Henry Crabb (1775–1867), man of letters, lawyer, and foreign correspondent, wrote voluminous diaries which provide fascinating information on the political and cultural life of nineteenth-century Britain.

Rousseau, Jean-Jacques (1712–78), French philosopher, championed liberty and equality in political writings such as the *Social Contract* (1762). His progressive views, however, did not extend to women, whom he regarded as physically, intellectually, and morally inferior to men.

Scott, Walter (1771–1832), Scottish poet and hugely successful novelist, was an incisive and generous critic of Austen.

Sheridan, Richard Brinsley (1751–1816), Irish-born playwright and Whig politician, is best remembered for *The Rivals* (1775) and *The School for Scandal* (1777).

Smith, Adam (1723–90), economist and philosopher, was a major figure of the Scottish Enlightenment, and a friend of David Hume and Edmund Burke. His most influential works are *The Theory of Moral Sentiments* (1759) and *The Wealth of Nations* (1776).

Twain, Mark (1835–1910), American author, is best known for *The Adventures of Tom Sawyer* (1876) and *The Adventures of Huckleberry Finn* (1884).

Wollstonecraft, Mary (1759–97) was one of the most famous radical voices of her day, and a passionate advocate of educational and social equality for women. Her *Vindication of the Rights of Men* (1790) was a caustic and principled reply to Edmund Burke's condemnation of the French Revolution in *Reflections on the*

Revolution in France, while her *Vindication of the Rights of Woman* (1792) argued that true political freedom meant equality of the sexes.

Woolf, Virginia (1882–1941) was one of the leading members of the so-called 'Bloomsbury Group', an informal association of artists, writers, and philosophers. Her major novels include *Mrs. Dalloway* (1925), *To the Lighthouse* (1927), and *Orlando* (1928), while her brilliant literary criticism is collected in volumes such as *The Common Reader* (1925). In *A Room of One's Own* (1929), Woolf describes the difficulties encountered by women writers in a man's world.

Wordsworth, William (1770–1850), English poet, was best known in Austen's lifetime for *Lyrical Ballads* (1798; co-written with Samuel Taylor Coleridge) and *The Excursion* (1814).

2

Interpretations

Critical History

'I began a commentary on the works of Jane Austen', declares Morris Zapp in **David Lodge's**[1] campus novel *Small World*, 'the aim of which was to be utterly exhaustive, to examine the novels from every conceivable angle – historical, biographical, rhetorical, mythical, structural, Freudian, Jungian, Marxist, existentialist, Christian, allegorical, ethical, phenomenological, archetypal, you name it' (see Novelists on *Pride and Prejudice*, **p. 69**). The extracts in this section are by no means 'utterly exhaustive', but they cover many of the angles listed by Zapp, and demonstrate the remarkably varied and incisive nature of some of the best criticism that has appeared on *Pride and Prejudice* from its original publication until the present.

The Early Critical Reception of the novel came in both published reviews and private letters and diaries. Lord Byron's future wife **Annabella Milbanke** thought *Pride and Prejudice* 'the *most probable* fiction I have ever read' (see **p. 56**), though the anonymous reviewer in the *British Critic* (like many subsequent critics) pointed to inconsistencies in the character of Darcy, whose 'easy unconcern and fashionable indifference, somewhat abruptly changes to the ardent lover' (see **p. 55**). **Henry Crabb Robinson** recommended the novel for 'the perfectly colloquial style of the dialogue' (see **p. 57**), but **Jane Davy** snobbishly disapproved because its 'picture of vulgar minds and manners [. . .] is unrelieved by the agreeable contrast of more dignified and refined characters' (see **p. 57**). The *Critical Review* was decidedly impressed: *Pride and Prejudice*, it concluded, 'rises very superior to any novel we have lately met with in the delineation of domestic scenes' (see **p. 56**).

From the outset, some of the most insightful criticism of the novel has come from other novelists. Austen's 'chief admirers have always been those who write novels themselves', noted Virginia Woolf, 'and from the time of Sir Walter Scott [. . .] she has been praised with unusual discrimination'.[2] Novelists on *Pride and Prejudice* contains the comments of fourteen novelists extending from **Mary Russell Mitford** in the early nineteenth century to Martin Amis in the late twentieth century. These writers explore Austen's commonplace and uneventful

---

1   As noted in previous sections, figures whose names appear in bold are included in the Biographical Directory, **pp. 44–8**.
2   *The Essays of Virginia Woolf*, ed. Andrew McNeillie, 4 vols (London: Hogarth Press, 1986 – continuing), vol. iii, p. 268.

world, compare her to other novelists, and reflect on a wide-ranging series of issues, including her selflessness, satire, realism, politics, language, readability, and inexhaustibility. Despite Woolf's enthusiasm, however, some novelists have responded coolly to Austen. **Charlotte Brontë** found her straitlaced and passionless while, notoriously, every time **Mark Twain** read *Pride and Prejudice* he wanted to dig up Austen and 'beat her over the skull with her own shin-bone!' (see **p. 64**).

Modern Criticism of Austen is usually said to commence with Mary Lascelles's *Jane Austen and her Art* (1939), which is the first detailed and penetrating study of her novels. Lascelles concludes her book with warm words on the intimacy and affection that exists between Austen and her readers. 'What distinguishes Jane Austen's manner of inviting us to share in the act of creation but a greater delicacy of intimation?', writes Lascelles. '[. . .] It is implicit in all her dealings with us'.[3] D. W. Harding's 'Regulated Hatred: An Aspect of the Work of Jane Austen' appeared only one year later, and like Lascelles he proved himself a thorough and attentive reader of Austen. But the conclusions of the two critics could hardly have been more different. Harding represented Austen as a distinctly twentieth-century figure, neither a prudish and demure spinster nor a delicate and warm-hearted ironist, but an alienated and modern subversive bent on ridiculing the very people who embrace the world she represents. Previous readings of Austen had too often found comedy and twinkle. Harding recognized her anger and isolation. In *Jane Austen: Irony as Defense and Discovery*, Marvin Mudrick developed and expanded Harding's views, portraying Austen as a tough-minded writer who used irony to protect herself from both the demands of her society and the depths of her own feelings. Other commentators paid increasing attention to the political, economic, and linguistic dimensions of Austen's work. Like Harding and Mudrick, David Daiches firmly rejected representations of Austen as 'escapist', for his Marxist reading demonstrates that she knew all about the harsh economic realities of spinsterhood and the marriage market. Similarly, Mark Schorer finds that the humour in *Pride and Prejudice* is generated by alienation and injustice, as the aristocrats cling to what the bourgeois desire. Dorothy Van Ghent's focus is on language. Harding describes Mr. Collins as a 'comic monster' because he shows clearly how 'economic and social institutions have such power over the values of personal relationships' (see **p. 72**). Van Ghent comes from a very different angle, but arrives at much the same conclusion. Mr. Collins is a 'moral monstrosity', though in this instance 'Language is the mirror of his degeneracy' (see **p. 76**). Howard Babb is also interested in Austen's language, and explores the ways in which Elizabeth and Darcy communicate their intentions and insights through a complex series of social rituals and rhetorical codes.

Innovative, diverse, and searching criticism of *Pride and Prejudice* has continued in recent decades. Alistair Duckworth's *The Improvement of the Estate* analyses Austen's novels as responsive to the political and moral controversies of her age, and represents her as a conservative writer who is deeply invested in traditional values and responsibilities, and who looks with apprehension at a contemporary world of recklessness, innovation, mobility, and social disorder.

---

3   Mary Lascelles, *Jane Austen and her Art* (Oxford: Clarendon Press, 1939), p. 219.

Pride and Prejudice has often been celebrated for its brightness and warmth, but feminist critics such as Nina Auerbach find it a shadowland that women inhabit as they wait for men. The case of Charlotte Lucas, observes Robert Polhemus, 'must concern anyone who thinks seriously about the history of women', and he proceeds to show how economic and social pressures force Charlotte into the life of a respectable prostitute (see **p. 89**). Mary Bennet has often been read as silly or humorous, but Steven Scott finds her an almost tragic figure who 'lives for herself and the part of the world that she touches', and who in this sense deserves to be admired as a 'precursor of a modern woman' (see **p. 98**). For Mary Poovey, *Pride and Prejudice* exposes the acute vulnerability of women like Elizabeth Bennet, but Austen did not have the strength of her own feminist insights, and so she opted for a fairytale conclusion that was aesthetically satisfying rather than politically responsible. Several other critics agree. Judith Lowder Newton argues that the novel is a fantasy in which Elizabeth seems to retain power even as she crumples into a wife. Using Freudian theory, Susan Fraiman reveals that in the male-dominated world of *Pride and Prejudice*, Elizabeth briefly finds power and security as a kind of surrogate son to her father, but ultimately he must betray her by turning her into a gift and handing her over to a husband. To other critics, however, such arguments are misguided and unjust, both to Elizabeth and to Austen. At stake here is whether or not in *Pride and Prejudice* Austen capitulated to the power structures of patriarchy and aristocracy, or whether she defied these structures in favour of self-assertion, bourgeois aspiration, and the dignity of women. Elizabeth does not become aristocratic. Darcy is democratized. Alison Sulloway asserts that he learns to divest himself of the aristocratic myths of privilege and entitlement, and Elizabeth finds herself loved by a man who respects her. In a battle of the sexes shot through with irony and misconception, argues Allan Bloom, the marriage of Elizabeth and Darcy unites two equals, two 'equivalent centres of self' as John Wiltshire (quoting George Eliot) observes in his psychoanalytic reading (see **p. 97**). From a very different vantage point, Douglas Murray makes an analogous assertion, using the theorizations of Michel Foucault to demonstrate that in *Pride and Prejudice* Elizabeth is closely associated with eyes, and her 'resistance and independence of mind amid powerful forces of conformity' (see **p. 95**) mean that she is equal to even the sternest aristocratic stare. Similarly, Claudia Johnson declares that Austen looked squarely at the political situation of the day, and she reached a conclusion that pushes forward into social criticism, not backward into wish fulfilment. In *Pride and Prejudice*, the apparently private sphere bristles with political resonance. Elizabeth and Darcy are mutually transformed through the agency of candid and extended debate as Austen re-imagines a form of conservatism capable of embracing and legitimating subversive demands and beliefs.

The Novel in Performance section features three discussions of the 1995 BBC film of *Pride and Prejudice*. Colin Firth, who played Darcy, explains his understanding of the role, and offers interesting qualifications to the judgements of literary critics. Cheryl Nixon explores the crucial differences between Austen's presentation of Darcy and screenwriter Andrew Davies's transformation of the character for the film. Lisa Hopkins describes how the film illuminates the 'need' in which 'we most want to believe' (see **p. 107**).

The excerpts in this section of the sourcebook present *Pride and Prejudice* from many different – and sometimes diametrically opposed – points of view. Depending on the critical perspective, *Pride and Prejudice* is a comedy, a fantasy, a nightmare. For some it ignores the contemporary political scene while for others it speaks directly to the Napoleonic Wars. One critical camp contends that Elizabeth compels Darcy's interest with her energy and impertinence, while another declares that she waits in a darkening limbo land for his approval. Does Elizabeth stand up to patriarchy or is she humiliated by it? Does marriage reduce her or does it make her whole? Is she is a lover, a savage, an instructor, a temptress, a servant, a gold-digger, or a partner? Is the novel finally about money, love, women, class, patriarchy, individualism, democracy, or defeat? The excerpts throughout this section explore many such questions and paradoxes, and reveal the exciting and remarkable range of readings the novel has produced. Test your own ideas against these critical debates and assessments, and use them to develop readings of your own that are nuanced, broadminded, and incisive.

Many of the articles in this section comment directly on the scenes and dialogues found in the Key Passages section, and are cued there by a series of cross-references. Several articles also link back to the work of the writers collected in the Contemporary Documents section, and are similarly cross-referenced.

Early Critical Reception

From **Anonymous, '*Pride and Prejudice*'** in *British Critic*, 41, February 1813, pp. 189–90

> The *British Critic* was founded in 1793, and was firmly committed to Tory principles in Church and State. Half of this brief review was devoted to plot summary, but the anonymous critic also commented revealingly on character. Like the similarity in the openings of Amelia Opie's *Temper* and Austen's *Pride and Prejudice* (see Contemporary Documents, **pp. 40–1**), Mr. Collins and Lydia Bennet can seem strikingly original to us, but they represented well-known types in Austen's England.

It is very far superior to almost all the publications of the kind which have lately come before us [. . .] Of the characters, Elizabeth Bennet, the heroine, is supported with great spirit and consistency throughout; there seems no defect in the portrait; this is not precisely the case with Darcy her lover; his easy unconcern and fashionable indifference, somewhat abruptly changes to the ardent lover. The character of Mr. Collins, the obsequious rector, is excellent. Fancy presents us with many such, who consider the patron of exalted rank as the model of all that is excellent on earth, and the patron's smiles and condescension as the sum of human happiness. Mr. Bennet, the father of Elizabeth, presents us with some novelty of character; a reserved, acute, and satirical, but indolent personage, who sees and laughs at the follies and indiscretions of his dependents, without making any exertions to correct them. The picture of the younger Miss Bennets, their perpetual visits to the market town where officers are quartered, and the result, is perhaps exemplified in every provincial town in the kingdom.

From **Anonymous, 'Pride and Prejudice'** in *Critical Review*, fourth series, 3.3, March 1813, pp. 318–24

> The *Critical Review* was founded in 1756. During Austen's day it was liberal in its politics but 'old school' in its literary criticism, disapproving of innovation and championing the virtues of decorum, propriety, and consistency. Its anonymous review of *Pride and Prejudice* was positive but largely devoted to plot summary. It recognized the complicated nature of Mr. Bennet, for his 'amusement in absurdity [. . .] is by no means of advantage to his five daughters'. Like Mary Wollstonecraft, it too warned of 'the danger' young women incurred in associating with officers (see Contemporary Documents, **p. 37**).

Though Mr. Bennet finds amusement in absurdity, it is by no means of advantage to his five daughters, who, with the help of their silly mother, are looking out for husbands. Jane, the eldest daughter, is very beautiful, and possesses great feeling, good sense, equanimity, cheerfulness, and elegance of manners [. . .] Mary is a female pedant, affecting great wisdom, though saturated with stupidity [. . .] Kitty is weak-spirited and fretful; but Miss Lydia [. . .] is mad after the officers who are quartered at Meryton [. . .]

Although these young ladies claim a great share of the reader's interest and attention, none calls forth our admiration so much as Elizabeth, whose archness and sweetness of manner render her a very attractive object in the family piece. She is in fact the *Beatrice* of the tale; and falls in love on much the same principles of contrariety.[1] [. . .] An excellent lesson may be learned from the elopement of Lydia: – the work also shows the folly of letting young girls have their own way, and the danger which they incur in associating with the officers, who may be quartered in or near their residence [. . .]

We cannot conclude, without repeating our approbation of this performance, which rises very superior to any novel we have lately met with in the delineation of domestic scenes.

From **Annabella Milbanke (later Lady Byron) to her mother, Judith Noel, the Hon. Lady Milbanke, 1 May 1813** in Malcolm Elwin, *Lord Byron's Wife* (New York: Harcourt, Brace & World, 1963), p. 159

I have finished the Novel called Pride & Prejudice, which I think a very superior work. It depends not on any of the common resources of Novel writers, no drownings, nor conflagrations, nor runaway horses, nor lapdogs & parrots, nor chambermaids & milliners, nor rencontres and disguises. I really think it the *most probable* fiction I have ever read. It is not a crying book, but the interest is very strong, especially for Mr. Darcy. The characters which are not amiable are diverting, and all of them are consistently supported. I wish much to know who is the author or *ess* as I am told.

---

1   Beatrice is the sharp and cynical heroine in Shakespeare's comedy *Much Ado About Nothing*. She and Benedick engage in a war of wits, but eventually fall in love.

From **Jane Davy, letter to Sarah Ponsonby, 14 May 1813** in *The Hamwood Papers of the Ladies of Llangollen and Caroline Hamilton*, ed. Mrs. G. H. Bell (London: Macmillan, 1930), p. 351

'Pride and Prejudice' I do not very much like. Want of interest is the fault I can least excuse in works of mere amusement, and however natural the picture of vulgar minds and manners is there given, it is unrelieved by the agreeable contrast of more dignified and refined characters occasionally captivating attention. Some power of new character is, however, ably displayed, and Mr. Bennet's indifference is in truth not exaggeration.

From **Henry Crabb Robinson, diary entry for 12 January 1819** in *Henry Crabb Robinson on Books and Their Writers*, ed. Edith J. Morley, 3 vols (London: Dent, 1938), vol. i, p. 227

I sat up till two [. . .] to finish *Pride and Prejudice*. This novel I consider as one of the most excellent of the works of our female novelists. Its merit lies in the characters, and in the perfectly colloquial style of the dialogue. Mrs. Bennet, the foolish mother, who cannot conceal her projects to get rid of her daughters, is capitally drawn. There is a thick-headed servile parson, also a masterly sketch. His stupid letters and her ridiculous speeches are as delightful as wit. The two daughters are well contrasted – the gentle and candid Jane and the lively but prejudiced Elizabeth, are both good portraits, and the development of the passion between Elizabeth and the proud Darcy, who at first hate each other, is executed with skill and effect.

From **Henry Crabb Robinson, letter to Mrs. William Pattisson, 1 February 1819** in *Henry Crabb Robinson on Books and Their Writers*, ed. Edith J. Morley, 3 vols (London: Dent, 1938), vol. iii, p. 851

The merit [of *Pride and Prejudice*] lies in the perfect truth of the painting. The dialogue is exquisitely in character and the characters, tho' not ideal, are charming. The women especially are drawn after the life and Mrs. Bennet is a very jewel [. . .] Mr. Collins too, the sneaking and servile parson, is quite a masterpiece. The heroines (for there are a brace of them) are as natural as beauties can be and as beautiful as any successful portrait can be.

Novelists on *Pride and Prejudice*

From **The Life of Mary Russell Mitford**, ed. A. G. L'Estrange, 3 vols (London: Richard Bentley, 1870), vol. i, pp. 300 and 305–6

Mary Russell Mitford was an ambivalent admirer of Austen. In the first letter, she offers qualified praise of *Pride and Prejudice*, but sounds like the aristocratically snobbish Caroline Bingley when she pronounces Elizabeth's manners 'a mixture of pride and impertinence', and finds Elizabeth herself has 'no stile' and 'no taste'.[1] In the second letter, Mitford remembers her mother's account of Austen as a young, silly, husband-hunting girl. The description recalls Lydia Bennet, and forms a striking contrast to reports of the older, 'unbending' spinster who published *Pride and Prejudice*. Mitford's letter reminds us that Austen began *Pride and Prejudice* when she was twenty, but published it when she was thirty-seven. Claire Tomalin writes that Mitford's tone in the second letter is 'patently malicious, but this does not mean she is wholly wrong in what she says'.[2] Figure 5 (see **p. 59**) is a portrait of Austen around 1811, two years before the publication of *Pride and Prejudice* and four years before Mitford describes her as 'perpendicular, precise, taciturn'. Martin Amis declares that 'Elizabeth Bennet is Jane Austen with added spirit, with subversive passion, and, above all, with looks [. . .] The dull fact of Jane Austen's spinsterhood – her plainness, her childlessness, her virgin death – invests her comedies with disappointment',[3] a disappointment that is perhaps visible in this portrait.

From **Mary Russell Mitford to Sir William Elford, 20 December 1814**

The want of elegance is almost the only want in Miss Austen. [. . .] It is impossible not to feel in every line of 'Pride and Prejudice,' in every word of 'Elizabeth,' the entire want of taste which could produce so pert, so worldly a heroine as the

1   Jane Austen, *Pride and Prejudice*, ed. R. W. Chapman (Oxford: Clarendon Press, 1923), Volume I, Chapter 8, p. 35.
2   Claire Tomalin, *Jane Austen: A Life* (London: Viking, 1997), p. 312.
3   Martin Amis, 'Miss Jane's Prime' in *The Atlantic*, 265.2 (February 1990), p. 101.

Figure 5 **Sketch of Jane Austen by her sister Cassandra, c. 1811. This is the single extant image of Austen's face drawn from life.**

beloved of such a man as Darcy. Wickham is equally bad. Oh! they were just fit for each other, and I cannot forgive that delightful Darcy for parting them. Darcy should have married Jane. He is of all the admirable characters the best designed and the best sustained.

From *Mary Russell Mitford to Sir William Elford, 13 February 1815*

A propos to novels, I have discovered that our great favourite, Miss Austen, is my countrywoman; that mamma knew all her family very intimately; and that she herself is an old maid (I beg her pardon – I mean a young lady) with whom mamma before her marriage was acquainted. Mamma says that she was then the prettiest, silliest, most affected, husband-hunting butterfly she ever remembers; and a friend of mine, who visits her now, says that she has stiffened into the most perpendicular, precise, taciturn piece of 'single blessedness'[4] that ever existed, and that, till 'Pride and Prejudice' showed what a precious gem was hidden in that unbending case, she was no more regarded in society than a poker or a fire-screen, or any other thin upright piece of wood or iron that fills its corner in peace and quietness. The case is very different now; she is still a poker – but a poker of whom every one is afraid.

From *The Journal of Walter Scott,* ed. W. E. K. Anderson (Oxford: Clarendon Press, 1972), p. 114

Walter Scott was a steadfast Tory and the author of the hugely successful Waverley novels, which typically placed a large number of vivid and diverse characters in a tumultuous historical setting, and dramatically enacted the momentous collision of different classes, cultures, regions, and societies. In the following extract, Scott revealingly compares the 'Big Bow wow' method of his own novels to the 'exquisite touch' of Austen's.

Sir Walter Scott's Journal, entry for 14 March 1826

Also read again and for the third time at least Miss Austen's very finely written novel of *Pride and Prejudice*. That young lady had a talent for describing the involvements and feelings and characters of ordinary life which is to me the most wonderful I ever met with. The Big Bow wow strain I can do myself like any now going but the exquisite touch which renders ordinary common-place things and characters interesting from the truth of the description and the sentiment is denied to me. What a pity such a gifted creature died so early!

From **Harriet Martineau, *Society in America*,** 2 vols (New York: Saunders and Otley, 1837), vol. ii, pp. 275–6

Harriet Martineau was a committed radical who campaigned vigorously on behalf of political reform, the abolition of the slave trade, and the rights of women. She considered Austen 'a glorious novelist',[1] and re-read all of Austen before she began work on her best-known novel, *Deerbrook* (1839),[2] a study of

---

4   'Single blessedness' is 'the unmarried state' (*Oxford English Dictionary*). Mitford draws on Shakespeare, *A Midsummer Night's Dream*, I.i.78: 'Grows, lives, and dies in single blessedness'.

1   Deborah Anna Logan, *The Hour and the Woman: Harriet Martineau's 'Somewhat Remarkable' Life* (DeKalb: Northern Illinois University Press, 2002), p. 22.
2   Margaret Kirkham, *Jane Austen, Feminism and Fiction* (Sussex: The Harvester Press, 1983), p. 169.

English provincial life that unsurprisingly reminded several contemporaries of Austen. Mary Shelley observed that, 'without Miss Austen's humour', Martineau has 'all her vividness & correctness. To compensate for the absence of humour she has higher philosophical views'.[3] The *Edinburgh Review* concluded that in Martineau and Austen 'there is the same microscopic observation of foibles – the same quick sense of the ridiculous, especially as displayed in affectation and pretension; both avoid the leaven of romance; and both draw their scenes among country society of the middle classes'.[4] In *Society in America*, Martineau discussed *Pride and Prejudice*, and invoked the distinction between democratic America and aristocratic Britain. If the Bennets were American, 'the superior minds of the family would take the lead'. But the Bennets are English, and so the parents' authority is viewed 'as a right' that is theirs no matter how 'lenient they may be in the use of it'.

A question was asked me, oftener than once, which indicates the difference between family manners in England and America. I was asked whether it was possible that the Bennet family would act as they are represented in 'Pride and Prejudice:' whether a foolish mother, with grown up daughters, would be allowed to spoil the two youngest, instead of the sensible daughters taking the case into their own hands. It is certainly true that in America the superior minds of the family would take the lead; while in England, however the domestic affairs might gradually arrange themselves, no person would be found breathing the suggestion of superseding the mother's authority. The most remarkable difference is, that in England the parents value the authority as a right, however lenient they may be in the use of it. In America, the parent disapproves of it, as a matter of reason: and, if he acts rationally, had rather not possess it.

From ***The Letters of Charlotte Brontë,*** ed. Margaret Smith, 2 vols (Oxford: Clarendon Press, 1995 – continuing), vol. ii, p. 10

In *Jane Eyre*, Charlotte Brontë combined Gothicism with moral realism and an impassioned statement of woman's claim to independence. Brontë was – perhaps not surprisingly – unimpressed by *Pride and Prejudice*, and her views have often been taken as a rallying cry for the critical camp that finds Austen's world narrow, flat, and uninteresting. Brontë 'provides the key statement of the Romantic case against Jane Austen', B. C. Southam notes, 'a case determined as much by a personal, temperamental incompatibility as by the moment of history'.[1] In the

---

3   *The Letters of Mary Wollstonecraft Shelley*, ed. Betty Bennett, 3 vols (Baltimore: Johns Hopkins University Press, 1980–8), vol. ii, p. 314.
4   'Deerbrook; A Novel. By Harriet Martineau' in *Edinburgh Review*, 69 (July 1839), pp. 495–6 (this review has been attributed to the minor novelist Thomas Henry Lister, though not definitively).

1   B. C. Southam, 'Introduction' in *Jane Austen: The Critical Heritage*, ed. B. C. Southam, 2 vols (London: Routledge & Kegan Paul, 1968–1987), vol. i, p. 24.

following extract, Tony Tanner stresses Brontë's 'preponderant vocabulary of boundaries – "accurate", "carefully fenced, highly cultivated gardens", "neat borders", "elegant but confined houses". Her own impulse is towards the "open country" and the boundless "air"'.[2]

From **Charlotte Brontë to George Henry Lewes,** 12 January 1848

Why do you like Miss Austen so very much? I am puzzled on that point.

What induced you to say that you would rather have written 'Pride & Prejudice' or 'Tom Jones' than any of the Waverley Novels?[3]

I had not seen 'Pride & Prejudice' till I read that sentence of yours, and then I got the book and studied it. And what did I find? An accurate daguerreotyped portrait of a common-place face; a carefully-fenced, highly cultivated garden with neat borders and delicate flowers – but no glance of a bright vivid physiognomy – no open country – no fresh air – no blue hill – no bonny beck. I should hardly like to live with her ladies and gentlemen in their elegant but confined houses. These observations will probably irritate you, but I shall run the risk.

From **George Henry Lewes, 'A Word about *Tom Jones*'** in *Blackwood's Edinburgh Magazine*, 87 (March 1860), pp. 331–41

George Henry Lewes wrote often of Austen, and sometimes with a condescension typical of much nineteenth-century criticism of her. 'Miniatures are not frescoes', he declared, 'and her works are miniatures. Her place is among the Immortals; but the pedestal is erected in a quiet niche of the great temple'.[1] Yet he felt an intense admiration for Austen, championing her to Charlotte Brontë and George Eliot, and praising her in an important series of articles: 'First and foremost', Lewes wrote in 1852, 'let Jane Austen be named, the greatest artist that has ever written, using the term to signify the most perfect mastery over the means to her end'.[2] His thoughts on *Pride and Prejudice* are characteristic in their emphasis on the subtlety and unity of Austen's art, where design and meaning inform what seems only 'the ordinary life of everyday'.

Pride and Prejudice is a finely-constructed work, and shows what a fine artistic sense Miss Austen had. The ease and naturalness of the evolution of the story are so perfect, that only very critical readers are aware of its skill in selection. Take it

2   Tony Tanner, *Jane Austen* (Cambridge, Mass.: Harvard University Press), pp. 138–9.
3   Brontë refers to George Henry Lewes's December 1847 *Fraser's Magazine* review of *Jane Eyre*. The great eighteenth-century novelist Henry Fielding wrote *Tom Jones* (1749); Walter Scott, the most popular novelist of Austen's day, wrote the Waverley novels.

1   George Henry Lewes, 'The Novels of Jane Austen' in *Blackwood's Edinburgh Magazine*, 86 (July 1859), p. 113.
2   George Henry Lewes, 'The Lady Novelists' in *Westminster Review*, 58 (July 1852), 134.

to pieces, examine the characters, scenes, and dialogues, in relation to each other and to the story, and you will find that there is nothing superfluous – that all this variety is secretly tending to one centre; that all this ease of nature, which looks so like the ordinary life of every day, is subordinate to the principles of Economy and Selection; and that nothing is dragged in, nothing is superfluous.

From **Margaret Oliphant, 'Miss Austen and Miss Mitford'** in *Blackwood's Edinburgh Magazine*, 107 (March 1870), pp. 290–313

As her interest in Austen and Mitford (see Novelists on *Pride and Prejudice*, **pp. 58–60**) suggests, **Margaret Oliphant** wrote often of domestic life, and with insight, sympathy, and humour. Her literary criticism on Austen is most notable as an early challenge to the 'Janeite' school, which reads Austen as cuddly, comfy escapism. For Oliphant, Austen's writings contain a 'fine vein of feminine cynicism' and a 'stinging yet soft-voiced contempt'. In *Pride and Prejudice*, she singles out Austen's realism, and her portrait of Mr. Collins, which combines 'the most genuine comedy' with 'consistent remorseless ridicule'.

It is a very difficult thing to realise how a brain of one-and-twenty could have identified such a family as the Bennets, such a character as Mr. Collins, and could have willingly filled up her background with figures such as those of the female Bingleys, Wickham, Lady Catherine, and the rest. Nothing could be more lifelike, more utterly real. The household is not described, but rises vividly before us as if we had visited it yesterday, with all its rusticity and ignorance, its eager thirst for pleasure, and incapacity to perceive the bad taste and futility of its own efforts. The first wonder that occurs to us is how Jane and Elizabeth should have found a place in such a family. The eldest is all sweetness and grace and beauty; the second brightly intelligent, quick to perceive, and equally quick to take up false impressions, but clever and affectionate and honest to the highest degree; while every one else in the house is a study of absurdity and vulgarity of one sort or another [. . .] It is all so common – never rising above the level of ordinary life, leaving nothing (so think the uninstructed) to imagination or invention at all – and yet what other hand has ever been able to detach such a group from the obscure level of their ordinary fate? Mr. Collins, for instance, who is the heir of Mr. Bennet's entailed estate, and who, with a certain quaint sense of justice which enhances his self-importance, comes prepared to propose to one of the daughters, whom he is obliged to deprive of their inheritance [. . .] The sublime and undisturbed complacence of his arrival, when he compliments Mrs. Bennet on having so fine a family of daughters, 'and added that he did not doubt her seeing them all in time well disposed of in marriage,' is inimitable [. . .] When he receives Elizabeth's refusal to marry him with undisturbed complacency, attributing it to 'your wish of increasing my love by suspense, according to the usual practice of elegant females,' the situation rises to one of the most genuine comedy.[1] [. . .]

---

1 See Key Passages, **p. 127.**

Miss Austen does not even let her victim escape her when he is married and has left the central scene [. . .] And when we take our parting glance of Mr. Collins, watching the country road from his 'book-room', and hastening to inform his wife and her friends every time Miss De Burgh drives by in her phaeton, we feel that the power of consistent remorseless ridicule can no further go. There is not a moment's faltering, nor the ghost of an inclination on the part of the author to depart from her wonderful conception. He stands before us tall and grave and pompous, wrapt in a cloud of solemn vanity, servility, stupidity, and spitefulness, but without the faintest gleam of self-consciousness or suspicion of the ridiculous figure he cuts; and his author, with no pity in her heart, walks round and round him, giving here and there a skilful touch to bring out the picture. It is amazing in its unity and completeness – a picture perhaps unrivalled, certainly unsurpassed, in its way. It is, we repeat, cruel in its perfection.

From **Mark Twain's Letters,** ed. Albert Bigelow Paine, 2 vols (New York: Harper, 1917), vol. ii, p. 667; the last sentence does not appear in Paine's edition, and was added in **Brander Matthews, 'Mark Twain and the Art of Writing'** in *Harper's Magazine*, 141 (October 1920), p. 642

Mark Twain is perhaps Austen's most famous detractor, and he damned her writings – especially *Pride and Prejudice* – with witty but heart-felt disgust. 'Twain's rabid discomfort with Austen's paradise' aligns him with 'a familiar story about the American literary tradition', Mary Favret observes: 'its aversion to domesticity and social convention; its fascination with the individual, the loner; its yearning for open spaces, unclaimed vistas, Huck Finn lighting out for the territories. This is a distinctly masculine tradition, uneasy about any contact with the feminine'.[1]

From **Mark Twain to Rev. J. H. Twichell,** 13 September 1898

I haven't any right to criticise books, and I don't do it except when I hate them. I often want to criticise Jane Austen, but her books madden me so that I can't conceal my frenzy from the reader; and therefore I have to stop every time I begin. Every time I read *Pride and Prejudice* I want to dig her up and beat her over the skull with her own shin-bone!

---

1   Mary Favret, 'Free and Happy: Jane Austen in America' in *Janeites: Austen's Disciples and Devotees*, ed. Deidre Lynch (Princeton: Princeton University Press, 2000), p. 168.

From **William Dean Howells, 'Jane Austen's Elizabeth Bennet'** in
Heroines of Fiction, 2 vols (New York: Harper, 1901), vol. i, pp. 37–48

> **William Dean Howells** and Mark Twain were close friends, fellow Americans, and leading literary figures, yet their attitude toward Austen could hardly have been more different. In contrast to Twain's contempt, Howells was an outspoken enthusiast, and one of the preeminent Janeites. In *Heroines of Fiction* he described Austen as 'the greatest of the gifted women', and reported that 'the story of *Pride and Prejudice* has of late years become known to a constantly, almost rapidly, increasing cult, as it must be called, for the readers of Jane Austen are hardly ever less than her adorers: she is a passion and a creed, if not quite a religion'. Yet Howells's admiration of Austen's 'delightful talent' did not prevent him from recognizing the subversive qualities of *Pride and Prejudice*, particularly in the famous scene between Elizabeth Bennet and Lady Catherine, where 'the value of humanity' hits back against 'the pretensions of rank'.

In all this the heroine easily gets the better of her antagonist not only in the mere article of *sauce*, to which it must be owned her lively wit occasionally tends, but in the more valuable qualities of person dignity.[1] She is much more a lady than her ladyship, as the author means she shall be; but her superiority is not invented for the crisis; it springs from her temperament and character, cool, humorous, intelligent and just: a combination of attributes which renders Elizabeth Bennet one of the most admirable and attractive girls in the world of fiction. It is impossible, however, not to feel that her triumph over Lady de Burgh is something more than personal: it is a protest, it is an insurrection, though probably the discreet, the amiable author would have been the last to recognize or to acknowledge the fact. An indignant sense of the value of humanity as against the pretensions of rank, such as had not been felt in English fiction before, stirs throughout the story.

From **G. K. Chesterton, *The Victorian Age in Literature*** (London:
Williams and Norgate, 1913), pp. 109–10

> **G. K. Chesterton** was a determined supporter of Austen, and understood that her intense concentration on a small section of society led to large insights about the predicaments of women and the motives of men. In *Pride and Prejudice*, he was especially impressed by her knowledge of Darcy. Chesterton found him far more compelling than the heroes of the Brontës or George Eliot.

Jane Austen was born before those bonds which (we are told) protected woman from truth, were burst by the Brontës or elaborately untied by George Eliot. Yet the fact remains that Jane Austen knew much more about men than either of

---

1   See Key Passages, **pp. 150–6.**

them. Jane Austen may have been protected from truth: but it was precious little of truth that was protected from her. When Darcy, in finally confessing his faults, says, 'I have been a selfish being all my life, in practice *though not in theory*,' he gets nearer to a complete confession of the intelligent male than ever was even hinted by the Byronic lapses of the Brontës' heroes or the elaborate exculpations of George Eliot's. Jane Austen, of course, covered an infinitely smaller field than any of her later rivals; but I have always believed in the victory of small nationalities.

From **Virginia Woolf, A Room of One's Own** (London: The Hogarth Press, 1929), pp. 101–2, 104

Virginia Woolf was one of the most distinguished novelists and critics of her time. In *A Room of One's Own*, a landmark in feminist literature, her discussion of Austen takes as its starting point a passage from the memories of Austen's nephew James Edward Austen-Leigh in which he describes how his aunt wrote her novels 'upon small sheets of paper which could easily be put away, or covered with a piece of blotting paper. There was, between the front door and the offices, a swing door which creaked when it was opened; but she objected to having this little inconvenience remedied, because it gave her notice when anyone was coming'.[1] Yet despite having no room of her own, Woolf stresses that Austen wrote 'without hate, without bitterness'. Following nineteenth-century critics such as Thomas Macaulay and George Henry Lewes, she compares Austen to Shakespeare.[2] Similarly, like G. K. Chesterton, Woolf discusses 'the narrowness of life' imposed upon Austen, and tellingly contrasts Austen's selflessness and clarity with Charlotte Brontë's egotism and rage (see Novelists on *Pride and Prejudice*, **pp. 61–2, 65–6**).

One would not have been ashamed to have been caught in the act of writing *Pride and Prejudice*. Yet Jane Austen was glad that a hinge creaked, so that she might hide her manuscript before anyone came in. To Jane Austen there was something discreditable in writing *Pride and Prejudice*. And, I wondered, would *Pride and Prejudice* have been a better novel if Jane Austen had not thought it necessary to hide her manuscript from visitors? I read a page or two to see; but I could not find any signs that her circumstances had harmed her work in the slightest. That, perhaps, was the chief miracle about it. Here was a woman about the year 1800 writing without hate, without bitterness, without fear, without protest, without preaching. That was how Shakespeare wrote, I thought, looking at *Antony and Cleopatra*; and when people compare Shakespeare and Jane Austen, they may mean that the minds of both had consumed all impediments; and for that reason

1 James Edward Austen-Leigh, *A Memoir of Jane Austen and Other Family Recollections*, ed. Kathryn Sutherland (Oxford: Oxford University Press, 2002), pp. 81–2.
2 Thomas Macaulay, 'The Diary and Letters of Mme D'Arblay' in *Edinburgh Review*, 76 (January 1843), pp. 561–2. George Henry Lewes, 'The Fair Carew' in *The Leader* (22 November 1851), p. 1115.

we do not know Jane Austen and we do not know Shakespeare, and for that reason Jane Austen pervades every word that she wrote, and so does Shakespeare. If Jane Austen suffered in any way from her circumstances it was in the narrowness of life that was imposed upon her. It was impossible for a woman to go about alone. She never traveled; she never drove through London in an omnibus or had luncheon in a shop by herself. But perhaps it was the nature of Jane Austen not to want what she had not. Her gift and her circumstances matched each other completely. But I doubt whether that was true of Charlotte Brontë, I said, opening *Jane Eyre* and laying it beside *Pride and Prejudice* [. . .] [Brontë] will write in a rage where she should write calmly. She will write foolishly where she should write wisely. She will write of herself where she should write of her characters. She is at war with her lot. How could she help but die young, cramped and thwarted?

From **W. Somerset Maugham, '*Pride and Prejudice*'** in *Atlantic Monthly,* 181 (May 1948), p. 104

> **W. Somerset Maugham** regarded Darcy's proposal to Elizabeth as 'the most dramatic scene' in *Pride and Prejudice*, and commented discerningly on issues of rank and class as they relate to Elizabeth, Lady Catherine, and Mr. Collins. Above all, he lauded Austen's immense readability. Why, when *Pride and Prejudice* is so well known, are we eager to read it over and over and over again? For Maugham, the answer lies in Austen's immense interest in her characters.

Darcy has been generally regarded as a fearful cad. His first offense was his refusal to dance with people he didn't know and didn't want to know at a public ball to which he had gone with a party. Not a very heinous one. It is true that when he proposes to Elizabeth it is with an unpardonable insolence, but pride, pride of birth and wealth, was the predominant trait of his character and without it there would have been no story to tell. The manner of his proposal, moreover, gave Jane Austen opportunity for the most dramatic scene in the book.[1] It is conceivable that with the experience she gained later Jane Austen might have been able to indicate Darcy's feelings in such a way as to antagonize Elizabeth without putting into his mouth speeches so improbable as to shock the reader.

There is perhaps some exaggeration in the drawing of Lady Catherine and Mr. Collins, but to my mind little more than comedy allows. Comedy sees life in a light more sparkling, but colder, than that of common day, and a touch of exaggeration, that is of farce, is often no disadvantage. A discreet admixture of farce, like a sprinkle of sugar on strawberries, may well make comedy more palatable.

With regard to Lady Catherine one must remember that in Jane Austen's day rank gave its possessors a sense of immense superiority over persons of inferior station, and these persons accepted the position without resentment. If Lady Catherine looked upon Elizabeth as so much white trash, let us not forget that

---

1 See Key Passages, **pp. 132–8.**

Elizabeth looked upon her Aunt Phillips, because she was the wife of an attorney, as very little better. In my own youth, a hundred years after Jane Austen wrote, I knew great ladies whose sense of importance, though not quite so blatant, was not far removed from Lady Catherine's. And as for Mr. Collins, who has not known even today men with that combination of pomposity and sycophancy? [. . .]

I have said nothing yet of what to my mind is the greatest merit of this charming book: it is wonderfully readable – more readable than some greater and more famous novels. As Scott said, Miss Austen deals with commonplace things, the involvements, feelings, and characters of ordinary life; nothing very much happens and yet when you reach the bottom of a page you eagerly turn it in order to know what will happen next; nothing very much does and again you turn the page with the same eagerness. The power of making you do this is the greatest gift a novelist can have and I have often wondered what creates it. Why is it that even when you have read the novel over and over again your interest never flags? I think with Jane Austen it is because she was so immensely interested in her characters and in what happened to them and because she profoundly believed in them.

From **V. S. Pritchett, *George Meredith and English Comedy*** (London: Chatto & Windus, 1970), p. 28

In his study of the English novelist George Meredith, **V. S. Pritchett** rejected the notion of Austen's world as 'small' and 'cosy', and described her as a novelist aware of the 'horror outside', and one whose work was shaped by the most pressing economic and political concerns of the day. 'What calm lives they had, those people!', British Prime Minister Winston Churchill exclaimed of Austen's characters. 'No worries about the French Revolution, or the crashing struggle of the Napoleonic wars'.[1] Pritchett eloquently disagrees.

Our perfect novelist of comedy, Jane Austen, is often presented as an example of the felicity of living in a small, cosy world, with one's mind firmly withdrawn from the horror outside. This has always seemed to me untrue. I think of her as a war-novelist, formed very much by the Napoleonic wars, knowing directly of prize money, the shortage of men, the economic crisis and change in the value of capital. I have even seen a resemblance of that second visit to Darcy's house as a naval battle; for notice there how the positions of the people in the drawing room are made certain, where Elizabeth like a frigate has to run between the lines. Militancy and vigilance are the essence of comedy; it brings the enemies within, into the open: pride meets prejudice, sense meets sensibility, the interchange is sharp. The end is clarification and [. . .] it enacts the myth or illusion of a perennial rebirth.

---

1   F. B. Pinion, 'Background' in *A Jane Austen Companion* (London: Macmillan, 1973), p. 24.

From **David Lodge, *Small World*** (London: Secker & Warburg, 1984), pp. 28–9

David Lodge has worked extensively on Austen, and in his irreverent 'academic romance', *Small World*, he has the high-flying American professor Morris Zapp explain both the frustration and exhilaration of studying her texts. Austen's novels appeal to critics from across the theoretical spectrum, from those interested in the traditional approaches of biography and history to those who exploit the theoretical paradigms of psychoanalysis, Marxism, existentialism, and phenomenology. Zapp is thwarted in his attempts to say the last word on Austen both by his post-structuralist awareness of the instability and indeterminacy of language, and by the deceptive and remarkable inexhaustibility of her novels.

'I used to be a Jane Austen man. I think I can say in all modesty I was *the* Jane Austen man. I wrote five books on Jane Austen, every one of which was trying to establish what her novels meant – and, naturally, to prove that no one had properly understood what they meant before. Then I began a commentary on the works of Jane Austen, the aim of which was to be utterly exhaustive, to examine the novels from every conceivable angle – historical, biographical, rhetorical, mythical, structural, Freudian, Jungian, Marxist, existentialist, Christian, allegorical, ethical, phenomenological, archetypal, you name it. So that when each commentary was written, there would be *nothing further to say* about the novel in question.

Of course, I never finished it. The project was not so much Utopian as self-defeating. By that I don't just mean that if successful it would have eventually put us all out of business. I mean that it couldn't succeed because it isn't possible, and it isn't possible because of the nature of language itself, in which meaning is constantly being transferred from one signifier to another and can never be absolutely possessed.

From **Martin Amis, 'Miss Jane's Prime'** in *The Atlantic*, 265.2 (February 1990), p. 102

'After a long immersion in [Austen's] work', writes Martin Amis, 'I find that her thought rhythms entirely invade my own'.[1] Amis is fascinated by Austen's language. Perhaps more than any other single factor, it illuminates her polite and hierarchical world, and the ways in which her characters' assertions of desperation and desire must be kept within 'the bounds of propriety', as Howard Babb explains (see Modern Criticism, **p. 79**). Austen's language of civility and restraint both attracts us to her world, and reveals our distance from it.

1   Martin Amis, 'Jane's World' in *The New Yorker*, 71.41 (8 January 1996), p. 34.

How do we get a sense of this society, this universe, with its inhibition, its formality, its echelonized emotions? It comes to us most clearly, perhaps, in its language. Mr. Darcy's first name is Fitzwilliam, which is a nice name – but Elizabeth will never use it. She will call him 'Mr. Darcy' or, occasionally, 'My dear Mr. Darcy'. You call your mother 'Madam' and your dad 'Sir'. When the dance floor is 'crouded', young ladies may get a 'headach'. You may 'teaze' a gentleman, should you 'chuse', and should he consent to be 'laught' at. If it be the sixth of October, then 'Michaelmas' will have been celebrated 'yesterday se'night'. 'La', what 'extacies' we were in! Everyone is much 'incumbered' by 'secresy' and the need to watch their 'expences'. A rich man must marry a rich girl, to avoid 'degradation' or even 'pollution'. But a poor man must marry a rich girl too, in order to achieve a 'tolerable independence'. So who is to marry all the *poor* girls – the poor girls, how will they find 'an husband'? How will they swerve between passion and prudence, between sensibility and sense, between love and money?

Modern Criticism

From **D. W. Harding, 'Regulated Hatred: An Aspect of the Work of Jane Austen'** in *Scrutiny*, 8 (1939–40), pp. 346–62

Harding begins with a pat and broadly accepted view of Austen: 'she was a delicate satirist, revealing with inimitable lightness of touch the comic foibles and amiable weaknesses of the people whom she lived amongst and liked'. For Harding such a representation is 'seriously misleading', and he counters it with a portrait of Austen as a distinctly modern figure, an alienated and misunderstood person and artist who sought 'unobtrusive spiritual survival, without open conflict' through caustic and subversive ironies. Austen's comedy disguises her deep anger and disgust, and her 'books are, as she meant them to be, read and enjoyed by precisely the sort of people whom she disliked'. Mrs. Bennet is risible but also detestable, for her power within the family enables her to thwart and humiliate her daughters. The same is true of Mr. Collins. He is ludicrous, to be sure, and his proposal to Elizabeth is 'comic fantasy'. But harsh economic and social realities mean that there is tremendous pressure on her to accept him. His unwelcome addresses are for her 'a taste of the fantastic nightmare'.

One of Jane Austen's most successful methods is to offer her readers every excuse for regarding as rather exaggerated figures of fun people whom she herself detests and fears. Mrs. Bennet, according to the Austen tradition, is one of 'our' richly comic characters about whom we can feel superior, condescending, perhaps a trifle sympathetic, and above all heartily amused and free from care. Everything conspires to make this the natural interpretation once you are willing to overlook Jane Austen's bald and brief statement of her own attitude to her: 'She was a woman of mean understanding, little information, and uncertain temper.'[1] How many women amongst Jane Austen's acquaintance and amongst her most complacent readers to the present day that phrase must describe! How gladly they

---

1   Jane Austen, *Pride and Prejudice*, ed. R. W. Chapman (Oxford: Clarendon Press, 1923), Volume I, Chapter 1, p. 5.

enjoy the funny side of the situations Mrs. Bennet's unpleasant nature creates, and how easy it is made for them to forget or never observe that Jane Austen, none the less for seeing how funny she is, goes on detesting her. The thesis that the ruling standards of our social group leave a perfectly comfortable niche for detestable people and give them sufficient sanction to persist, would, if it were argued seriously, arouse the most violent opposition, the most determined apologetics for things as they are, and the most reproachful pleas for a sense of proportion.

Caricature served Jane Austen's purpose perfectly. Under her treatment one can never say where caricature leaves off and the claim to serious portraiture begins. Mr. Collins is only given a trifle more comic exaggeration than Lady Catherine de Bourgh, and by her standards is a possible human being. Lady Catherine in turn seems acceptable as a portrait if the criterion of verisimilitude is her nephew Mr. Darcy. And he, finally, although to some extent a caricature, is near enough natural portraiture to stand beside Elizabeth Bennet, who, like all the heroines, is presented as an undistorted portrait. The simplest comic effects are gained by bringing the caricatures into direct contact with the real people, as in Mr. Collins's visit to the Bennets and his proposal to Elizabeth.[2] But at the same time one knows that, though from some points of view caricature, in other directions he does, by easy stages, fit into the real world. He is real enough to Mrs. Bennet; and she is real enough to Elizabeth to create a situation of real misery for her when she refuses. Consequently the proposal scene is not only comic fantasy, but it is also, for Elizabeth, a taste of the fantastic nightmare in which economic and social institutions have such power over the values of personal relationships that the comic monster is nearly able to get her.

From **David Daiches, 'Jane Austen, Karl Marx, and the Aristocratic Dance'** in *The American Scholar*, 17 (1947–8), pp. 289–96

Marxist criticism, in its many formulations, is grounded in the economic and cultural theories expounded by Karl Marx (1818–83) and Friedrich Engels (1820–95) in works such as *The Communist Manifesto* (1848) and *Das Kapital* (1867, 1885, 1894). One of its principle assertions is that economic factors determine the key values and practices in a culture. The English poet W. H. Auden commented wittily on the Marxist element in Austen when he described her novels as demonstrating 'so frankly and with such sobriety / The economic basis of society'.[1] Similarly, Daiches describes Austen in *Pride and Prejudice* as 'in a sense a Marxist before Marx' because she saw so clearly the crucial role economics played in shaping the fate of the Bennet family. Daiches rejects the notion of Austen as 'escapist' in favour of a view of her as 'the most realistic novelist of her age', and like D. W. Harding (see Modern Criticism,

---

2 See Key Passages, **pp. 124–7.**

1 W. H. Auden, 'Letter to Lord Byron' in *Collected Poems*, ed. Edward Mendelson (London: Faber, 1994), p. 84.

pp. 71–2) he recognizes her ability to create characters who are simultaneously 'both amusing and disturbing'. In *Thoughts on the Education of Daughters*, Mary Wollstonecraft details the dreadful circumstances that await fashionable women who are 'left without a fortune' (see Contemporary Documents, **p. 33**). In *Pride and Prejudice*, economics demand that Charlotte Lucas marry Mr. Collins, and they put enormous stress on Mrs. Bennet, who must ensure that her young daughters do not become old maids. Martin Amis rightly observes that 'Mrs. Bennet (stupid, prattling, vulgar, greedy), is one of the greatest comic nightmares in all literature, yet we are scarcely less restrained than she in our fretful ambition for her daughters. Jane Austen makes Mrs. Bennets of us all'.[2]

In fact, if we read Jane Austen carefully enough, we find that she is not an 'escapist' novelist at all: she is the most realistic novelist of her age, and the only English novelist of stature who was in a sense a Marxist before Marx. She exposes the economic basis of social behavior with an ironic smile that is much more effective than the passionate outbursts of the propagandists. There is an iron delicacy about her presentation of social life that is both amusing and disturbing. Think of Charlotte Lucas in *Pride and Prejudice*, deliberately accepting the hand of a man she despises — the egregious Mr. Collins, a complacent fool of the most impossible kind — because she knows that if she does not close with that offer she will never get another, and the fate in store for her as an unmoneyed spinster in a genteel society is too tragic to contemplate. Critics have remarked that there is no real delineation of true love in Jane Austen, and that is true enough, for Miss Austen knew only too well that in that kind of society genteel young ladies cannot afford true love: their objective must be marriage, and marriage with someone *eligible*. In Jane Austen, only the poor can afford passion.

Her novels are usually described as social comedies, but the fact is that some of them come close to tragedy, though Miss Austen quickly retreats from the brink of the pit to which she has so gracefully led us. We are not allowed to consider Charlotte Lucas's plight too curiously. [. . .] Or consider the relations between Mr. and Mrs. Bennet in *Pride and Prejudice*. Mrs. Bennet had captured her man early, and assured herself of a proper context for her gentility. (She is not, it is true, as genteel as she might be — but that only means that she has a tendency to tell the truth about the economic objectives pursued by members of her class.) She had successfully fooled Mr. Bennet when she was young enough for her beauty to outweigh her silliness, and Mr. Bennet spent the rest of his life regretting it. It had clearly been no genuine love match, but a match between cool self-interest and male susceptibility. And silly though she is, Mrs. Bennet is realistic enough to know that by hook or by crook her daughters must be properly married off before their looks begin to fade. A genteel upbringing is impossible equipment for life unless you secure a wealthy husband. How much more necessary is marriage to the Bennet girls than to their servants!

2   Martin Amis, 'Miss Jane's Prime' in *The Atlantic*, 265.2 (February 1990), p. 100.

From **Marvin Mudrick, 'Irony as Discrimination: *Pride and Prejudice*'** in *Jane Austen: Irony as Defense and Discovery* (Princeton: Princeton University Press, 1952), pp. 94–126

For Mudrick, Austen uses irony as both a shield and an instrument of discovery, but when it comes to the topic of sex she is squeamish and stock. Elizabeth cannot laugh at Darcy and, more seriously, neither can Austen, with the result that she cannot animate him 'with her characteristic informing irony' in the way that she is almost always able to animate Elizabeth. The *British Critic* reviewer of *Pride and Prejudice* complained just after the novel was published that Darcy's character was inconsistent (see Early Critical Reception, **p. 55**). Mudrick agrees, and finds further that Darcy emerges 'out of inconsistency . . . into flatness' as the final third of the novel declines into predictabilities and convention. Mudrick is notoriously given to overstatement ('Jane Austen herself, routed by the sexual question she has raised, is concealed behind a fogbank of bourgeois morality'), but many critics have objected to Austen's prudery and patness. Virginia Woolf argues that the 'chief damage' which Austen's 'conservative spirit has inflicted on her art is that it tied her hands together when she dealt with men'.[1] For a very different view, however, see Colin Firth, who declares that Austen 'really did have an instinctive grasp of Darcy's inner self' (see The Novel in Performance, **p. 101**).

Darcy's function as the character most difficult for the heroine to interpret, and yet most necessary for her to interpret if *she* is to make a proper decision in the only area of choice her society leaves open, his simultaneous role as the heroine's puzzle and her only possible hero, is clearly marked out during the action. From Elizabeth's point of view, in fact, the process of the interpretation of Darcy's personality from disdain through doubt to admiration is represented with an extraordinarily vivid and convincing minuteness. Nevertheless, Darcy himself remains unachieved. [. . .] Why is he, among the major figures in *Pride and Prejudice*, the only one disturbingly derived and wooden?

The reason seems to be the same as that which compelled Jane Austen to falsify her tone and commentary concerning Wickham's seductions. [. . .] The socially unmanageable, the personally involving aspects of sex, Jane Austen can no longer treat with irony, nor can she as yet treat them straightforwardly. Darcy is the hero, he is the potential lover of a complex young woman much like the author herself; and as such Jane Austen cannot animate him with emotion, or with her characteristic informing irony. She borrows him from a book; and, though she alters and illuminates everything else, she can do nothing more with him than fit him functionally into the plot.

Even here the author is so uncharacteristically clumsy as to rely on inconsistencies of personality to move her story along. However difficult Elizabeth's task of interpreting Darcy, it is clear from the beginning that, in his consistent functional

---

1   *The Essays of Virginia Woolf*, ed. Andrew McNeillie, 4 vols (London: Hogarth Press, 1986 – continuing), vol. ii, p. 12.

impact upon the story, he is a proud man with a strong sense of at least external propriety and dignity, and with no taste whatever for his aunt's vulgar condescension or the kind of sarcasm dispensed by Mr. Bennet. Yet on his first appearance he initiates Elizabeth's prejudice by speaking with a simple vulgarity indistinguishable from his aunt's, and in a voice loud enough to be overheard by the object of his contempt.[2] [. . .] In spite of his rigid and principled reserve, in spite of Elizabeth's having just turned down his arrogant proposal, he makes his explanation to Elizabeth in a thoroughly frank and unreserved letter, which [. . .] seems an author's gesture of desperation to weight the scales in favor of her predetermined hero. [. . .]

Out of inconsistency, Darcy emerges into flatness. Only in his sparing with Elizabeth, and then only occasionally, does he establish himself with a degree of solidity, of independent reference. [. . .] In dialogue, at least when Elizabeth is an enlivening participant, Jane Austen seems able now and then to overcome her awkwardness in handling Darcy. Otherwise, however, she can only make him serve: he interests us chiefly because he is the centre of Elizabeth's interest; and because, in a book in which the individual must choose and in which marriage is the single area of choice, Darcy represents Elizabeth's only plausible, or almost plausible, mate. [. . .] And when Darcy is ironed out into the conventionally generous and altruistic hero, making devoted efforts to shackle Wickham to Lydia, expending thousands of pounds to restore peace of mind to Elizabeth's family, and all for the love of Elizabeth – when he does all this, with no more of personal depth than Jane Austen allows of moral depth in the whole Lydia-Wickham episode, he comes very close to forfeiting even the functional plausibility that Elizabeth's interest lends him.

The last third of the book [. . .] does in fact diminish suddenly in density and originality; that is, beginning with Lydia's elopement. We get a conventional chase by an outraged father, a friendly uncle, and a now impeccable hero; we get outbursts of irrelevantly directed moral judgment, and a general simplification of the problems of motive and will down to the level of the Burneyan novel. Jane Austen herself, routed by the sexual question she has raised, is concealed behind a fogbank of bourgeois morality; and the characters, most conspicuously Darcy, must shift for themselves, or, rather, they fall automatically into the grooves prepared for them by hundreds of novels of sentiment and sensibility.

Only Elizabeth does not. She may yield temporarily to a kind of homeless moralizing on Lydia's disgrace, she may be rather obvious and stiff in acquainting herself with Darcy's virtues at last; but the lapses are minor, and they never seriously dim her luminous vigour, her wit, curiosity, discrimination, and independence. If the novel does not collapse in the predictabilities of the denouement, it is because Elizabeth has from the outset been presented in a depth specific and vital enough to resist flattening, because she remains what she has been – a complex person in search of conclusions about people in society, and on the way to her unique and crucial choice.

---

2   See Key Passages, pp. 114–17.

From **Dorothy Van Ghent, 'On *Pride and Prejudice*'** in *The English Novel: Form and Function* (New York: Rinehart, 1953), pp. 99–111

The great American critic Lionel Trilling believed that the relationship of Elizabeth and Darcy expressed itself 'as a conflict and reconciliation of styles: a formal rhetoric, traditional and rigorous, must find a way to accommodate a female vivacity, which in turn must recognize the principled demands of the strict male syntax'.[1] Van Ghent is similarly interested in Austen's style as an index of character and behaviour. Mr. Collins aims at intellectual refinement but produces only elaborate affectation. When he proposes to Elizabeth, his rhetoric is tired and hollow, but his indifference to meaning is a substantial threat to her 'emotional intelligence and quickness of moral perception'. Like Elizabeth, Austen prizes expression that is vigorous, plain, precise. Mr. Collins's 'language is the mirror of his degeneracy'. In *Pride and Prejudice*, the style is the man.

We shall illustrate with a sentence from Mr. Collins's proposal to Elizabeth, where 'significant form' lies in elaborate rather than in modest phrasing. Mr. Collins manages to wind himself up almost inextricably in syntax.

> 'But the fact is, that being as I am, to inherit this estate after the death of your honoured father, (who, however, may live many years longer,) I could not satisfy myself without resolving to chuse a wife from among his daughters, that the loss to them might be as little as possible, when the melancholy event takes place – which, however, as I have already said, may not be for several years.'[2]

Fancy syntax acts here, not as an expression of moral and intellectual refinement (as Mr. Collins intends it to act), but as an expression of stupidity, the antithesis of that refinement. The elaborate language in which Mr. Collins gets himself fairly *stuck* is a mimesis of an action of the soul, the soul that becomes self dishonest through failure to know itself, and that overrates itself at the expense of the social context, just as it overrates verbalism at the expense of meaning. We have suggested that moral life, in an Austen novel, is identified with emotional intelligence; and it is precisely through failure of intelligence – the wit to know his own limitations – that Mr. Collins appears as a moral monstrosity. Language is the mirror of his degeneracy. Against Mr. Collins's elaborate style of speech we may place the neat and direct phrasing of a sentence such as 'It is a truth universally acknowledged . . .' where the balance of overt thesis and buried antithesis acts as a kind of signature of the intelligential life – its syntactical modesty conveying a very deft and energetic mental dance.

Similarly, elaborate epithet ('your honoured father,' 'the melancholy event') is suspect – the sign not of attention but of indifference, of a moldiness of spirit which, far from being innocuous, has the capacity of mold to flourish

---

1   Lionel Trilling, 'In Mansfield Park' in *Encounter*, 3.3 (September 1954), pp. 15–6.
2   See Key Passages, **p. 125**.

destructively and to engulf what is clean and sound, as such epithet itself devours sense. Comedy, let us say again, 'is a serious matter,' and what is serious in this scene of Mr. Collins's proposal is the engulfing capacity of the rapacious Mr. Collins, from whom Elizabeth escapes narrowly. The narrowness of the escape is underlined by the fact that Elizabeth's friend, Charlotte – herself, we assume, intelligent, inasmuch as she is Elizabeth's friend – complacently offers herself as host to this mighty mold. In the civilized community which is our area of observation, emotional intelligence and quickness of moral perception – as we see them, for instance, in Elizabeth – are profoundly threatened by an all-environing imbecility. It is through style that we understand the nature of this threat; for the simplicity and directness of the governing syntax of the book prepares us to find positive values in simplicity and directness, negative values in elaboration and indirection.

From **Mark Schorer, 'Pride Unprejudiced'** in *Kenyon Review*, 18 (1956), pp. 72–91

> Mr. Darcy 'is a gentleman; I am a gentleman's daughter; so far we are equal', Elizabeth tells Lady Catherine in a heated exchange toward the close of the novel (see Key Passages, **p. 154**). But as Lady Catherine and Schorer point out, Elizabeth's social standing is in fact decidedly below Darcy's and, in Schorer's formulation, the discrepancy between Darcy's 'aristocratic assumptions' and Elizabeth's 'bourgeois desires' produce a powerful ambivalence that simultaneously places both of them in the right. Darcy can hardly be expected to rejoice in the thought of uniting himself to the rudeness, folly, and indolence of the Bennet family. But Elizabeth is understandably repulsed at the idea of marrying into Darcy's family, for he himself behaved rudely at their first meeting, and in many instances his aunt Lady Catherine seems even more foolish, vulgar, and scheming than Mrs. Bennet. These ambiguities generate both comic and impassioned effects, but are 'transcended' by the marriage of Darcy and Elizabeth, which merges two distinct social classes.

In large part, the comedy of *Pride and Prejudice* arises out of a basic historic discrepancy that is not in itself comic at all, the discrepancy between aristocratic assumptions of social place that are becoming unreal and therefore seem merely boorish, and bourgeois desires for social place that are not yet quite realizable, and therefore, when they do not arouse our pity, seem merely foolish. This discrepancy that lies at the heart of the book leads to an enormous ambiguity which, when the hero and heroine are finally merged in marriage, is transcended. The ambiguity arises from the fact that the author herself accepts one code as proper and at the same time aspires with the other.

Says Darcy:

> '. . . Nor am I ashamed of the feelings I related. They were natural and just. Could you expect me to rejoice in the inferiority of your connections? To congratulate myself on the hope of relations, whose condition in life is so decidedly beneath my own?'

Replies Elizabeth:

> 'You are mistaken, Mr. Darcy, if you suppose that the mode of your declaration affected me in any other way, than as it spared me the concern which I might have felt in refusing you, had you behaved in a more gentleman-like manner.'[1]

Our hearts, of course, go out to Elizabeth, because she has nothing on her side (no money, no family, no tradition) – nothing but her splendid intelligence; but the author's mind is divided between these two, for it is her observing social *eye* that sees and gives them the world they live in, even if it is her imaginative heart that, ultimately, judges them in relation to that world. For – ask yourself: is Elizabeth not perfectly correct? Darcy's 'arrogance ... conceit, and ... selfish disdain of the feelings of others' could only provide 'that groundwork of disapprobation, on which succeeding events have built so immoveable a dislike.' But is Darcy any less correct? Mrs. Bennet is a transparently scheming boor 'of mean understanding, little information, and uncertain temper';[2] Mr. Bennet, for all his amiable intelligence and wit, is a demoralized man; their daughter Lydia is a cheap flibber-ti-gibbet, with Kitty close behind her; Mary is a foolishly pontificating young bore; so who – with all this tastelessness and weakness so obvious at a glance – who could know about Jane? who, on first meeting, could know even about Lizzy?

From **Howard S. Babb, '*Pride and Prejudice*: Vitality and a Dramatic Mode'** in *Jane Austen's Novels: The Fabric of Dialogue* (Columbus: Ohio State University Press, 1962), pp. 113–44

The world of *Pride and Prejudice* is an elaborately coded one in which expressions of emotional and sexual attraction must work through complicated mediations of dance, gesture, dress, and dialogue. Babb is interested in 'performance', and the ways in which Elizabeth and Darcy treat literal situations metaphorically, keeping up the appearance of social propriety while at the same time betraying their most intense emotions. At Rosings, Darcy ostensibly comments on Elizabeth's piano playing, but he is actually expressing 'his deepest attachment' to her.

Elizabeth finally resorts to her literal performance on the piano in order to carry the day. She uses it metaphorically so that her thrust may seem decorously oblique, yet she aims her words straight at Darcy's stubbornness:

> 'My fingers ... do not move over this instrument in the masterly manner which I see so many women's do. They have not the same force or

---

1   See Key Passages, **p. 137.**
2   Jane Austen, *Pride and Prejudice*, ed. R. W. Chapman (Oxford: Clarendon Press, 1923), Volume I, Chapter 1, p. 5.

rapidity, and do not produce the same expression. But then I have always supposed it to be my own fault – because I would not take the trouble of practising. It is not that I do not believe *my* fingers as capable as any other woman's of superior execution.'[1]

At the same time, of course, this is one of Elizabeth's typical self-displays. But there is a further point: since Elizabeth creates the metaphor consciously, making the social situation into a vehicle for illustration, she must still be thinking of *performance* in its flattest sense.

This allegiance on her part fills Darcy's reply with reverberations:

Darcy smiled and said, 'You are perfectly right. You have employed your time much better. No one admitted to the privilege of hearing you, can think any thing wanting. We neither of us perform to strangers.'

He expresses his deepest attachment to her in these sentences. The first refuses to dispute her judgment of him, which is to say that Darcy cheerfully sacrifices the real motives he has been explaining. His second sentence must be sheer feeling, for it contradicts the logic both of Elizabeth's metaphor and of what Darcy himself has said earlier: after all, he praises his sister at the beginning of the scene because she 'practises very constantly,' and Elizabeth has just reproached herself for not practicing more often. Darcy can only mean that her behaviour toward him, no matter how prejudiced, is more valuable than her piano-playing. In the third sentence he reverts to the metaphor by 'hearing you,' which plainly stands for 'being with you,' but only to keep his extravagant generalization about her charm within the bounds of propriety. Yet his last sentence crowns the others. Perhaps, as a gallant gesture, he is straining to use 'perform' in Elizabeth's narrow sense – straining fearfully, if he really wants this meaning, for she is indeed playing to 'strangers.' But actually, I think, Darcy is calling here on his deeper sense of the word while uttering his most impassioned plea for intimacy, a plea all the more fervent in that it quite irrationally disregards – as a paraphrase shows – the blindness which has marked Elizabeth all along: 'We reserve our fullest selves, perfectly understood by both of us, for each other'. It is his final, almost desperate attempt before the first proposal to come to terms with her.

From **Alistair M. Duckworth, '*Pride and Prejudice*: The Reconstitution of Society'** in *The Improvement of the Estate: A Study of Jane Austen's Novels* (Baltimore: The Johns Hopkins Press, 1971), pp. 115–43

According to Duckworth, Darcy embodies some of the fundamental components of conservatism as it was powerfully expounded by Edmund Burke in *Reflections on the Revolution in France* (see Contemporary Documents, **pp. 34–5**). Darcy represents 'old money' as the owner of a great estate, and has a proper reverence for ancestry, tradition, custom, and duty, as seen in his attitude toward his library. By contrast, Bingley's 'new money' comes from trade, and he seems unaware that his wealth brings responsibilities, as seen in his negligent attitude toward his library. Mr. Bennet is, in relative terms, much poorer than either Darcy or Bingley, and his library provides 'no emblem of trusteeship, but is instead a refuge from responsibility'. Duckworth insists, however, that Austen's conception of a healthy society is dynamic and not narrowly conservative, for she recognizes that the allegiances and traditions of Darcy must embrace the aspirations and energies of individuals like Elizabeth.

A contemporary context may be given to Darcy's attitudes if one turns to Burke, whose advice Jane Austen might have followed in her portrayal of Darcy. 'High and worthy notions of . . . function and destination',[1] to introduce a phrase from the *Reflections*, explain Darcy's stiff posture and uncompromising demands. Like Burke's responsible official, Darcy does not 'look to the paltry pelf[2] of the moment, nor to the temporary and transient praise of the vulgar, but to a solid, permanent existence, in the permanent part of [his] nature'.[3] Again, it might be argued that it is his manifest desire to save traditional customs and usages from 'prophanation and ruin'[4] which accounts for the acerbity of some of his remarks to Bingley, a man who has not yet chosen his permanent role, who has not yet discovered his stage of action. Moreover, though Darcy is constantly and appropriately associated with judgment and justice (his favourite uncle was a judge), there is in his outlook something of the Burkean 'prejudice', which 'renders a man's virtue his habit and not a series of unconnected acts. Through just prejudice, his duty becomes part of his nature'.[5]

That Darcy has a Burkean regard for the wisdom of his ancestors is shown on several occasions in the novel. [. . .] Darcy's pride in his library is the proper pride of the responsible owner of a large house who is conscious of his responsibilities as trustee and who is aware (in Burkean terms) that he is not the 'entire master' but only the 'life-renter' of Pemberley. In 'the modes of holding property [and] exercising function'[6] Darcy is an instructive contrast not only to the idle and negligent Bingley but to Mr. Bennet himself, whose library can provide no emblem of trusteeship, but is instead a refuge from responsibility, a subjective retreat which he is 'anxious to . . . have . . . to himself.'[7] [. . .] In pointing to the Burkean content of Darcy's 'proper pride', I do not mean to suggest any passive or mechanical acceptance on Jane Austen's part of the given rightness of the social

1   Edmund Burke, *Reflections on the Revolution in France*, ed. J. C. D. Clark (Stanford: Stanford University Press, 2001), p. 256.
2   'Money, wealth, riches [. . .] "filthy lucre"' (*Oxford English Dictionary*).
3   Edmund Burke, *Reflections on the Revolution in France*, ed. J. C. D. Clark (Stanford: Stanford University Press, 2001), p. 257.
4   Ibid., p. 256.
5   Ibid., p. 252.
6   Ibid., p. 260.
7   Jane Austen, *Pride and Prejudice*, ed. R. W. Chapman (Oxford: Clarendon Press, 1923), Volume I, Chapter 15, p. 71.

status quo. [. . .] A properly constituted society, Jane Austen insists, emerges only from the interaction of cultural discipline and individual commitment, and only when inherited forms receive the support of individual energy do they carry value. Conversely, however [. . .] individual energy must be generated within social contexts, for, lacking social direction and control, it turns too easily to withdrawal from society, or to irresponsibility and anarchy.

From **Nina Auerbach, 'Pride and Prejudice'** in *Communities of Women* (Cambridge, Mass.: Harvard University Press, 1978), pp. 38–55

Feminist criticism comes in many forms, but it takes as one of its central tenets the conviction that the Western world is male-dominated or 'patriarchal', and that it has been organized in such a way as to ensure that women remain economically, politically, artistically, and socially subordinate to men. Auerbach demonstrates how in *Pride and Prejudice* women live shadowy, fraught, and indeterminate lives that only take on some form of coherence when a man is present. Far from being a fairy tale, the novel shows the oppressive reality of women's lives in early nineteenth-century Britain. Men command. Women wait. Men inherit. Women wait. Men enjoy. Women wait.

> Anxious and uneasy, the period which passed in the drawing-room, before the gentlemen came, was wearisome and dull to a degree, that almost made her uncivil. She looked forward to their entrance, as the point on which all her chance of pleasure for the evening must depend.[1]

Since Elizabeth Bennet has passed her life in a world of waiting women, and we have passed it with her for much of the previous two volumes of the novel, this passage need describe such a world only as a temptation to lose one's temper. The story, the glow, will begin with the opening of the door.

In an earlier description of a similar situation we are given a chance, not so much to hear what women say to each other during this excruciating period, as to have our attention called to the distrust and emotional pressure that forbid their saying anything:

> Elizabeth soon saw that she was herself closely watched by Miss Bingley, and that she could not speak a word, especially to Miss Darcy, without calling her attention. This observation would not have prevented her from trying to talk to the latter, had they not been seated at an inconvenient distance; but she was not sorry to be spared the necessity of saying much. Her own thoughts were employing her. She expected every moment that some of the gentlemen would enter the room. She wished, she feared that the master of the house might be

---

1 Jane Austen, *Pride and Prejudice*, ed. R. W. Chapman (Oxford: Clarendon Press, 1923), Volume III, Chapter 12, p. 341.

amongst them; and whether she wished or feared it most, she could scarcely determine.[2]

Darcy has gently commanded that Elizabeth and his sister like each other, but his absent presence is the only emotional point of reference for all three women. Waiting for the entrance of the gentlemen, their shared world is a limbo of suspension and suspense, which cannot take shape until it is given one by the opening of the door.

The unexpressed intensity of this collective waiting for the door to open and a Pygmalion[3] to bring life into limbo defines the female world of *Pride and Prejudice*; its agonized restraint is reflected microcosmically in the smaller community of the Bennet family, and macrocosmically in the larger community of England itself. [. . .] In presenting these drawing rooms full of women watching the door and watching each other, Jane Austen tells us what an observant, genteel woman has to tell about the Napoleonic Wars: she writes novels about waiting.

As her England is in large part a country of women whose business it is to wait for the return of the men who have married them or may do so, so her heroine's family has occupied much of its history in waiting, with increasing hopelessness, for a male to enter it:

> When first Mr. Bennet had married, economy was held to be perfectly useless; for, of course, they were to have a son. This son was to join in cutting off the entail,[4] as soon as he should be of age, and the widow and younger children would by that means be provided for. Five daughters successively entered the world, but yet the son was to come; and Mrs. Bennet, for many years after Lydia's birth, had been certain that he would. This event had at last been despaired of, but it was then too late to be saving. Mrs. Bennet had no turn for economy, and her husband's love of independence had alone prevented their exceeding their income.[5]

In the family microcosm, the male whom all await can alone bring substance; by inheriting the estate, he will ensure the family the solidity and continuity of income and land. Without him, their emotional and financial resources, and ultimately the family itself, can only evaporate. The quality of the Bennet household is determined by the Beckett-like[6] realization that the period of protracted waiting is not a probationary interim before life begins: waiting for a male is life itself.

---

2   Ibid., Volume III, Chapter 3, p. 268.
3   In Roman mythology, Pygmalion made a statue representing his ideal of womanhood, and then fell in love with it. The goddess Venus brought the statue to life in answer to Pygmalion's prayers.
4   For the importance of the law of entail in *Pride and Prejudice*, see Contemporary Documents, pp. 31–2.
5   Jane Austen, *Pride and Prejudice*, ed. R. W. Chapman (Oxford: Clarendon Press, 1923), Volume III, Chapter 8, p. 308.
6   Samuel Beckett (1906–89), Irish-born author best known for *Waiting for Godot*, a play often linked with the Theatre of the Absurd.

From **Judith Lowder Newton, 'Pride and Prejudice'** in *Women, Power, and Subversion: Social Strategies in British Fiction, 1778–1860* (Athens: University of Georgia Press, 1981), pp. 55–85

> Like Mudrick (see Modern Criticism, **pp. 74–5**), Newton finds the final third of *Pride and Prejudice* the least impressive as the informing ironies collapse and conventionality takes hold. Elizabeth's marriage is a mixed blessing at best, and requires some Austenian sleight-of-hand. From one perspective the lessons Elizabeth learns from and about Darcy require her to 'dwindle by degrees into a wife'. But from another she retains her vitality and depth from start to finish. Austen convinces us of 'the fantasy of Elizabeth's power', but the novel at its core is wish-fulfillment: Elizabeth's subjugation is made to seem her success, and her decline into marriage an ascent into happiness.

Austen's difficulties with Elizabeth's reward, her attempt to give her marriage but to alter what marriage means, her attempt to balance love and quest, her tinkering with heroine and hero must account for the fact that most readers of *Pride and Prejudice* find the end less satisfactory than the beginning. On the one hand, the charge that Elizabeth, as witty heroine, is now too inclined to moralize and be grateful owes much to the fact that marriage requires her to dwindle by degrees into a wife. On the other hand, the observation that Darcy as hero is less convincing than as villain owes much to the requirements of Austen's fantasy, which are that Elizabeth not dwindle too far, that she maintain her equality with if not her ascendancy over her husband. Darcy, therefore, though he must demonstrate all the economic privilege and social authority of the traditional hero – which are plenty – may not have everything; he may not have Pemberley, £10,000 a year, rank, looks, intelligence, flexibility, wit, and a convincing reality as well. There is some point, though an unconscious point, to his stiffness and unreality, for both function at some level to preserve the fantasy of Elizabeth's power.

The end of *Pride and Prejudice*, nevertheless, witnesses a decline in Elizabeth Bennet, for in *Pride and Prejudice* as in much of women's fiction the end, the reward, of woman's apprenticeship to life is marriage, and marriage demands resignation even as it prompts rejoicing, initiates new life while it confirms a flickering suspicion that the best is over. Given the ambivalent blessing of marriage as a happy ending, it is a tribute to Austen's genius that what we take from *Pride and Prejudice* is not a sense of Elizabeth's untimely decline but a tonic impression of her intelligence, her wit, and her power, and it is an even greater tribute that we believe in her power, that we do not perceive it as fantasy. For Austen's brilliant construction of her heroine's world, her recognition and subtle subversion of economic forces, the mobile intelligence of the heroine herself, the ironies directed at that intelligence, the complexities of Elizabeth's failure in vision and of her recovery complicate what is at base a wish fulfillment, give it an air of credibility which lends force to the spell of the fantasy upon us.

As one of my students put it, we need more fantasies like Elizabeth.

From **Mary Poovey, 'Ideological Contradictions and the Consolations of Form: The Case of Jane Austen'** in *The Proper Lady and the Woman Writer* (Chicago: University of Chicago Press, 1984), pp. 172–207

Poovey explores Elizabeth's vulnerability. When Darcy rejects her as a dance partner, she may react with characteristic pluck, but the incident unnerves her because it clearly exposes the most distressing aspects of her predicament. She fantasizes about Darcy as a partner, but the marked inferiority of her financial and social position makes such fantasies acts of 'imaginative presumption'. More worryingly, his dismissal of her suggests there may be further slights, and presses a dreadful question on Elizabeth: 'What if I am not handsome enough to attract a wealthy man?' Perhaps the moment marks the first time that Elizabeth confronts the possibility that her 'tolerable' beauty may not attract a desirable and permanent partner, and that she stands much closer than she realized to a fate of spinsterhood and servitude.

The action of *Pride and Prejudice* generally reveals that, despite what looks like a generous overflow of irrepressible energy, Elizabeth's 'liveliness' is primarily defensive. More specifically, her 'impertinence' is a psychological defense against the vulnerability to which her situation as a dependent woman exposes her. Elizabeth's prejudice against Darcy is so quickly formed and so persistent because, at the first assembly, he unthinkingly confronts her with the very facts that it is most in her interest to deny. 'She is tolerable', Darcy concedes, rejecting Bingley's overtures on Elizabeth's behalf, 'but not handsome enough to tempt *me*; and I am in no humour at present to give consequence to young ladies who are slighted by other men'.[1]

Despite the fact that Elizabeth's 'playful disposition' enables her to turn this 'ridiculous' remark against Darcy, his cool observation continues to vex and haunt her for much of the novel and to govern not only her anger toward Darcy but also her 'mortification' at the antics of her family. It has this effect for two closely related reasons. First of all, in spite of her professed unconcern, Elizabeth, like everyone else, is immediately attracted to this handsome, eminently eligible bachelor, and, if only for a short time, he engages her natural romantic fantasies. We discover this later, when Darcy offers to make her dream come true and Elizabeth retorts by acknowledging that, though she once considered him as a possible husband, she no longer does so: 'I had not known you a month', she exults, inadvertently acknowledging the longevity of her fantasy, 'before I felt that you were the last man in the world whom I could ever be prevailed on to marry'.[2] But, given Elizabeth's social position and economic situation, even to dream of marrying Darcy is an act of imaginative presumption. The second reason for her lingering pain, then, is that Darcy's rejection deflates not only her romantic fantasies of marriage to a handsome aristocrat but, more important, the image of herself upon which such fantasies are based.

---

1   See Key Passages, **p. 117.**
2   See Key Passages, **p. 137.**

Darcy's casual remark suggests that the fact that Elizabeth is momentarily without a partner indicates that she will always be so 'slighted', that her 'tolerable' beauty will never attract the permanent partner she desires. And this remark strikes very close to home. For the inevitable result of an entail in a household more blessed with daughters than frugality is, at best, a limited choice of suitors; at worst, the Bennet's shortage of money for dowries and their equivocal social position foretell spinsterhood, dependence on a generous relative, or, most ominous of all, work as a governess or lady's companion.[3] Austen never lets the reader or Elizabeth forget how very likely such a future is. Darcy lays the groundwork for this scenario when, alluding to their uncles in trade and law, he remarks that such connections 'must very materially lessen [the sisters'] chance of marrying men of any consideration in the world'.[4] Even closer to home, when Charlotte Lucas rejects romance, she does so for its opposite, the matter-of-fact assessment that a 'comfortable home'[5] is more substantial than romantic fantasies. Elizabeth's mother is even more brutally frank. 'If you take it into your head', she warns Elizabeth, 'to go on refusing every offer of marriage in this way, you will never get a husband at all – and I am sure I do not know who is to maintain you when your father is dead.'[6] In the context of such dark realism, even Mr. Collins's compensatory retaliation sounds ominously like a self-evident truth. 'Your portion is unhappily so small', he smugly informs Elizabeth, 'that it will in all likelihood undo the effects of your loveliness and amiable qualifications.'[7]

From **Claudia L. Johnson, '*Pride and Prejudice* and the Pursuit of Happiness'** in *Jane Austen: Women, Politics, and the Novel* (Chicago: University of Chicago Press, 1988), pp. 73–93

Linda Colley views *Pride and Prejudice* as 'a deliberate essay in fantasy'.[1] Similarly, Mary Poovey (in a different part of her argument than the passage quoted above; see Modern Criticism, **pp. 84–5**) finds that the novel exposes complex social problems and then wishes them away in a happy ending that is satisfying but unrealistic and 'politically irresponsible'. Such conceptions, however, are challenged by Annabella Milbanke, who read the novel when it first appeared and thought it 'the *most probable* fiction I have ever read' (see Early Critical Reception, **p. 56**; Milbanke's italics). Johnson too contests such views, arguing that in the marriage of Elizabeth and Darcy Austen imagines a version of conservatism that allows for debate and is 'capable of transformation'. In bringing Elizabeth and Darcy together, she merges what Mark Schorer describes as

---

3   Compare Mary Wollstonecraft's observations on becoming 'an humble companion', a 'teacher at a school', or a 'governess to young ladies' (Contemporary Documents, **p. 33**).
4   See Key Passages, **p. 119**.
5   See Key Passages, **p. 130**.
6   Jane Austen, *Pride and Prejudice*, ed. R. W. Chapman (Oxford: Clarendon Press, 1923), Volume I, Chapter 20, p. 113.
7   See Key Passages, **p. 127**.

1   Linda Colley, 'Why Darcy would not have married Elizabeth Bennet' in *London Review of Books*, 20.17 (3 September 1998), p. 10.

Darcy's 'aristocratic assumptions' and Elizabeth's 'bourgeois desires' (see Modern Criticism, **pp. 77–8**). The ending of the novel points, not to never-never land, but to an immediate future in which conservatism would have to broaden and reinvent itself in order to survive.

To some, *Pride and Prejudice* has a markedly fairy-tale-like quality which, while accounting for much of the novel's enduring popular success, is politically suspect. One of Austen's recent critics observes that the novel's wishful, though aesthetically satisfying, 'romantic conclusion' fudges the ideological contradictions uncovered earlier between the 'individualistic perspective inherent in the bourgeois value system *and* the authoritarian hierarchy retained from traditional, paternalistic society.'[2] By this account, the happy ending of *Pride and Prejudice* is an 'aesthetic solution' that cannot really address the 'social problems' the novel itself uncovers, and indeed that actually conceals their depth. But while these objections are partly true, we should not let our own rather modern preference for ideological conflict predispose us to undervalue Austen's achievement in *Pride and Prejudice*. To imagine versions of authority responsive to criticism and capable of transformation is not necessarily to 'escape' from urgent problems into 'romance' and to settle for politically irresponsible 'consolations of form' which offer us a never-never land and leave the structures of the 'real world' unchanged.[3] When we recall that Austen's preceding novel[4] could locate her protagonists' contentment only in a retreat from and renunciation of power, Austen's decision here to engage her exceptionally argumentative antagonists in direct, extensive, and mutually improving debates can just as well be viewed as a step towards, rather than an 'escape' from, constructive political commentary.

While it is thus indeed true that the happy ending of *Pride and Prejudice* 'dismisses the social and psychological realism with which the novel began' – dodging, for example, such dire issues as the destitution we are told the Bennet sisters would otherwise expect after their father's death – nevertheless the novel as a whole certainly does not evade or neutralize social criticism out of a fond or unquestioning allegiance to established forms and the attractive men who embody them. In fact, the 'conservatism' of *Pride and Prejudice* is an imaginative experiment with conservative myths, and not a statement of faith in them as they had already stood in anti-Jacobin[5] fiction. To be sure, by using these myths, even to hedge, qualify, and improve them, Austen is also [. . .] unavoidably used by them. But throughout the course of the novel those myths become so transformed that they are made to accommodate what could otherwise be seen as subversive

---

2   [Johnson's note] Mary Poovey, *The Proper Lady and the Woman Writer* (Chicago: University of Chicago Press, 1984), p. 205.

3   [Johnson's note] Ibid., p. 207. For a discussion of *Pride and Prejudice* as a powerful female fantasy, see Tania Modleski, *Loving With a Vengeance* (Hamden, Conn.: Archon, 1982), pp. 36, 49–51.

4   Austen's first novel, *Sense and Sensibility* (1811).

5   The Jacobins were the most famous political group of the French Revolution, and became identified with extreme equalitarianism and violence. English conservatives used the term to smear radicals like William Godwin and Mary Wollstonecraft. Anti-Jacobin fiction embraced the status quo and deplored revolutionary energies.

impulses and values, and in the process they themselves become the vehicles of incisive social criticism.

From **Alison G. Sulloway, 'Voices and Silences: The Province of the Drawing Room and the War of Debates'** in *Jane Austen and the Province of Womanhood* (Philadelphia: University of Pennsylvania Press, 1989), pp. 160–85

As Sulloway observes, Elizabeth Bennet is surrounded by irresponsibility, cynicism, greed, temerity, conceit, and dishonesty, and she must somehow try to find her way to success as both a person and a marriage partner. In the complicated patriarchal world of *Pride and Prejudice*, it is often difficult to determine where aristocratic privilege ends and 'earned worthiness' begins. Darcy is an educated and intelligent man, but even he initially treats Elizabeth 'as an object of his sexual lust who is little better than a whore'. Gradually he comes to recognize her as a person, not a commodity, and to divest himself of the arrogant presumptions and conduct-book formulations that have hampered his own growth as a person. Darcy elevates Elizabeth through a highly advantageous marriage, but it is equally the case that Elizabeth elevates Darcy. Though he grows ashamed of his first proposal, her cutting rejection showed him 'how insufficient were all my pretensions to please a woman worthy of being pleased' (see Key Passages, **p. 157**).

Elizabeth is surrounded by immature people – by parents who are morally irresponsible toward daughters, three sisters equally irresponsible toward the community, another sister who is afraid to make unflattering judgments, one intimate woman friend who is cynical about marriage, with good reasons, and close neighbors in the Lucas family, who are all governed entirely by the cash ethic and by the same lust for social prestige that corrupts her cousin, Mr. Collins. [. . .] Much as she and her uncle, Mr. Gardiner, admire each other, their relationship is hardly close, nor does she see him often, and it is symbolic that readers are treated to no dialogues between them, in stark contrast to the witty, affectionate, and sometimes serious debates between Elizabeth and her aunt, Mrs. Gardiner.

Elizabeth must largely teach herself the way of the masculine world, in common with all Austen's heroines. [. . .] She must try to uncover truths, both bitter and liberating, and to distinguish between those truths and the myths and fictions of innate and earned worthiness, which people with many privileges to protect and lesser creatures to fend off, tend to weave around themselves. Eventually she does learn that Darcy is capable of stripping himself, at least in private, of his own myths about his right to arrogance, whereas Wickham is not capable of that moral learning. Eventually Elizabeth finds herself loved by a man who does not now treat her as a fool, as a marriage commodity for sale, and as an object of his sexual lust who is little better than a whore. The automatic masculine conduct-book association between articulate women and fornicating women does indeed partly explain Darcy's initial behavior, but nothing quite excuses it. He is intelligent enough to assume that Elizabeth can only be forced to provide him the sexual satisfaction he wants if he marries her; but he has assumed that her articulate self-confidence is nothing more than the sexual bait commonly claimed for it: 'I believed you to be wishing, expecting my addresses,' he later admits in shame.[1]

From **Robert M. Polhemus, 'The Fortunate Fall: Jane Austen's** *Pride and Prejudice'* in *Erotic Faith: Being in Love from Jane Austen to D. H. Lawrence* (Chicago: University of Chicago Press, 1990), pp. 28–54

'Without an unusual share of natural sensibility, and very peculiar good fortune', John Gregory declares in *A Father's Legacy to his Daughters*, 'a woman in this country has very little probability of marrying for love' (see Contemporary Documents, **p. 30**). Elizabeth Bennet, however, insists upon it, though the contrasting fates of Charlotte Lucas and Lydia Bennet demonstrate both the unnerving reality of Gregory's proclamation and the fragile and highly contingent nature of Elizabeth's romantic idealism. Polhemus defines 'erotic faith' as 'an emotional conviction, ultimately religious in nature, that meaning, value, hope, and even transcendence can be found through love [. . .] the kind of love we mean when we say that people are in love'. Austen enacts her notion of erotic faith in Elizabeth's relationship with Darcy, but she also explores the irony, tension, and bitterness in relationships that lack such faith. Charlotte weds a fool for security, and her predicament as an intelligent but ageing and unmarried woman invokes Austen's own. Her eagerness to marry Collins 'is a kind of socially respectable prostitution'. Lydia weds a rake, for her youthful eroticism leads not to romantic faith but to licentious fantasy. Her undifferentiated eagerness for men reveals a 'pornographic imagination'. Love transforms Elizabeth and Darcy, and creates a marriage of faith and desire. Lack of love debases Charlotte and Lydia, and creates marriages of hollowness and indifference.

Austen sets out her ideal of erotic faith in the process and end that she imagines for Elizabeth. But the contrasting figures of Charlotte Lucas and Lydia Bennet, between whom she places her heroine, show how dubious and difficult the subject of romantic love could be for women in the author's milieu. You may be committed to the idea of intelligent love, but economics and libido can make a mockery of that commitment. Charlotte is all head, Lydia all hormones. One, plain and aging, calculates that she had best marry a fool rather than no one, and the other, ruled by 'high animal spirits',[1] falls for a seducer. Austen makes them both in different ways sex objects and slaves to materialism. And though their behavior points up very serious problems surrounding love for women in this society, these characters ironically show why erotic faith could appeal, like most religions, to people who cannot or do not want to live by bread or flesh alone. Without love,

---

1   See Key Passages, **p. 157**.

1   Jane Austen, *Pride and Prejudice*, ed. R. W. Chapman (Oxford: Clarendon Press, 1923), Volume I, Chapter 9, p. 45.

the object of marriage tends to become a matter of accounting (Collins) or lust and greed (Wickham).

Charlotte's case must concern anyone who thinks seriously about the history of women:

> Mr. Collins to be sure was neither sensible nor agreeable; his society was irksome, and his attachment to her must be imaginary. But still he would be her husband. – Without thinking highly either of men or of matrimony, marriage had always been her object; it was the only honourable provision for well-educated young women of small fortune, and however uncertain of giving happiness, must be their pleasantest preservative from want. This preservative she had now obtained; and at the age of twenty-seven, without having ever been handsome, she felt all the good luck of it.[2]

Irony shimmers in that prose, and put so baldly, Charlotte's views may look cynical; but her situation is a fearful one, as the unmarried author of those bitter words well knew. Austen sees with more sympathy and ambivalence than her heroine, who quickly condemns her friend, the dilemma facing the woman who cannot get a man of means or promise – a man she might be able to love – to fall in love with her. It's too easy to do as Elizabeth and certain Austen critics do and simply dismiss or fudge the issue.[3] The point is not that Charlotte is a sellout, but that she lives in a narrow, desperate, feminine world of financial constraint, like some poor entrant in a ritualized beauty contest that determines your fate while drying up your soul. Articulate and intelligent, she in fact has affinities with her author, which may explain Elizabeth's sharp intolerance about Charlotte's choice: defensive reflex. Marriage to Collins is a kind of socially respectable prostitution in which Charlotte acquiesces. Love is not going to come to her, and lacking it, she seeks refuge in the security of substance. There is no mystery of life for her, no vision of ecstasy or sweet companionship. She has little chance to do what seems necessary for happiness and faith in Austen's fiction: aestheticize and sanctify life by aestheticizing and sanctifying marriage with love. [. . .]

Although she draws Lydia as a shallow materialist, at one key point she shifts her tone abruptly and imagines, with startling empathy, Lydia's inner life. Just before Lydia goes off with Wickham, we get this amazing passage:

> In Lydia's imagination, a visit to Brighton comprised every possibility of earthly happiness. She saw with the creative eye of fancy, the streets of that gay bathing place covered with officers. She saw herself the object of attention, to tens and to scores of them at present unknown. She saw all the glories of the camp; its tents stretched forth in beauteous uniformity of lines, crowded with the young and the gay, and dazzling with

---

2   See Key Passages, p. 129.
3   [Polhemus's note] See Susan Morgan's excellent study of Austen, *In the Meantime: Character and Perception in Jane Austen's Fiction* (Chicago: University of Chicago Press, 1980), pp. 92–9, for a different interpretation.

scarlet; and to complete the view, she saw herself seated beneath a tent, tenderly flirting with at least six officers at once.[4]

These words are full of the tension between the creative power of erotic faith and the destructive promiscuity to which romantic desire can lead. No one who pays close attention to this prose would say that Jane Austen did not know the flash of sexual fantasy and the pull of eroticism, and only someone insensitive to language could miss the appeal of Lydia's vision, ironic and insidious as it turns out to be. Suddenly Austen chooses to lay bare the mind of an ignorant girl at the beginning of the nineteenth century – a mind we hardly thought existed – and we see there historically and psychologically revealing imagery of desire. She gets at the impulse behind the pornographic imagination, which seeks for the self a sensually realized, beautiful, but undifferentiated and impersonal *more*. Lydia typically wants an endless supply of lovers. Erotic desire becomes limitless and, without reason or discipline, loses the power of distinction: humanity becomes imaginary, an army of fantasy whose mission it is to make the self feel infinitely desirable. The picture, enticing with its youth, joy, color, bustle, pattern, and amorousness, shows us another, more sinister version of Venus disarming Mars.[5]

From **Allan Bloom, 'Austen, *Pride and Prejudice*'** in *Love and Friendship* (New York: Simon and Schuster, 1993), pp. 191–208

Bloom emphasizes irony as a touchstone in Austen's writings, and one of the central features of *Pride and Prejudice*. Austen's use of irony promotes the virtue of moderation, and enables her both to embrace and critique her characters. Irony pervades Darcy's first proposal to Elizabeth. He congratulates himself on separating Bingley from the Bennet family at the same time that he seeks a similar connection for himself. His younger sister has wealth, talent, and virtue, but she commits the same folly as Elizabeth's younger sister: she agrees to elopement with Wickham. Darcy's censure of Elizabeth's family leaves her in a double-bind, for whether it proceeds from aristocratic snobbishness or genuine moral insight, the result is the same: she is ashamed of her family, and ashamed of her shame. Darcy's words hurt because, though she protests otherwise, he attracts her, even as she fiercely rejects him. Collins's proposal of marriage was equally tactless, but Elizabeth let him off with a firm refusal. She attacks Darcy, however, because even at this point he matters to her, and she both wants and resents him for it. She has to learn dependence at the same time that she believes in her own mastery. The same holds true for him. Edward Neill argues that 'despite Elizabeth's outward defiance there is an inner crumpling' in her attitude toward Darcy.[1] Maaja Stewart takes such claims even further,

---

4   Jane Austen, *Pride and Prejudice*, ed. R. W. Chapman (Oxford: Clarendon Press, 1923), Volume II, Chapter 18, p. 232.

5   In Roman mythology, Venus is the god of love, Mars the god of war.

1   Edward Neill, *The Politics of Jane Austen* (London: Macmillan, 1999), p. 52.

contending that 'large patterns of power [. . .] render Elizabeth completely help-less'.[2] Bloom disagrees. 'Elizabeth would never marry a man whom she con-sidered her inferior, while she hates a man who considers himself her superior', he contends. 'Equality of the partners would seem to be the answer, and it is.'

One thing all critics agree upon is that Jane Austen's prevailing tone is ironical. In a gentle way, she ridicules practically everything, not only the pretensions of inferior persons like Mr. Collins or the Bingley sisters with their concerns for money and place, but also the self-deceptions of her protagonists, and even the hopes and expectations attendant upon the marriages that seem to be their ful-fillment. And it is this irony that perhaps most links her to the classical tradition. Real irony has a lot to do with the virtue missing in modern thought, moderation. It is the tone of superiority politely exposing inferiority without wounding it, leaving things in their place while nevertheless understanding them. It is a certain art of deception, the mode of radical thought that accepts conventional life while itself remaining free. Irony flourishes on the disproportion between the way things are and the way they should be while accepting the necessity of this disproportion. [. . .]

In the gripping drama of Darcy's first proposal and [Elizabeth's] furious rejec-tion of it,[3] she gives a mixture of good and bad reasons to justify her rejection. She has discovered that Darcy has played a critical role in preventing his friend Bing-ley from marrying her beloved and truly wonderful elder sister, Jane. He has done so on two grounds, her horrible family and Jane's apparent indifference to Bing-ley. The connection with the Bennets is evidently unsuitable in Darcy's eyes, although he himself seeks such a connection. But he does so, as he believes, out of an almost tragic necessity. And he can interpret Jane's motives as stemming out of the desire only for a comfortable situation. Both reasons actually have a certain basis in fact. Elizabeth has herself criticized Jane for not expressing her attraction to Bingley more openly.[4] Jane's reticence is due to good taste and modesty, but the misinterpretation is an excusable one. Moreover, Elizabeth's family is, with the exception of Jane and Elizabeth, indeed rather repulsive. We have had ample opportunity to see this with our own eyes, and their behavior at Bingley's ball was mortifying to Elizabeth herself. Their mother is mindless, social-climbing, taste-less, and without any self-control. The three younger sisters are each in her own way equally unappealing. They appear to be a tight band of marriageable pred-ators. Even Mr. Bennet, who is so bright and witty, from the point of view of severe virtue can be understood to be irresponsible and even frivolous. Elizabeth has experienced that most excruciating of pains for a decent person, being ashamed of one's family, being ashamed of one's shame, and the disagreeable

---

2 Maaja Stewart, *Domestic Realities and Imperial Fictions* (Athens: University of Georgia Press, 1993), p. 40.
3 See Key Passages, **pp. 132–8.**
4 For example, Elizabeth 'felt that Jane's feelings, though fervent, were little displayed, and that there was a constant complacency in her air and manner not often united with great sensibility' (see Key Passages, **p. 144**).

uncertainty whether the criticism is in fact justified or is merely an acceptance of the conventional opinions of others. This ambiguity is in Darcy himself. It is not clear whether his strictures stem from the merely social unacceptability of the Bennets, or a real insight into their inferiority. His relative, Catherine de Bourgh, is at least as vulgar as any of the Bennets, and compounds her vulgarity with abuse of her high station. And however different the cases, Darcy's sister agrees to an elopement with Wickham, as does Lydia. A part of Darcy's education in this novel is his coming to clarity about this issue. But Elizabeth responds with the angry defense of her own relations in a way characteristic of proud persons. Aristotle says that a gentleman is ironic to inferiors and insolent to superiors.[5] In this respect, Elizabeth is very much a gentleman.

The second objection to Darcy is his mistreatment of Wickham, whom he is alleged to have cheated out of his rightful inheritance as determined by Darcy's father in his love for his godson. Here the charge is not only pride or prejudice but strictly immoral conduct. Darcy appears to be not only a man contemptuous of others because he is born to high position but also simply a bad man, a breaker of faith and a moral hypocrite.

There is no doubt that Elizabeth believes what she says to Darcy and is truly indignant at his behavior, but her indignation masks the fact that these are only excuses for her dislike of Darcy. Collins's manners are at least as bad, but the passions of her soul do not combine in a passionate attack on him. With him she is objective and detached, or, at most, irritated. But with Darcy she is enraged because of his hold over her, the fact that his opinion really does count. She must make him think that it does not and that she is really independent of him. She has to get to him. If he thinks she is independent, maybe she will be able to believe that she is independent. [. . .] The real objection to Darcy is his taking her for granted and the hopeless inferiority that a marriage with him would entail. All the power is in his hands, and his only attachment to her appears to be an uncontrollable attraction without the support of either the conventional standards or a reverence for her virtue. Throughout a marriage that began in this way, he would have the advantage in every disagreement, for she would merely be a siren who entrapped him counter to all the good reasons for permanent moral attachment. Her accusations help her to avoid admitting the less than noble reasons for her resentment. Her education in the novel is learning to accept her dependence. Marriage between these two savages requires the acceptance by each of slavery to the other, while each thinks that he or she ought to be the master. Elizabeth would never marry a man whom she considered her inferior, while she hates a man who considers himself her superior. Equality of the partners would seem to be the answer, and it is. But the establishment of equality between two strong-willed individuals is not such an easy thing and probably requires each to think the other is superior. The fact is that Elizabeth would very much like to marry Mr. Darcy, and she must only persuade herself that she is taming her own will rather than being tamed by Darcy and that Darcy requires her for substantial and enduring reasons. The correctives to pride and prejudice, and progress in self-knowledge, result from the combative engagement of these two doubting warriors.

5   [Bloom's note] Aristotle, *Nicomachean Ethics*, 1124b18–20, 1124b30–1.

From **Susan Fraiman, 'The Humiliation of Elizabeth Bennet'** in
Unbecoming Women: British Women Writers and the Novel of Development
(New York: Columbia University Press, 1993), pp. 59–87

Sigmund Freud (1856–1939) established the theoretical framework for what is
known as 'psychoanalysis', a mode of criticism and inquiry centrally concerned
with the nature of the unconscious mind. According to Freud, we all have
repressed desires and fears, and one of the most common is the childhood wish
for sexual involvement with the parent of the opposite sex, and a corresponding
sense of rivalry with the parent of the same sex. This complex of feelings Freud
called 'oedipal', a term he derived from Sophocles's tragedy *Oedipus the King*,
where Oedipus unwittingly murders his father and marries his mother. Fraiman
centres her argument on the relationship between Mr. Bennet and Elizabeth,
and Elizabeth's role as an 'honorary boy' and 'surrogate son' who 'reaps the
spoils of maleness' and gains power through her alliance with her father. Ultimately, though, the male bond between father and daughter crumbles, for marriage means that Mr. Bennet withdraws his support and Elizabeth finds herself
returned to the disempowered sphere of the female. In psychoanalytic terms,
the world of *Pride and Prejudice* is 'phallocentric' (centred on the masculine
point of view), and fathers give their daughters away.

Like so many heroines in women's fiction, Elizabeth has a special relationship to
her father. She is immediately distinguished, both as a family member and as a
character, by his preference for her and hers for him. Entail aside, she is in many
respects his heir, for Mr. Bennet bequeaths to Elizabeth his ironic distance from
the world, his habit of studying and appraising those around him, his role of
social critic. Colleagues in this role, father and daughter scan Mr. Collins's letter
together, dismissing man and letter with a few, skeptical words. Mr. Bennet
enables Elizabeth, in short, by sharing with her an authorial mandate that is
Austen's own: the need and ability to frame a moral discourse and to judge
characters accordingly. Through her father, Elizabeth gains provisional access to
certain authorial powers. But Mr. Bennet also shares with her, illogically enough,
his disdain for women. He respects Elizabeth only insofar as she is unlike other
girls, so that bonding with him means breaking with her mother or even reneging
on femaleness altogether. In this sense Elizabeth is less a daughter than a surrogate
son: like a son, by giving up the mother and giving in to the father, she reaps the
spoils of maleness. Freud's charting of female development supplies an alternative
view. In this scheme, girls turn, disillusioned, from the mother to the father out of
penis envy. To complete their oedipal task, however, they must cease to identify
with the powerful father, come to accept their own 'castration', and learn to desire
a baby as a substitute for the phallus.[1] In these terms the cocky Elizabeth of the

---

1   [Fraiman's note] The relevant essays are 'The Dissolution of the Oedipus Complex' (1924), 'Some
     Psychical Consequences of the Anatomical Distinction between the Sexes' (1925), 'Female Sexual-
     ity' (1931), and 'Femininity' (1932). Nancy Chodorow [in *The Reproduction of Mothering* (Berke-
     ley: University of California Press, 1978), pp. 94–9)] offers a helpful recapitulation of Freud on
     fathers and daughters [...]

book's first half is charmingly arrested in the early phase of male-identification, victim of what Freud would call a 'masculinity complex'. And in either case – whether one sees her as an honourary boy who has completed his oedipal task or as a backward, wayward girl who refuses to complete hers – Elizabeth's discursive power arises from an alliance and identification with her father. As the scene with Mr. Collins shows, the force of her words is highly contingent, any authority she has merely borrowed.[2] Like a woman writing under a male pseudonym, Elizabeth's credibility depends on her father's signature. [. . .] For in Austen the male bonding between father and daughter is set up to collapse. Sooner or later, what Adrienne Rich calls 'compulsory heterosexuality'[3] – a conspiracy of economic need and the ideology of romance – forces Elizabeth out of the library, into the ballroom, and up to the altar. The father's business in this ritual is, in every sense, to give the daughter away. If Mr. Bennet is supportive up to a point, her marriage obliges him to objectify Elizabeth and hand her over. At this juncture, he not only withdraws his protection and empowerment but also gives away her true 'castrated' gender, revealing her incapacity for action in a phallocentric society.[4] This ceremony – posing father as giver, daughter as gift – could be said to underlie and ultimately to belie the relation of fathers to daughters in *Pride and Prejudice*.

From **Douglas Murray, 'Gazing and Avoiding the Gaze'** in *Jane Austen's Business: Her World and Her Profession*, eds Juliet McMaster and Bruce Stovel (London: Macmillan, 1996), pp. 44–5

Douglas Murray applies the insights of the French philosopher and historian Michel Foucault to *Pride and Prejudice*. Murray argues that highly efficient networks of surveillance enable Mrs. Bennet and Lady Catherine to keep a close eye on what is happening around them. Elizabeth attracts the male gaze, but she also returns it, for her ability to look others in the eye is a measure of her independence and strength. As is so often the case in *Pride and Prejudice*, objects of aesthetic beauty also signify powerfully in terms of politics and class. Darcy appreciates Elizabeth's 'fine eyes' for their beauty, but it is those same eyes that look straight into the implacable aristocratic gaze of Lady Catherine and refuse to close or conform (see Key Passages, **pp. 119, 150–6**). Lady Catherine looks for submission but Elizabeth does not blink.

In *Discipline and Punish: The Birth of the Prison* (*Surveiller et Punir*, 1975), Foucault enumerates the increased mechanisms of surveillance which arose

---

2   See Key Passages, **pp. 124–7**.
3   Adrienne Rich, 'Compulsory Heterosexuality and Lesbian Existence', in *Signs*, 5 (1980), pp. 631–60.
4   [Fraiman's note] In a letter to a favourite niece, Austen more explicitly and bitterly represents marriage as a loss, for women, ushering in a period of inactivity: 'Oh! what a loss it will be, when you are married. You are too agreable in your single state, too agreable as a Neice. I shall hate you when your delicious play of Mind is settled down into conjugal & maternal affections' (Jane Austen, 'Letter to Fanny Knight: 20–21 February 1817, Chawton' in *Jane Austen's Letters*, ed. Deirdre Le Faye (Oxford: Oxford University Press, 1995), p. 329).

during the Enlightenment.[1] He locates in Austen's era the institution of what he calls panopticism: unavoidable, universal, ceaseless surveillance [. . .] He argues that Enlightenment institutions used the knowledge gained by surveillance to discipline and normalize, to make individuals 'useful' for society, to 'strengthen the social force', to order 'human multiplicities' [. . .] Visibility, then, had its costs, but it insured full citizenship, since in the Enlightenment, to be was to be seen [. . .]

In *Pride and Prejudice*, spies are everywhere and news travels fast. By the opening scene, everyone in the vicinity of Netherfield Hall knows much about Charles Bingley – his approximate income, his mode of transportation, etc. In the past, these first chapters have been read as misogynistic satire of female gossip, but it is difficult to maintain this interpretation. Mrs. Bennet is the centre of a remarkably efficient and accurate network for the sharing of information: her 'solace was visiting and news'[2] – in other words, discovery and dissemination. And, of course, the men are simultaneously conducting their own surveys: Charles Bingley takes Netherfield Hall so that he can hunt game birds *and* find a suitable marriage partner.

In a novel full of powerful information centres, the most knowledgeable and potentially the most powerful is Lady Catherine de Bourgh, whom I label the 'panoptic centre' of the novel. She gathers information first by noticing – in fact, the word 'notice' is often used to accompany her appearances – second, by asking questions – the interrogative is her favoured form of the sentence – and, last, through the use of the Rev. William Collins, whose career suggests the upper class's use of the lower orders as spies and manipulators. Her centre of intelligence is Rosings, which appropriately features numerous windows expensively glazed.

But if Lady Catherine is an information centre, we should not forget her defeat at the hand of the triumphant and independent gazer Elizabeth Bennet, who throughout the novel is symbolically associated with the eye. An attentive reader will find that, in Volume I, Austen mentions Elizabeth's eyes with almost predictable frequency, every ten pages or so. Elizabeth's abilities to attract more than a cursory gaze and to return others' gaze indicate her resistance and independence of mind amid powerful forces of conformity. It is this central core of resistance which allows Elizabeth to withstand the powerful gaze of Lady Catherine – or, as the cliché puts it, to look her in the eye.

From **John Wiltshire, '*Pride and Prejudice*, love and recognition'** in *Recreating Jane Austen* (Cambridge: Cambridge University Press, 2001), pp. 99–124

Like Fraiman (see Modern Criticism, **pp. 93–4**), Wiltshire uses Freudian psychoanalysis to gain insight into one of the key relationships in the novel.

---

1   A general term applied to the movement of intellectual liberation that developed in Western Europe in the seventeenth century and climaxed in the eighteenth in the works of writers such as Jean-Jacques Rousseau, and the political ideals of the American and French Revolutions.
2   Jane Austen, *Pride and Prejudice*, ed. R. W. Chapman (Oxford: Clarendon Press, 1923), Volume I, Chapter 1, p. 5.

Elizabeth and Darcy project their own resentments and wishes onto one another. Each is a part of the other's psychological landscape, but neither is present to the other as a distinct being. Elizabeth denies her own shortcomings and displaces them onto Darcy, repeatedly ascribing to him what is coming from her: she condemns his pride and prejudice with pride and prejudice. Similarly, a desire for domination means that Darcy regards Elizabeth only as an object or vehicle for his own powerful psychic desires and discontents. When he proposes to her for the first time, he does not recognize her as an individual being, so that rather than reaching out to her, he conducts a kind of disastrously inner dialogue with himself. For both, the self sees only self, and their relationship is mired in solipsism until each perceives in the other a vital and separate presence.

The traditional focus of psychoanalysis on the processes occurring within the individual psyche can certainly throw some light on *Pride and Prejudice*. Its understanding of projection, in which 'the subject attributes tendencies, desires etc., to others that he refuses to recognize in himself' is an example.[1] This might suggest why Elizabeth makes no progress in her avowed design of understanding Darcy, of painting a portrait or taking a sketch of his nature. Her declared aim is always being undercut and subverted by her unconscious wishes. One might say that Elizabeth denies Darcy's subjectivity at the same time as she professes to invite it to speak. Elizabeth disowns parts of herself and bestows them instead on Darcy. For it is plain that Elizabeth, who is 'determined to dislike' Darcy (as she tells Charlotte, in half-jest), herself enacts just that 'implacable resentment'[2] she attributes to him – building on that first insult and making everything else she hears from or about him, feed into this original orientation. In a series of encounters Elizabeth attributes to Darcy the very emotions that are driving her – pride and prejudice among them.[3] Her anger at his words about her family's behaviour enables her to forget or displace her own sense of shame, or rather it converts that shame into anger against him. Her hatred of her mother, for example, which Darcy's presence makes her experience most keenly, is naturally projected onto him. Thus this 'Mr. Darcy' is for Elizabeth not someone who is perceived in his own right (so to speak) but someone who plays a role in her psychological life, as receptacle of her own projections and needs.

And to an extent less illuminated by the text, it seems the same is true of Darcy's relation to Elizabeth. In a different way, he attributes his own desires to her, so that up to the proposal, as he later confesses, he believes that she wishes for, and is even 'expecting [his] addresses'.[4] Just as it was taken for granted

---

1   [Wiltshire's note] J. Laplanche and J.-B. Pontalis, *The Language of Psychoanalysis* (London: Karnac, 1973), p. 351.
2   See Key Passages, **p. 123**.
3   [Wiltshire's note] Similar observations are made by Marilyn Butler, *Jane Austen and the War of Ideas* (Oxford: Clarendon Press, 1975), p. 105.
4   See Key Passages, **p. 157**. Alison Sulloway also examines Darcy's belief that Elizabeth is 'expecting [his] addresses' (see Modern Criticism, **p. 88**).

that a young man in possession of a fortune would seek a wife, Darcy assumes that a young lady in want of a fortune would accept a husband with one: but this is not all. As Elizabeth realises, listening to him in the proposal scene, she has no real presence to him: he is, in effect, though speaking in her company, conducting an inner dialogue with himself. His passion for her contains no element of perception of her as an independently existing being (hence, as in the formality of his proposal address, what Johnson calls its 'appalling resemblance'[5] to Mr. Collins's).[6]

It is such processes – the way that selves make use of other selves, fantasizing about them, incorporating them into their own psychic life – that psychoanalysis classically studied and illuminated. It is as if the self radiates out, and the phenomena of the external world, other people, were only visible in its own light. But through psychoanalysis's intense focus on the individual in whom they are enacted, the discourse itself tended to reproduce precisely that solecism – the focus on the operations of the monadic individual psyche – in its own theoretical writings. It seemed to suggest that this is all that need be said about normal human relations, that others exist for a human subject wholly as receptacles and vehicles for their psychic needs, or as 'objects' for their impulses. Jessica Benjamin argues that this concentration on 'object relations' very largely does reflect the nature of human psychological life. But, she insists, there are moments when we get beyond this – when we see others as existing outside ourselves with their own 'equivalent centres of self' (a phrase from George Eliot[7] she uses as an epigraph).[8] Drawing on Hegel's concept of the master-slave relation,[9] she argues that, most of the time, our relationships with others are relations of 'domination', in which we make psychological (ab)use of them. Darcy is using Elizabeth in this way in his first proposal – he addresses her not as an individual being but, as Rachel Brownstein puts it, as just another girl with a vulgar mother.[10] He is in 'the bonds of love', so overwhelmed by 'the utmost force of passion'[11] that he is in fact oblivious to the person he is addressing – a classic instance of love as domination.

5   [Wiltshire's note] Claudia L. Johnson, *Jane Austen: Women, Politics, and the Novel* (Chicago: University of Chicago Press, 1988), p. 82.
6   Compare Collins's proposal to Elizabeth (Key Passages, **pp. 124–7**) with Darcy's first proposal to her (Key Passages, **pp. 132–8**).
7   George Eliot (1819–80), English novelist whose major works include *Adam Bede* (1859), *The Mill on the Floss* (1860), and *Middlemarch* (1871–2).
8   [Wiltshire's note] Jessica Benjamin, *Like Subjects, Love Objects: Essays on Recognition and Sexual Difference* (New Haven: Yale University Press, 1995), p. 27.
9   Georg Wilhelm Friedrich Hegel (1770–1831), German philosopher who in the most famous section of his *Phenomenology* (1807) argues the interaction between master and slave is the product of an uncompleted fight to the death for 'recognition'. The battle is characterized by an inverted logic in which master and slave switch roles.
10 [Wiltshire's note] Rachel M. Brownstein, *Becoming a Heroine: Reading about Women in Novels* (New York: Columbia University Press, 1994), p. 116.
11 See Key Passages, **p. 140**.

From **Steven Scott, 'Making Room in the Middle: Mary in *Pride and Prejudice*'** in *The Talk in Jane Austen* (Edmonton: University of Alberta Press, 2002), pp. 225–36

In *Pride and Prejudice*, humour often disguises fear and disappointment. The Bennets' middle daughter Mary is easy to miss or mock. Her father's treatment of her is snide and uncharitable. In 1813, the *Critical Review* described her as 'a female pedant, affecting great wisdom, though saturated with stupidity' (see Early Critical Reception, **p. 56**). Film adaptations have repeatedly turned her character to caricature. Scott, however, finds Mary an almost tragic figure who rejects many of the same norms and notions that the novel itself rejects. Throughout *Pride and Prejudice* Austen packs depth and suggestive detail into even the most apparently minor characters and scenes.

Mr. Bennet, in fact, goes out of his way in the novel and in the film adaptations to single out Mary for ridicule. I would suggest that the best explanation for that singling out is that Mary is the first real disappointment of the Bennet family. The Bennets expected to have a son and break the entail on their estate. The first two daughters were treated as valued children, and Jane and Elizabeth act like cherished children; Mary, however, was clearly supposed to be a boy. The parents seem to have given up with the youngest two, who have no sense whatsoever and are essentially clones of their very foolish mother. Mary is the disappointment. This also explains why it is that Mary spends so much time reading. She would like to please a father who spends all of his time in the library. This explanation, of course, moves Mary from being silly and a comic character to being a sad, nearly tragic one. [. . .]

The novel clearly condemns Mary as socially inept, someone who has spent too much time inside her own head and not nearly enough time in the company of good society. Accordingly, Mary's speech is of a curious kind. She does not speak easily or very well because speech is a social activity, along with walks, dancing, and cards, and she does not know how to play that game well: she really doesn't care to. She lives for herself and the part of the world that she touches. That seems to be enough for her. It seems to me that she displays the marks of a post-Romantic heroine and that, in her pursuits and interests and goals, Mary deserves not to be parodied, but admired as a precursor of a modern woman. In a sense, the novel has created a woman who is beyond itself. It condemns Mary for not following many of the social norms that it itself condemns at the same time. Mary seems, remarkably, capable of picking and choosing and making her own society. That individual capacity for self-determination is a fact of modern life that we now take for granted; I find it fascinating to discover it here, in this most unlikely of places.

The Novel in Performance

Introduction

There have been seven film versions of *Pride and Prejudice*,[1] among which the following three are the best-known:

1 The 1940 MGM production written by Aldous Huxley and Jane Murfin, directed by Robert Z. Leonard, and featuring Greer Garson as Elizabeth Bennet and Laurence Olivier as Mr. Darcy (see Figure 6, **p. 100**). The film 'was to be what Hollywood called a woman's picture', writes Rachel Brownstein, 'with Darcy's beautiful marble face as its focus'.[2] The dresses from the film are clearly in the style of those in *Gone With the Wind* (1939), for 'they feature tight bodices, tight natural waists, huge puffed sleeves, and billowing hooped skirts', as Sue Parrill observes.[3] The script condensed the novel into just under two hours, and turned it into a comedic romp. The advertising campaign warned, 'Bachelors Beware! Five Gorgeous Beauties are on a Madcap Manhunt'.[4]
2 The 1979 BBC version written by Fay Weldon, directed by Cyril Coke, and featuring Elizabeth Garvie as Elizabeth Bennet and David Rintoul as Mr. Darcy.
3 The 1995 BBC version written by Andrew Davies, directed by Simon Langton, and featuring Jennifer Ehle as Elizabeth Bennet and Colin Firth as Mr. Darcy (see Figure 10, **p. 146**).

The following three selections concentrate on the 1995 film, and in particular the character of Darcy. Firth explains how he approached the role; Nixon shows how Davies rewrites Austen's Darcy; and Hopkins explores watching us watching Darcy watching Elizabeth.

1 For full details, see Sue Parrill, *Jane Austen on Film and Television* (Jefferson, NC: McFarland, 2002), pp. 191–5.
2 Rachel Brownstein, 'Out of the Drawing Room, Onto the Lawn' in *Jane Austen in Hollywood*, eds Linda Troost and Sayre Greenfield (Lexington: University of Kentucky Press, 1998), p. 13.
3 Parrill, *Jane Austen on Film and Television*, p. 55.
4 Ibid., p. 49.

Figure 6 **Greer Garson as Elizabeth Bennet and Laurence Olivier as Mr. Darcy in the 1940 MGM version of** *Pride and Prejudice.*

From **Sue Birtwistle and Susie Conklin, 'A Conversation with Colin Firth'** in *The Making of Pride and Prejudice* (London: Penguin, 1995), pp. 97–105

In this interview Colin Firth comments frankly and suggestively on Darcy's key scenes and motivations. Many critics, including Mudrick (see Modern Criticism, **pp. 74–5**), argue that Darcy's character is inconsistent, but Firth contends otherwise. Darcy's 'real crime [. . .] is silliness', Firth observes. When he first proposes to Elizabeth he is anxious she does not think him 'a reckless school-boy'. He has to learn that Elizabeth is 'his equal, if not his superior, in terms of wit, intellectual agility and sense of personal dignity'.

Did Andrew's scripts[1] help you to understand Darcy's character?

Yes, I think they were a wonderful way into Jane Austen because he doesn't have that absurd, academic reverence that people sometimes have for a great work of literature. He treated it like a vastly enjoyable story. Had I started with the novel, I might not have become involved. I think Andrew's earthiness, and the fact that he sometimes made things a lot more specific than Jane Austen does, were very helpful. He offers very strong suggestions as to what Darcy is thinking when he's looking, poker-faced, at the people in a crowd scene, and that helps Darcy to become more than simply an image.

What's interesting when you're doing a part like this is if you can find fluidity from moment to moment. When something is somehow not truthful, it jars because you've got to try to force your imagination to think up justifications for what you're doing. I never had to do that with Darcy – or very rarely – and it suddenly hit me that Jane Austen really did have an instinctive grasp of Darcy's inner self, even though she didn't have the arrogance to write it. But she writes the outer man so logically that the inside 'plays'.

Can you think of a specific example?

I remember thinking that it makes sense when Darcy slights Elizabeth at the Meryton assembly.[2] I agree to go to a party with my friend Bingley. He encourages me: 'Come on, it'll be a great party with lots of women.' I arrive. I'm terribly shy – terribly uneasy in social situations anyway. This is not a place I'd normally go to, and I don't know how to talk to these people. So I protect myself behind a veneer of snobbishness and rejection. Bingley immediately engages with the most attractive woman in the room, and that makes me feel even less secure. He comes bounding over with a big, enthusiastic smile and tells me I should be dancing. I say, 'You've got the best-looking girl in the room,' and he replies, 'Well, never mind – what about the less attractive sister?' and this exacerbates the position I've put myself in. Then I say, 'She's okay, but not good enough for me,' but what I'm really saying is: 'Look, I'm supposed to be better than you, so don't give me the plain sister. I'm not even going to consider her.' By keeping this in mind when filming, I found that the scene actually played itself.

At the end of the story Darcy tells Lizzy that he doesn't know when he first fell in love with her. But you would have needed to plot his journey more specifically.

Yes, it's very interesting to watch out for the triggers that lead to Darcy's falling in love. Of course, love often starts with something trivial that attracts your

---

1   Andrew Davies wrote the screenplay for the film.
2   See Key Passages, pp. 114–17.

attention. In Darcy's case, very little had ever attracted his attention. So I think the first trigger is the moment when Elizabeth rejects him so impertinently – when she overhears him saying, 'She's tolerable, I suppose, but not handsome enough to tempt *me*.'[3] When she walks past and gives him a cheeky look, Andrew was very helpful here in writing: 'Darcy was used to looking at other people like that, but was not used to being looked at like that himself.' So at that moment, I think, he notices her simply out of bewilderment and curiosity; he becomes intrigued by her, which, I suspect, is the first time he has ever been intrigued by a woman, and he has to know a little bit more about her. It strikes me that you can be on a fatal course from a moment like that whether you know it or not. [. . .]

You had to film Darcy's first proposal scene in the second week of filming. How did that affect you?
It seemed a catastrophe at first. Everybody knows how important the scene is.[4] For scheduling reasons we had to film a lot of Darcy's later scenes first – where he appears a much nicer person – and then do this scene with him at breaking point. Because it's so inappropriate to do it early and it's so nerve-racking, we gave it a tremendous amount of attention and got a degree of adrenalin working up to it. So that perhaps it's invested with something that it would never have had if we had done it later, when everyone had settled in. It was a case of jumping in at the deep end, and Simon Langton[5] handled it brilliantly.

How did you approach this scene?
I asked myself some extremely basic questions about what it was I wanted to do in the scene. I asked, 'What's my character trying to get?' and then, 'How will he overcome any obstacles that are in the way?' In this case, the main question was: 'How is Elizabeth going to make it difficult for me, and how am I going to make it difficult for myself?' If you address problems like these, you come up with ways and means that help to make the approach clear.

I felt, for instance, that when Darcy goes into that room and says those shocking things – 'I'm too good for you, but will you marry me anyway?' – if I played it as if I knew I were being shocking and arrogant, it would never work. I realized that I had to make it the most reasonable thing in the world to say, but I wondered, 'How do I do that? How do I turn that extraordinary speech about her family connections being utterly disastrous into something reasonable?' And I thought, 'Okay, let's think ourselves into the time for a moment, into 1813,' and from Jane Austen's perspective this business about appropriate and inappropriate marriages made an awful lot of sense. It might be a disaster to cross class barriers; it could lead to all sorts of misery and unhappiness; the social fabric of the time was threatened by it, and so on.

He is also arrogant enough to think he has bestowed an enormous gift on her. Every woman he has ever met would say 'yes' to a proposal from him. It would be insane for Lizzy to say 'no', not because he assumes she finds him attractive – I don't think that's the reason – but because it's the most practical offer that even

3   See Key Passages, p. 117.
4   See Key Passages, pp. 132–8.
5   Simon Langton directed the film.

someone considerably her social superior could ever hope to receive. I think he assumes, as everybody would at that time, that it would be a Cinderella ending for her.

And so Darcy is coming in with a very imprudent proposal, as he sees it. He's saying to her, 'I'm going to put to you a proposal that may make me seem rash, irresponsible and even, possibly, juvenile, but I don't want you to believe I'm those things. I have thought through every detail of this; I know that my family will be angry, that people will frown on us and that our social positions are very different. So don't think that I haven't dealt with these issues – don't imagine that I'm just some reckless schoolboy. Nevertheless, having thought it all through, I find that my love for you is so overwhelming that these objections are rendered insignificant.' And, from that point of view, it's a terribly romantic proposal. I was a bit hurt when we filmed it, and everybody thought I was saying something terrible: I had got myself so far into the notion that he had come in with a really charming thing to say. Of course, when you watch it, you don't see it from his point of view. You see a self-important man entering and expressing these pompous sentiments as if they were the most natural reactions in the world and then having the gall to be astonished by Elizabeth's rejection – and I think that's right. But I couldn't have played that astonishment without approaching it the way I did.

He doesn't see her again until he unexpectedly runs into her at Pemberley. What's he trying to do at this stage?
Jane Austen is rather vague in her description of Darcy during this period, and I found myself foraging for clues about how he is supposed to come across. There are contradictions. People often ask whether Darcy changes in the course of the story or whether we find out what he is really like. I think it is a mixture of the two. His housekeeper talks affectionately of him and reveals that he has always looked after his sister and taken care of his household in a very kindly way. He hasn't suddenly turned into a good man; I think that he has always been a good man underneath that stiff exterior.

I realized that when he runs into Elizabeth at Pemberley he needs to prove a great deal to her in a short space of time.[6] He needs to show her in about three minutes flat that he is prepared to be apologetic and tender and amenable and unsnobbish. He's just got to get a foot in the door and prove that he has tried to change those aspects of his nature that alienated her before. He wants her to love him: but how do you make somebody love you in just a few minutes? And how do you do that while still being true to Darcy's character?

Does Lizzy's rejection effect any real changes in Darcy, then?
Oh, yes. You cannot think that Darcy is simply going to return to the way he was. The fact that he writes her a letter explaining himself and disclosing some very personal information – which is ostensibly a tremendously out-of-character thing to do – suggests this.[7] I think he suffers enormously as a result of her rejection

6 See Key Passages, pp. 145–9.
7 See Key Passages, pp. 138–43.

because he loves her. I think he endures torment because a lifetime's behaviour, even his very character, has been thrown into relief by her words.

His real crime, I think, is silliness. I know that's a terribly undignified way to look at him, but I believe his failing is foolish, superficial, social snobbery, and that's the bitter lesson he has to learn. And I think in that sense he does change. He actually says in the book that his father instilled in him good values but also taught him to think meanly of the world outside his own social circle. He is rather afraid of anything outside his immediate experience and is quite convinced that he will encounter nothing but barbarianism. People do make assumptions about other areas of civilization, and that's precisely what Darcy does. It's ignorance.

He learns his lesson when he falls in love with one of those barbarians and realizes that she's at least his equal, if not his superior, in terms of wit, intellectual agility and sense of personal dignity. He is so profoundly challenged by her that his old prejudices cannot be upheld. I still think he'll always have something of the old view – he'll always be disgusted by ridiculous, boring people who talk too much. I don't think he'll ever learn to adore Mrs. Bennet or develop an enormous admiration for Sir William Lucas.

And, of course, he hasn't quite learned to laugh at himself. He's learned to criticize himself, which is probably the first step, but he doesn't yet know how to find himself ridiculous and enjoy it. With Lizzy as a partner, however, married life will be a matter of survival, and it's plain that he's going to learn *that* lesson before too long.

From **Cheryl Nixon, 'Balancing the Courtship Hero: Masculine Emotional Display in Film Adaptations of Austen's Novels'** in *Jane Austen in Hollywood*, eds Linda Troost and Sayre Greenfield (Lexington: University of Kentucky Press, 1998), pp. 22–43

Nixon demonstrates the ways in which the Darcy of Austen's novel undergoes a 'radical revision' in Davies's screenplay. In the novel Darcy's first proposal to Elizabeth is a passionate and sudden outburst from a man who has shown little emotion up to that point. In the film, a series of additional scenes of physical activity reveal the intensity of Darcy's feelings, while his brooding and staring demonstrate his inability to speak of those feelings. 'Is Darcy's proposal too expressive, as the novel might have it', Nixon asks, 'or not expressive enough, as the film has it?' The answer, she concludes, 'is both'.

In Davies's screenplay of *Pride and Prejudice*, Darcy is cast as an awkward hero tortured by an excess of emotions he cannot express. With his tousled dark hair, smoldering eyes that stare deeply into middle space, and a pained self-consciousness in social situations, he is convincingly reimagined as a vaguely Byronic hero.[1] A brooding loner who can neither physically contain nor verbally

---

1   Lord Byron (1788–1824) was the most famous literary figure of Austen's day. Several of his poems featured a proudly defiant but self-tormenting outcast known as 'the Byronic hero'.

express his inner emotional battles, Darcy engages in a roster of physical activities that do not appear in the novel but which convey these battles to the viewer. The film's additions envision Darcy playing billiards, bathing, fencing, and swimming. As Darcy's pursuit of Elizabeth becomes more certain, his physical activities are increasingly replaced by meditative stares which, in turn, become increasingly direct; this expression of longing peaks when he spends a tumultuous night pacing back and forth to his window while attempting to write a response to her rejection of his marriage proposal. Darcy's physical activities reveal the violence of his emotions while his longing stares restate his inability to express verbally those emotions. [. . .]

After Elizabeth rejects his marriage proposal, Darcy turns to physical exercise as if to chastise the flesh for its desires. When placed in the context of earlier scenes, this physical behavior can only be an expression of his continuing love and not an exorcising of it. In a most noticeable addition to Austen, Darcy engages in an intense fencing match with his fencing master. He fights with great force and noise, sweating and panting with exertion. After being praised by his master, he turns away with a brooding stare. Looking deep into himself and speaking only to himself, he exclaims, 'I shall conquer this.' It is obvious that Darcy is expressing his desire to conquer his love for Elizabeth – not, say, to conquer a weakness in his fencing technique. This emotional dialogue with the self is best expressed by physical exertion. Unlike the film, the novel does not express Darcy's continued emotional struggle; when he and Elizabeth are separated, the reader learns nothing of his thoughts or actions. While the novel leaves the reader, like Elizabeth, uncertain of Darcy's emotions, the BBC adaptation allows no such questioning of the relationship. [. . .]

The 'extra Darcy' presented in these scenes is extra emotion. Darcy's added physical display of emotion provides a radical revision of the masculine balance Austen advocates between personal expression and social restraint. For example, in the film adaptation, Elizabeth's rejection of Darcy's first marriage proposal can be read as a rejection due to his inability to voice his full emotions. Compared with his doting stares, billiard playing, bathing, fencing, and swimming, Darcy's proposal seems restrained; although he expresses his love, he is unable to put his hidden emotions into a verbal vocabulary that matches the intensity of his physical vocabulary. His private desires are held back by public considerations of social inequality. Viewing the film, we feel Elizabeth is right to reject him; he has not given full expression to the depth of the emotions we, the audience, know him to have. In contrast, the novel can be read as constructing the scene according to completely opposite dictates. Darcy's proposal is rejected because he has displayed too much of his emotions rather than too little. Darcy does not show proper courtship restraint and propose according to proper social form; after Elizabeth rejects him, he himself says, 'These bitter accusations might have been suppressed, had I with greater policy concealed my struggles, and flattered you into the belief of my being impelled by unqualified, unalloyed inclination [. . .] But disguise of every sort is my abhorrence. Nor am I ashamed of the feelings I related'.[2] In contrast to the film, which places the same verbal expression within

---

2 See Key Passages, p. 137.

the context of emotionally charged physical expression, the text positions this verbal expression as an unexpected outburst from a character who has displayed almost no emotion in any form. Austen's Darcy has suddenly displayed too much emotional freedom: he expresses his love openly and then openly states the frustrating barriers his love has overcome. Is Darcy's proposal too expressive, as the novel might have it, or not expressive enough, as the film has it? The answer is both; he exists as both in two different *Pride and Prejudice* texts. Masculine emotional display has been envisioned differently by each; it provides a telling example of how Austen's 'balance' has been reformulated and paradoxically maintained by today's audience, an audience that expects masculinity to evidence balance through emotional display.

From **Lisa Hopkins, 'Mr. Darcy's Body: Privileging the Female Gaze'** in Jane Austen in Hollywood, eds Linda Troost and Sayre Greenfield (Lexington: University of Kentucky Press, 1998), pp. 111–21

Hopkins is interested in the iconography of Davies's adaptation, and the erotic energy that builds up as Darcy stares repeatedly at Elizabeth. In the first half of the film, Darcy is a figure of glances, profiles, and side-shots. But after his first proposal to Elizabeth, the presentation of him changes, and he become visually central. We gaze at Darcy as Darcy gazes at Elizabeth, and while the adaptation fetishizes Darcy's looks, it is his need to look at Elizabeth that holds us most powerfully. *Pride and Prejudice* privileges the female gaze, and enacts a fantasy in which a man loves a woman with an intensity that we worry may not exist for real men in everyday lives.

From the bath scene onwards, Darcy looking at Elizabeth becomes a recurrent and compelling image, used both to provide a crucial insight into his character and to build up a powerful erotic charge, of which he is clearly the center. When Elizabeth and Jane leave Netherfield, Darcy watches their departure from a window. The moment recapitulates his earlier gazing out of windows, as for instance when he is bored by Mrs. Bennet on her visit to Netherfield, but with a significant difference: this time, we know what he is looking at and are invited to decode the meaning of his gaze. When she returns to Netherfield for the ball, Elizabeth looks around for Wickham. Heads part to show Mr. Darcy in profile – and he then turns to look at her. However, the fact that we are by no means drawing toward the end of the story is clearly signaled by the persistence of some of the earlier iconography. When he and Colonel Fitzwilliam visit Hunsford parsonage, Darcy looks out of the window, and on his first trip alone there, he sits sideways on, revealing only his profile. Most crucially, for the first proposal scene he is again, as at Lucas Lodge, standing at first by a mirror; when rejected, he immediately moves into profile, walks agitatedly, and then returns to the mirror, standing sideways on. Though his propensity to look out of windows as well as into mirrors may acquit him of simple vanity, the iconography nevertheless insistently suggests that he has, as yet, not looked fully either at what lies within him or at the woman who sits in front of him.

After the first proposal – the moment when, in the video version, the first part comes to an end – the presentation of Darcy shifts: from being a figure of side-shots and glances away, he becomes one of iconic centrality for both visual and narrative imperatives. The opening shot shows the immediate aftermath of the rejection, but it focuses, notably, not on Elizabeth, but on Darcy. The first thing we see is him striding away from the parsonage, with Elizabeth's dismissal of him heard in voice-over, obviously still ringing in his ears. When her accusations reach the subject of Wickham, he says aloud, 'Well at least in *that* I may defend myself.' Returning to his aunt's house, he immediately rushes upstairs, excusing himself to Colonel Fitzwilliam. We follow him into his bedroom and see him at once begin to write the letter, which we hear him reading in voice-over. As the voice-over continues, he moves away from the desk and looks out of the window, through which we see a flashback to his Cambridge days. Darcy, in cap and gown, is walking down a college cloister; he opens a door and finds Wickham *in flagrante*[1] with a young woman. Looking disgusted, Darcy closes the door, and we revert to the present, with the older Darcy, his shirt now open, throwing back his head in his chair. The light picks out his throat, so vulnerable in this position. Next, with his shirt still further thrust open, he plunges his face into a basin of water [. . .]

During Darcy's writing of the letter,[2] the visual imagery is structured by a heady mingling of two *leitmotifs*: heat and sex. There is a particularly telling counter-point between the heated contemporary Darcy and the buttoned-up younger self who bursts in on Wickham: Wickham's animalistic copulation may be deplored, but a subtler eroticism is not. The episode also inflects the next section of the letter, in which we cut from Darcy writing to Elizabeth reading, as we hear of his comments on the Bingley episode and particularly on Jane's apparent lack of response. Not only is our awareness of Darcy's qualifications to judge responsiveness heightened, but the whole question of sexual attraction and female desire is thus sharply highlighted. [. . .]

In the world of romance in general, women authors have delighted in creating male characters who crave the love of the heroines with an intensity which, we may fear, real men rarely experience. Perhaps the deepest appeal of *Pride and Prejudice* lies in the extent to which it has exploited the medium of television to lend physical actuality to that fantasy. What we want to see, I think, is not just Darcy in the abstract: it is Darcy looking – particularly at Elizabeth but also, on other occasions, at images which have been contextualized as being poignantly redolent of her absence. These looks too can signify his need. And we look back in a silent collusion, because it is in that need that we most want to believe.

1   'in the midst of sexual activity'.
2   See Key Passages, **pp. 138–43**.

3

Key passages

Introduction

The text for these Key Passages is taken from the first edition of *Pride and Prejudice*, which Austen herself received on 27 January 1813, and which seems to have been first advertised in the *Morning Chronicle* for 28 January 1813 (see Contemporary Documents, **p. 41**).[1] The plot of the novel is usefully summarized by A. Walton Litz.[2] Figure 7 (see **p. 112**) is a map for *Pride and Prejudice*, and gives the various locations for the major events in the novel, including London, Brighton, Pemberley, Longbourn, Netherfield, and Rosings. Each Key Passage in this section is introduced by a headnote that draws attention to its importance in the novel, and to the writers and critics whose ideas illuminate it. Where necessary, footnotes translate foreign phrases, cue cross-references, and identify contemporary usages, activities, and place names. The task of choosing the passages has of course not been an easy one, but I hope this selection provides useful insights into the novel's central predicaments, themes, and anxieties.

1   See also R. W. Chapman, 'Introductory Note to *Pride and Prejudice*' in Jane Austen, *Pride and Prejudice*, ed. R. W. Chapman (Oxford: Clarendon Press, 1923), p. xi.
2   A. Walton Litz, '*Pride and Prejudice*' in *The Jane Austen Handbook*, ed. J. David Grey (London: The Athlone Press, 1986), pp. 334–5.

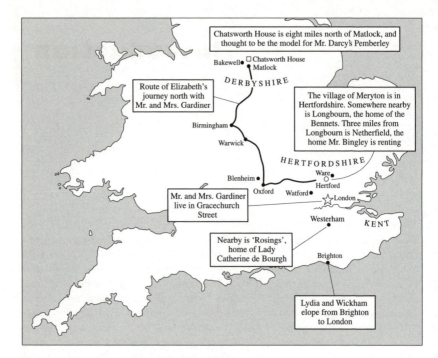

Figure 7 **A map for *Pride and Prejudice.***

Key Passages

Volume I, Chapter One

Pride and Prejudice contains perhaps the most famous opening sentence in English literature. 'It is a truth universally acknowledged, that a single man in possession of a good fortune, must be in want of a wife'. Critics have pointed at length to the economy and irony of the sentence, and the ways in which the novel's sparkling wit and darker undertones emerge simultaneously out of it. According to Judith Lowder Newton, the opening sentence helps to establish how 'economic inequity shapes male and female power'.[1] John Wiltshire declares that in it the narrator assumes 'a voice in order to expose how widespread is the attribution to others of what we ourselves wish. The Mrs. Bennets of this world bestow their own desires on the young men who are their object'.[2] For Nina Auerbach, the key is '*must be*'. These two words, she argues, 'take us out of the novelistic sphere of contingent, palpable reality into a world of wish and vision, somewhere between injunction and hope, command and prayer'.[3] Mark Schorer rewrites the sentence by inverting it: 'It is a truth universally acknowledged, that a single woman without a fortune, must be in want of a husband who has one'. Failing this, he states, 'marriage to an imbecile (Mr. Collins) dependent on the fortune of a pretentious termagant (Lady Catherine) is a plausible second-best. And if even this is impossible, then marriage to anyone at all, marriage if necessary to a scoundrel (Wickham), but under any circumstances, marriage, marriage!'[4] Dorothy Van Ghent finds the sentence contains similar kinds of inversions and antagonisms, and inducts us 'into the Austen language, the ironical Austen attack, and the energy, peculiar to an Austen novel, that arises from the compression between a barbaric subsurface

1   Judith Lowder Newton, *Women, Power, and Subversion: Social Strategies in British Fiction, 1778–1860* (Athens: University of Georgia Press, 1981), p. 56.
2   John Wiltshire, *Recreating Jane Austen* (Cambridge: Cambridge University Press, 2001), p. 101.
3   Nina Auerbach, *Communities of Women* (Cambridge, Mass.: Harvard University Press, 1978), pp. 41–2.
4   Mark Schorer, 'Pride Unprejudiced' in *Kenyon Review*, 18 (1956), p. 82.

marital warfare and a surface of polite manners and civilized conventions'.[5] A. Walton Litz charts the ways in which the sentence shapes the entire novel. In the opening chapters its ironies are 'directed at economic motives for marriage', he writes, 'but as the action develops the implications of the opening sentence are modified and extended, until by the end of the novel we are willing to acknowledge that both Bingley and Darcy were "in want of a wife." Thus the sentence is simultaneously a source for irony and a flat statement of the social and personal necessities which dominate the world of *Pride and Prejudice*'.[6]

Volume I, Chapter Three

In this scene, Bingley, Darcy and their party arrive at the Meryton ball. Bingley dances the entire evening and pays special attention to Jane. Darcy dances rarely and snubs Elizabeth, who is 'tolerable; but not handsome enough to tempt *me*'. Amelia Opie exploits a very similar scenario in the opening chapter of her novel *Temper*, published just one year before *Pride and Prejudice* (see Contemporary Documents, **pp. 40–1**). Poovey notes that 'Darcy's casual remark suggests that the fact that Elizabeth is momentarily without a partner indicates that she will always be so "slighted", that her "tolerable" beauty will never attract the permanent partner she desires' (see Modern Criticism, **p. 85**). But Firth, who played Darcy in the 1995 BBC film, mounts a partial defense of Darcy's conduct by emphasizing that his remarks are intended to put Bingley in his place, rather than to slight Elizabeth. 'I say, "She's okay, but not good enough for me," but what I'm really saying is: "Look, I'm supposed to be better than you, so don't give me the plain sister. I'm not even going to consider her"' (see The Novel in Performance, **p. 101**). The incident fixes Elizabeth in her dislike of Darcy, though within days he is asking her to dance and praising her 'fine eyes'.[1] As Wiltshire observes, 'it is plain that Elizabeth [. . .] enacts just that "implacable resentment" she attributes to [Darcy] – building on that first insult and making everything else she hears from or about him, feed into this original orientation' (see Modern Criticism, **p. 96**).

In Figure 8 (see **p. 115**), Bingley and his party enter. Darcy is in the lead, presumably with Caroline Bingley, while Bingley follows, chatting with Mrs. Hurst. The couples are turned inward, and not yet ready to speak with others. Only Mr. Hurst looks out into the room. Bingley appears amicable enough, but

5   Dorothy Van Ghent, *The English Novel: Form and Function* (New York: Rinehart, 1953), pp. 100–1.
6   A. Walton Litz, *Jane Austen: A Study of her Artistic Development* (New York: Oxford University Press, 1965), p. 107.

1   Jane Austen, *Pride and Prejudice*, ed. R. W. Chapman (Oxford: Clarendon Press, 1923), Volume I, Chapter 6, p. 27.

Darcy's eyes are cast down and to the side, and the decidedly snooty expression on his face indicates both his lofty sense of his own importance and his discomfort at finding himself in such a provincial setting. He is prepared to dance with Caroline and Mrs. Hurst, but to stand up with anyone else at 'such an assembly as this [. . .] would be insupportable'.

A report soon followed that Mr. Bingley was to bring twelve ladies and seven gentlemen with him to the assembly. The girls grieved over such a number of

"When the party entered"

Figure 8 '**When the party entered**': Hugh Thomson's 1894 illustration from *Pride and Prejudice*.

ladies; but were comforted the day before the ball by hearing, that instead of twelve, he had brought only six with him from London, his five sisters and a cousin. And when the party entered the assembly room, it consisted of only five altogether; Mr. Bingley, his two sisters, the husband of the eldest, and another young man.

Mr. Bingley was good looking and gentlemanlike; he had a pleasant countenance, and easy, unaffected manners. His sisters were fine women, with an air of decided fashion. His brother-in-law, Mr. Hurst, merely looked the gentleman; but his friend Mr. Darcy soon drew the attention of the room by his fine, tall person, handsome features, noble mien; and the report which was in general circulation within five minutes after his entrance, of his having ten thousand a year.[2] The gentlemen pronounced him to be a fine figure of a man, the ladies declared he was much handsomer than Mr. Bingley, and he was looked at with great admiration for about half the evening, till his manners gave a disgust which turned the tide of his popularity; for he was discovered to be proud, to be above his company, and above being pleased; and not all his large estate in Derbyshire could then save him from having a most forbidding, disagreeable countenance, and being unworthy to be compared with his friend.

Mr. Bingley had soon made himself acquainted with all the principal people in the room; he was lively and unreserved, danced every dance, was angry that the ball closed so early, and talked of giving one himself at Netherfield. Such amiable qualities must speak for themselves. What a contrast between him and his friend! Mr. Darcy danced only once with Mrs. Hurst and once with Miss Bingley, declined being introduced to any other lady, and spent the rest of the evening in walking about the room, speaking occasionally to one of his own party. His character was decided. He was the proudest, most disagreeable man in the world, and every body hoped that he would never come there again. Amongst the most violent against him was Mrs. Bennet, whose dislike of his general behaviour, was sharpened into particular resentment, by his having slighted one of her daughters.

Elizabeth Bennet had been obliged, by the scarcity of gentlemen, to sit down for two dances; and during part of that time, Mr. Darcy had been standing near enough for her to overhear a conversation between him and Mr. Bingley, who came from the dance for a few minutes, to press his friend to join it.

'Come, Darcy,' said he, 'I must have you dance. I hate to see you standing about by yourself in this stupid manner. You had much better dance.'

'I certainly shall not. You know how I detest it, unless I am particularly acquainted with my partner. At such an assembly as this, it would be insupportable. Your sisters are engaged, and there is not another woman in the room, whom it would not be a punishment to me to stand up with.'

'I would not be so fastidious as you are,' cried Bingley, 'for a kingdom! Upon my honour, I never met with so many pleasant girls in my life, as I have this evening; and there are several of them you see uncommonly pretty.'

---

2   It is notoriously difficult to compute contemporary equivalents of the sums of money named by Austen in her novels. For the best discussions, see James Heldman, 'How Wealthy is Mr. Darcy – Really?' in *Persuasions*, 12 (1990), pp. 38–49; and Mary Mogford, 'Darcy's Wealth: An Addendum' in *Persuasions*, 13 (1991), p. 49.

'*You* are dancing with the only handsome girl in the room,' said Mr. Darcy, looking at the eldest Miss Bennet.

'Oh! she is the most beautiful creature I ever beheld! But there is one of her sisters sitting down just behind you, who is very pretty, and I dare say, very agreeable. Do let me ask my partner to introduce you.'

'Which do you mean?' and turning round, he looked for a moment at Elizabeth, till catching her eye, he withdrew his own and coldly said, 'She is tolerable; but not handsome enough to tempt *me*; and I am in no humour at present to give consequence to young ladies who are slighted by other men. You had better return to your partner and enjoy her smiles, for you are wasting your time with me.'

Mr. Bingley followed his advice. Mr. Darcy walked off; and Elizabeth remained with no very cordial feelings towards him. She told the story however with great spirit among her friends; for she had a lively, playful disposition, which delighted in any thing ridiculous.

Volume I, Chapter Eight

In this chapter, Darcy revealingly aligns himself with both the conservatism of Edmund Burke and the feminism of Mary Wollstonecraft (see Contemporary Documents, Burke **pp. 34–6**, Wollstonecraft **pp. 33, 36–7**). Jane Bennet is ill and staying with the Bingleys at Netherfield. Elizabeth walks through muddy fields to visit her, much to the consternation of the Bingley sisters. The conversation in the evening concerns libraries, education, and female 'accomplishments'. Darcy endorses the Bingley sisters' assertion that Elizabeth and Jane's 'low connections' materially lessen their chances of marrying well, while Duckworth stresses that 'Darcy's pride in his library is the proper pride of the responsible owner of a large house who is conscious of his responsibilities as a trustee and who is aware (in Burkean terms) that he is not the "entire master" but only the "life-renter" of Pemberley' (see Modern Criticism, **p. 80**). Yet despite these conservative views, Darcy is drawn toward a woman with the kind of strength, independence, and intelligence so valued by Wollstonecraft. He does not join the Bingley sisters in their condemnation of Elizabeth's 'conceited independence', and he sets himself against both the sisters and writers such as Rousseau, Fordyce, and Gregory when he emphasizes that to the typical female accomplishments ('singing, drawing, dancing') a woman 'must yet add something more substantial, in the improvement of her mind by extensive reading' (see Contemporary Documents, **pp. 26–7, 29–31**). The comment is perhaps meant to provoke Elizabeth, who has just declared herself '*not* a great reader', but Darcy's emphasis on intelligence rather than accomplishments indicates his boredom with the vacuous and submissive females who surround him. Darcy is proud of his rank, property, and possessions, and clearly the product of an older, aristocratic world. But Elizabeth's wit, cleverness, and defiant unconventionality challenge his most cherished assumptions, and force him to acknowledge a newer world in which he must further extend and dramatically rethink his conception of an 'accomplished' woman. In *Pride and Prejudice*, declares Martin Amis, Darcy is 'chastened, deepened, and finally democratized by the force of love'.[1]

At five o'clock the two ladies retired to dress, and at half past six Elizabeth was summoned to dinner. To the civil enquiries which then poured in, and amongst which she had the pleasure of distinguishing the much superior solicitude of Mr. Bingley's, she could not make a very favourable answer. Jane was by no means better. The sisters, on hearing this, repeated three or four times how much they were grieved, how shocking it was to have a bad cold, and how excessively they disliked being ill themselves; and then thought no more of the matter: and their indifference towards Jane when not immediately before them, restored Elizabeth to the enjoyment of all her original dislike.

Their brother, indeed, was the only one of the party whom she could regard with any complacency.[2] His anxiety for Jane was evident, and his attentions to herself most pleasing, and they prevented her feeling herself so much an intruder as she believed she was considered by the others. She had very little notice from any but him. Miss Bingley was engrossed by Mr. Darcy, her sister scarcely less so; and as for Mr. Hurst, by whom Elizabeth sat, he was an indolent man, who lived only to eat, drink, and play at cards, who when he found her prefer a plain dish to a ragout,[3] had nothing to say to her.

When dinner was over, she returned directly to Jane, and Miss Bingley began abusing her as soon as she was out of the room. Her manners were pronounced to be very bad indeed, a mixture of pride and impertinence; she had no conversation, no stile, no taste, no beauty. Mrs. Hurst thought the same, and added,

'She has nothing, in short, to recommend her, but being an excellent walker. I shall never forget her appearance this morning. She really looked almost wild.'

'She did indeed, Louisa. I could hardly keep my countenance. Very nonsensical to come at all! Why must *she* be scampering about the country, because her sister had a cold? Her hair so untidy, so blowsy!'[4]

'Yes, and her petticoat; I hope you saw her petticoat, six inches deep in mud, I am absolutely certain; and the gown which had been let down to hide it, not doing its office.'[5]

'Your picture may be very exact, Louisa,' said Bingley; 'but this was all lost upon me. I thought Miss Elizabeth Bennet looked remarkably well, when she came into the room this morning. Her dirty petticoat quite escaped my notice.'

'*You* observed it, Mr. Darcy, I am sure,' said Miss Bingley; 'and I am inclined to think that you would not wish to see *your sister* make such an exhibition.'

'Certainly not.'

---

1   Martin Amis, 'Miss Jane's Prime' in *The Atlantic*, 265.2 (February 1990), p. 102.
2   'The fact or state of being pleased with a thing or person' (*Oxford English Dictionary*).
3   'A dish usually consisting of meat cut in small pieces, stewed with vegetables and highly seasoned' (*Oxford English Dictionary*).
4   There are two meanings that might apply here: 'flushed-looking' or 'dishevelled, frowzy' (*Oxford English Dictionary*).
5   The petticoat was an underskirt, designed to be seen and usually matching the overskirt.

'To walk three miles, or four miles, or five miles, or whatever it is, above her ancles in dirt, and alone, quite alone! what could she mean by it? It seems to me to shew an abominable sort of conceited independence, a most country town indifference to decorum.'

'It shews an affection for her sister that is very pleasing,' said Bingley.

'I am afraid, Mr. Darcy,' observed Miss Bingley, in a half whisper, 'that this adventure has rather affected your admiration of her fine eyes.'

'Not at all,' he replied; 'they were brightened by the exercise.' – A short pause followed this speech, and Mrs. Hurst began again.

'I have an excessive regard for Jane Bennet, she is really a very sweet girl, and I wish with all my heart she were well settled. But with such a father and mother, and such low connections, I am afraid there is no chance of it.'

'I think I have heard you say, that their uncle is an attorney in Meryton.'

'Yes; and they have another, who lives somewhere near Cheapside.'[6]

'That is capital,' added her sister, and they both laughed heartily.

'If they had uncles enough to fill *all* Cheapside,' cried Bingley, 'it would not make them one jot less agreeable.'

'But it must very materially lessen their chance of marrying men of any consideration in the world,' replied Darcy.

To this speech Bingley made no answer; but his sisters gave it their hearty assent, and indulged their mirth for some time at the expense of their dear friend's vulgar relations.

With a renewal of tenderness, however, they repaired to her room on leaving the dining-parlour, and sat with her till summoned to coffee. She was still very poorly, and Elizabeth would not quit her at all, till late in the evening, when she had the comfort of seeing her asleep, and when it appeared to her rather right than pleasant that she should go down stairs herself. On entering the drawing-room she found the whole party at loo,[7] and was immediately invited to join them; but suspecting them to be playing high[8] she declined it, and making her sister the excuse, said she would amuse herself for the short time she could stay below with a book. Mr. Hurst looked at her with astonishment.

'Do you prefer reading to cards?' said he; 'that is rather singular.'

'Miss Eliza Bennet,' said Miss Bingley, 'despises cards. She is a great reader and has no pleasure in any thing else.'

'I deserve neither such praise nor such censure,' cried Elizabeth; 'I am *not* a great reader, and I have pleasure in many things.'

'In nursing your sister I am sure you have pleasure,' said Bingley; 'and I hope it will soon be increased by seeing her quite well.'

Elizabeth thanked him from her heart, and then walked towards a table where a few books were lying. He immediately offered to fetch her others; all that his library afforded.

---

6   A commercial, rather than fashionable, district of London. Elizabeth's relations are judged as socially inferior because they are in business. Bingley and Darcy, on the other hand, live from the capital of income or land. Miss Bingley and Mrs. Hurst conveniently overlook the fact that their own fortunes come from trade.

7   A popular card game similar to bridge, except that up to twelve people are allowed to play.

8   The party is gambling and Elizabeth suspects that, while they would regard the stakes as quite low, she would find them uncomfortably high.

'And I wish my collection were larger for your benefit and my own credit; but I am an idle fellow; and though I have not many, I have more than I ever look into.'

Elizabeth assured him that she could suit herself perfectly with those in the room.

'I am astonished,' said Miss Bingley, 'that my father should have left so small a collection of books. – What a delightful library you have at Pemberley, Mr. Darcy!'

'It ought to be good,' he replied, 'it has been the work of many generations.'

'And then you have added so much to it yourself, you are always buying books.'

'I cannot comprehend the neglect of a family library in such days as these.'

'Neglect! I am sure you neglect nothing that can add to the beauties of that noble place. Charles, when you build *your* house, I wish it may be half as delightful as Pemberley.'

'I wish it may.'

'But I would really advise you to make your purchase in that neighbourhood, and take Pemberley for a kind of model. There is not a finer county in England than Derbyshire.'

'With all my heart; I will buy Pemberley itself if Darcy will sell it.'

'I am talking of possibilities, Charles.'

'Upon my word, Caroline, I should think it more possible to get Pemberley by purchase than by imitation.'

Elizabeth was so much caught by what passed, as to leave her very little attention for her book; and soon laying it wholly aside, she drew near the card-table, and stationed herself between Mr. Bingley and his eldest sister, to observe the game.

'Is Miss Darcy much grown since the spring?' said Miss Bingley; 'will she be as tall as I am?'

'I think she will. She is now about Miss Elizabeth Bennet's height, or rather taller.'

'How I long to see her again! I never met with anybody who delighted me so much. Such a countenance, such manners! and so extremely accomplished for her age! Her performance on the piano-forte is exquisite.'

'It is amazing to me,' said Bingley, 'how young ladies can have patience to be so very accomplished, as they all are.'

'All young ladies accomplished! My dear Charles, what do you mean?'

'Yes, all of them, I think. They all paint tables, cover skreens and net purses.[9] I scarcely know any one who cannot do all this, and I am sure I never heard a young lady spoken of for the first time, without being informed that she was very accomplished.'

'Your list of the common extent of accomplishments,' said Darcy, 'has too much truth. The word is applied to many a woman who deserves it no otherwise than by netting a purse, or covering a skreen. But I am very far from agreeing with you in your estimation of ladies in general. I cannot boast of knowing more than

---

9   A series of decorative but essentially frivolous feminine 'accomplishments'. 'Skreens' protected a woman's complexion from the heat of the fire.

half a dozen, in the whole range of my acquaintance, that are really accomplished.'

'Nor I, I am sure,' said Miss Bingley.

'Then,' observed Elizabeth, 'you must comprehend a great deal in your idea of an accomplished woman.'

'Yes; I do comprehend a great deal in it.'

'Oh! certainly,' cried his faithful assistant, 'no one can be really esteemed accomplished, who does not greatly surpass what is usually met with. A woman must have a thorough knowledge of music, singing, drawing, dancing, and the modern languages, to deserve the word; and besides all this, she must possess a certain something in her air and manner of walking, the tone of her voice, her address and expressions, or the word will be but half deserved.'

'All this she must possess,' added Darcy, 'and to all this she must yet add something more substantial, in the improvement of her mind by extensive reading.'

'I am no longer surprised at your knowing *only* six accomplished women. I rather wonder now at your knowing *any*.'

'Are you so severe upon your own sex, as to doubt the possibility of all this?'

'*I* never saw such a woman. *I* never saw such capacity, and taste, and application, and elegance, as you describe, united.'

Mrs. Hurst and Miss Bingley both cried out against the injustice of her implied doubt, and were both protesting that they knew many women who answered this description, when Mr. Hurst called them to order, with bitter complaints of their inattention to what was going forward. As all conversation was thereby at an end, Elizabeth soon afterwards left the room.

'Eliza Bennet,' said Miss Bingley, when the door was closed on her, 'is one of those young ladies who seek to recommend themselves to the other sex, by undervaluing their own; and with many men, I dare say, it succeeds. But, in my opinion, it is a paltry device, a very mean art.'

'Undoubtedly,' replied Darcy, to whom this remark was chiefly addressed, 'there is meanness in *all* the arts which ladies sometimes condescend to employ for captivation. Whatever bears affinity to cunning is despicable.'

Miss Bingley was not so entirely satisfied with this reply as to continue the subject.

Elizabeth joined them again only to say that her sister was worse, and that she could not leave her. Bingley urged Mr. Jones's being sent for immediately; while his sisters, convinced that no country advice could be of any service, recommended an express to town for one of the most eminent physicians. This, she would not hear of; but she was not so unwilling to comply with their brother's proposal; and it was settled that Mr. Jones should be sent for early in the morning, if Miss Bennet were not decidedly better. Bingley was quite uncomfortable; his sisters declared that they were miserable. They solaced their wretchedness, however, by duets after supper, while he could find no better relief to his feelings than by giving his housekeeper directions that every possible attention might be paid to the sick lady and her sister.

Volume I, Chapter Eleven

In this scene, Elizabeth and Darcy verbally spar, and Darcy acknowledges to himself the 'danger of paying Elizabeth too much attention'. Miss Bingley tries hard to please Darcy and initiates the discussion, but she is quickly left behind as Elizabeth and Darcy debate vanity, pride, and resentment. Darcy is stiff and self-important as he struggles to understand both himself and her, while Elizabeth remains fixed in her attitude toward him. He seems to offer her a good deal, but she hears only what she wants to hear. Fergus notes that 'the scene has under-currents of sexual antagonism and attraction not entirely contained by the comedy of misjudgment enacted on the surface'.[1] Young emphasizes that 'when at midpoint Elizabeth turns from her partner and audience to laugh to herself' she engages in 'a pleasure-filled, self-congratulatory gesture about her superior wit and understanding'. Young concludes that 'Elizabeth has so convinced her-self of the shortcomings of Darcy's character that she arrives at a hyperbolic assertion of his defect. Darcy turns Elizabeth's critique of him into a gentle, thoughtful retort about her defect: "And yours [. . .] is wilfully to misunderstand them." It is Darcy who ends their discourse with the pleasures of a smile'.[2]

Miss Bingley made no answer; and soon afterwards got up and walked about the room. Her figure was elegant, and she walked well; – but Darcy, at whom it was all aimed, was still inflexibly studious. In the desperation of her feelings she resolved on one effort more; and, turning to Elizabeth, said,

'Miss Eliza Bennet, let me persuade you to follow my example, and take a turn about the room. – I assure you it is very refreshing after sitting so long in one attitude.'

Elizabeth was surprised, but agreed to it immediately. Miss Bingley succeeded no less in the real object of her civility; Mr. Darcy looked up. He was as much awake to the novelty of attention in that quarter as Elizabeth herself could be, and unconsciously closed his book. He was directly invited to join their party, but he declined it, observing, that he could imagine but two motives for their chusing to walk up and down the room together, with either of which motives his joining them would interfere. 'What could he mean? she was dying to know what could be his meaning' – and asked Elizabeth whether she could at all understand him?

'Not at all,' was her answer; 'but depend upon it, he means to be severe on us, and our surest way of disappointing him, will be to ask nothing about it.'

Miss Bingley, however, was incapable of disappointing Mr. Darcy in any thing, and persevered therefore in requiring an explanation of his two motives.

'I have not the smallest objection to explaining them,' said he, as soon as she allowed him to speak. 'You either chuse this method of passing the evening because you are in each other's confidence and have secret affairs to discuss, or

1   Jan Fergus, *Jane Austen and the Didactic Novel* (Totowa, NJ: Barnes and Noble, 1983), p. 110.
2   Kay Young, 'Word-Work, Word-Play, and the Making of Intimacy in *Pride and Prejudice*' in *The Talk in Jane Austen* (Edmonton: University of Alberta Press, 2002), p. 67.

because you are conscious that your figures appear to the greatest advantage in walking; – if the first, I should be completely in your way; – and if the second, I can admire you much better as I sit by the fire.'

'Oh! shocking!' cried Miss Bingley. 'I never heard any thing so abominable. How shall we punish him for such a speech?'

'Nothing so easy, if you have but the inclination,' said Elizabeth. 'We can all plague and punish one another. Teaze him – laugh at him. – Intimate as you are, you must know how it is to be done.'

'But upon my honour I do *not*. I do assure you that my intimacy has not yet taught me *that*. Teaze calmness of temper and presence of mind! No, no – I feel he may defy us there. And as to laughter, we will not expose ourselves, if you please, by attempting to laugh without a subject. Mr. Darcy may hug himself.'

'Mr. Darcy is not to be laughed at!' cried Elizabeth. 'That is an uncommon advantage, and uncommon I hope it will continue, for it would be a great loss to *me* to have many such acquaintance. I dearly love a laugh.'

'Miss Bingley,' said he, 'has given me credit for more than can be. The wisest and the best of men, nay, the wisest and best of their actions, may be rendered ridiculous by a person whose first object in life is a joke.'

'Certainly,' replied Elizabeth – 'there are such people, but I hope I am not one of *them*. I hope I never ridicule what is wise or good. Follies and nonsense, whims and inconsistencies *do* divert me, I own, and I laugh at them whenever I can. – But these, I suppose, are precisely what you are without.'

'Perhaps that is not possible for any one. But it has been the study of my life to avoid those weaknesses which often expose a strong understanding to ridicule.'

'Such as vanity and pride.'

'Yes, vanity is a weakness indeed. But pride – where there is a real superiority of mind, pride will be always under good regulation.'

Elizabeth turned away to hide a smile.

'Your examination of Mr. Darcy is over, I presume,' said Miss Bingley; – 'and pray what is the result?'

'I am perfectly convinced by it that Mr. Darcy has no defect. He owns it himself without disguise.'

'No' – said Darcy, 'I have made no such pretension. I have faults enough, but they are not, I hope, of understanding. My temper I dare not vouch for. – It is I believe too little yielding – certainly too little for the convenience of the world. I cannot forget the follies and vices of others so soon as I ought, nor their offences against myself. My feelings are not puffed about with every attempt to move them. My temper would perhaps be called resentful. – My good opinion once lost is lost for ever.'

'*That* is a failing indeed!' – cried Elizabeth. 'Implacable resentment *is* a shade in a character. But you have chosen your fault well. – I really cannot *laugh* at it. You are safe from me.'

'There is, I believe, in every disposition a tendency to some particular evil, a natural defect, which not even the best education can overcome.'

'And *your* defect is a propensity to hate every body.'

'And yours,' he replied with a smile, 'is wilfully to misunderstand them.'

'Do let us have a little music,' – cried Miss Bingley, tired of a conversation in which she had no share. – 'Louisa, you will not mind my waking Mr. Hurst.'

Her sister made not the smallest objection, and the piano forte was opened, and Darcy, after a few moments recollection, was not sorry for it. He began to feel the danger of paying Elizabeth too much attention.

Volume I, Chapter Nineteen

In this scene, Collins proposes to Elizabeth and she repeatedly refuses him, though he does not give up easily, for he believes with Rousseau that 'the surest art for animating' a man's strength 'is to make it necessary by resistance. Then [. . .] the one triumphs in the victory that the other has made him win' (see Contemporary Documents, **p. 27**). But Collins cannot win Elizabeth. 'The elaborate language in which [he] gets himself fairly *stuck* is a mimesis of an action of the soul', observes Van Ghent, 'the soul that becomes self dishonest through failure to know itself, and that overrates itself at the expense of the social context, just as it overrates verbalism at the expense of meaning' (see Modern Criticism, **p. 76**). Harding examines the way in which Collins is both fool and menace. 'The proposal scene is not only comic fantasy', he writes, 'but it is also, for Elizabeth, a taste of the fantastic nightmare' (see Modern Criticism, **p. 72**). For Fraiman, Collins's proposal emphasizes that the force of Elizabeth's words 'is highly contingent, any authority she has merely borrowed. Like a woman writing under a male pseudonym, Elizabeth's credibility depends on her father's signature' (see Modern Criticism, **p. 94**).

The next day opened a new scene at Longbourn. Mr. Collins made his declaration in form. Having resolved to do it without loss of time, as his leave of absence extended only to the following Saturday, and having no feelings of diffidence to make it distressing to himself even at the moment, he set about it in a very orderly manner, with all the observances which he supposed a regular part of the business. On finding Mrs. Bennet, Elizabeth, and one of the younger girls together, soon after breakfast, he addressed the mother in these words,

'May I hope, Madam, for your interest with your fair daughter Elizabeth, when I solicit for the honour of a private audience with her in the course of this morning?'

Before Elizabeth had time for any thing but a blush of surprise, Mrs. Bennet instantly answered,

'Oh dear! – Yes – certainly – I am sure Lizzy will be very happy – I am sure she can have no objection. – Come, Kitty, I want you up stairs.' And gathering her work together, she was hastening away, when Elizabeth called out,

'Dear Ma'am, do not go. – I beg you will not go. – Mr. Collins must excuse me. – He can have nothing to say to me that any body need not hear. I am going away myself.'

'No, no, nonsense, Lizzy. – I desire you will stay where you are.' – And upon Elizabeth's seeming really, with vexed and embarrassed looks, about to escape, she added, 'Lizzy, I *insist* upon your staying and hearing Mr. Collins.'

Elizabeth would not oppose such an injunction – and a moment's consideration making her also sensible that it would be wisest to get it over as soon and as quietly as possible, she sat down again, and tried to conceal by incessant employment the feelings which were divided between distress and diversion. Mrs. Bennet and Kitty walked off, and as soon as they were gone Mr. Collins began.

'Believe me, my dear Miss Elizabeth, that your modesty, so far from doing you any disservice, rather adds to your other perfections. You would have been less amiable in my eyes had there *not* been this little unwillingness; but allow me to assure you that I have your respected mother's permission for this address. You can hardly doubt the purport of my discourse, however your natural delicacy may lead you to dissemble; my attentions have been too marked to be mistaken. Almost as soon as I entered the house I singled you out as the companion of my future life. But before I am run away with by my feelings on this subject, perhaps it will be advisable for me to state my reasons for marrying – and moreover for coming into Hertfordshire with the design of selecting a wife, as I certainly did.'

The idea of Mr. Collins, with all his solemn composure, being run away with by his feelings, made Elizabeth so near laughing that she could not use the short pause he allowed in any attempt to stop him farther, and he continued:

'My reasons for marrying are, first, that I think it a right thing for every clergyman in easy circumstances (like myself) to set the example of matrimony in his parish. Secondly, that I am convinced it will add very greatly to my happiness; and thirdly – which perhaps I ought to have mentioned earlier, that it is the particular advice and recommendation of the very noble lady whom I have the honour of calling patroness. Twice has she condescended to give me her opinion (unasked too!) on this subject; and it was but the very Saturday night before I left Hunsford – between our pools at quadrille, while Mrs. Jenkinson was arranging Miss de Bourgh's foot-stool, that she said, "Mr. Collins, you must marry. A clergyman like you must marry. – Chuse properly, chuse a gentlewoman for *my* sake; and for your *own*, let her be an active, useful sort of person, not brought up high, but able to make a small income go a good way. This is my advice. Find such a woman as soon as you can, bring her to Hunsford, and I will visit her." Allow me, by the way, to observe, my fair cousin, that I do not reckon the notice and kindness of Lady Catherine de Bourgh as among the least of the advantages in my power to offer. You will find her manners beyond any thing I can describe; and your wit and vivacity I think must be acceptable to her, especially when tempered with the silence and respect which her rank will inevitably excite. Thus much for my general intention in favour of matrimony; it remains to be told why my views were directed to Longbourn instead of my own neighbourhood, where I assure you there are many amiable young women. But the fact is, that being, as I am, to inherit this estate after the death of your honoured father, (who, however, may live many years longer,) I could not satisfy myself without resolving to chuse a wife from among his daughters, that the loss to them might be as little as possible, when the melancholy event takes place – which, however, as I have already said, may not be for several years. This has been my motive, my fair cousin, and I flatter myself it will not sink me in your esteem. And now nothing remains for me but to assure you in the most animated language of the violence of my affection. To fortune I am perfectly indifferent, and shall make no demand of that nature on your father, since I am well aware that it could not be complied with; and that one thousand pounds in the 4 per cents.[1] which will not be yours till after your mother's decease, is all that you may ever be entitled to. On that head, therefore, I shall be uniformly silent; and you may assure yourself that no ungenerous reproach shall ever pass my lips when we are married.'

It was absolutely necessary to interrupt him now.

'You are too hasty, Sir,' she cried. 'You forget that I have made no answer. Let me do it without farther loss of time. Accept my thanks for the compliment you are paying me. I am very sensible of the honour of your proposals, but it is impossible for me to do otherwise than decline them.'

'I am not now to learn,' replied Mr. Collins, with a formal wave of the hand, 'that it is usual with young ladies to reject the addresses of the man whom they secretly mean to accept, when he first applies for their favour; and that sometimes the refusal is repeated a second or even a third time. I am therefore by no means discouraged by what you have just said, and shall hope to lead you to the altar ere long.'

'Upon my word, Sir,' cried Elizabeth, 'your hope is rather an extraordinary one after my declaration. I do assure you that I am not one of those young ladies (if such young ladies there are) who are so daring as to risk their happiness on the chance of being asked a second time. I am perfectly serious in my refusal. – You could not make *me* happy, and I am convinced that I am the last woman in the world who would make *you* so. – Nay, were your friend Lady Catherine to know me, I am persuaded she would find me in every respect ill qualified for the situation.'

'Were it certain that Lady Catherine would think so,' said Mr. Collins very gravely – 'but I cannot imagine that her ladyship would at all disapprove of you. And you may be certain that when I have the honour of seeing her again I shall speak in the highest terms of your modesty, economy, and other amiable qualifications.'

'Indeed, Mr. Collins, all praise of me will be unnecessary. You must give me leave to judge for myself, and pay me the compliment of believing what I say. I wish you very happy and very rich, and by refusing your hand, do all in my power to prevent your being otherwise. In making me the offer, you must have satisfied the delicacy of your feelings with regard to my family, and may take possession of Longbourn estate whenever it falls, without any self-reproach. This matter may be considered, therefore, as finally settled.' And rising as she thus spoke, she would have quitted the room, had not Mr. Collins thus addressed her,

'When I do myself the honour of speaking to you next on this subject I shall hope to receive a more favourable answer than you have now given me; though I am far from accusing you of cruelty at present, because I know it to be the established custom of your sex to reject a man on the first application, and perhaps you have even now said as much to encourage my suit as would be consistent with the true delicacy of the female character.'

'Really, Mr. Collins,' cried Elizabeth with some warmth, 'you puzzle me exceedingly. If what I have hitherto said can appear to you in the form of

---

1   Government bonds which would provide Elizabeth with a very modest annual income of £40. With typical pomposity, Collins is informing Elizabeth that her father need not provide a dowry.

encouragement, I know not how to express my refusal in such a way as may convince you of its being one.'

'You must give me leave to flatter myself, my dear cousin, that your refusal of my addresses is merely words of course. My reasons for believing it are briefly these: – It does not appear to me that my hand is unworthy your acceptance, or that the establishment I can offer would be any other than highly desirable. My situation in life, my connections with the family of De Bourgh, and my relationship to your own, are circumstances highly in my favour; and you should take it into farther consideration that in spite of your manifold attractions, it is by no means certain that another offer of marriage may ever be made you. Your portion is unhappily so small that it will in all likelihood undo the effects of your loveliness and amiable qualifications. As I must therefore conclude that you are not serious in your rejection of me, I shall chuse to attribute it to your wish of increasing my love by suspense, according to the usual practice of elegant females.'

'I do assure you, Sir, that I have no pretension whatever to that kind of elegance which consists in tormenting a respectable man. I would rather be paid the compliment of being believed sincere. I thank you again and again for the honour you have done me in your proposals, but to accept them is absolutely impossible. My feelings in every respect forbid it. Can I speak plainer? Do not consider me now as an elegant female intending to plague you, but as a rational creature[2] speaking the truth from her heart.'

'You are uniformly charming!' cried he, with an air of awkward gallantry; 'and I am persuaded that when sanctioned by the express authority of both your excellent parents, my proposals will not fail of being acceptable.'

To such perseverance in wilful self-deception Elizabeth would make no reply, and immediately and in silence withdrew; determined, if he persisted in considering her repeated refusals as flattering encouragement, to apply to her father, whose negative might be uttered in such a manner as must be decisive, and whose behaviour at least could not be mistaken for the affectation and coquetry of an elegant female.

Volume I, Chapter Twenty-Two

In this scene, Collins proposes to Charlotte Lucas, who eagerly accepts what Elizabeth had flatly refused. Both women have small fortunes and face the threat of spinsterhood, but Charlotte is older, less attractive, and far more practical. Elizabeth is stunned by the news, for once again she has seriously misjudged the people around her, and in this instance she does not realize the extent to which her closest friend's 'opinion of matrimony was not exactly like her own'. In *Thoughts on the Education of Daughters*, Wollstonecraft examined the 'very

---

2   Compare Mary Wollstonecraft in *A Vindication of the Rights of Woman*: 'My own sex, I hope, will excuse me, if I treat them like rational creatures' (see Contemporary Documents, p. 36).

humiliating' options that face a 'fashionably educated' but single woman who must work to stave off poverty (see Contemporary Documents, **p. 33**). Elizabeth rejects Collins because she wants marriage with love. But Charlotte is 'not romantic you know. I never was'. Marriage, for her, is 'the only honourable provision for well-educated young women of small fortune, and however uncertain of giving happiness, must be their pleasantest preservative from want'. Poovey remarks that 'at worst, the Bennet's shortage of money for dowries and their equivocal social position foretell spinsterhood, dependence on a generous relative, or, most ominous of all, work as a governess or lady's companion. Austen never lets the reader or Elizabeth forget how very likely such a future is' (see Modern Criticism, **p. 85**). For Polhemus, 'the point is not that Charlotte is a sellout, but that she lives in a narrow, desperate, feminine world of financial constraint [. . .] Marriage to Collins is a kind of socially respectable prostitution in which Charlotte acquiesces' (see Modern Criticism, **p. 89**).

Charlotte's kindness extended farther than Elizabeth had any conception of; – its object was nothing less, than to secure her from any return of Mr. Collins's addresses, by engaging them towards herself. Such was Miss Lucas's scheme; and appearances were so favourable that when they parted at night, she would have felt almost sure of success if he had not been to leave Hertfordshire so very soon. But here, she did injustice to the fire and independence of his character, for it led him to escape out of Longbourn House the next morning with admirable slyness, and hasten to Lucas Lodge to throw himself at her feet. He was anxious to avoid the notice of his cousins, from a conviction that if they saw him depart, they could not fail to conjecture his design, and he was not willing to have the attempt known till its success could be known likewise; for though feeling almost secure, and with reason, for Charlotte had been tolerably encouraging, he was comparatively diffident since the adventure of Wednesday. His reception however was of the most flattering kind. Miss Lucas perceived him from an upper window as he walked towards the house, and instantly set out to meet him accidentally in the lane. But little had she dared to hope that so much love and eloquence awaited her there.

In as short a time as Mr. Collins's long speeches would allow, every thing was settled between them to the satisfaction of both; and as they entered the house, he earnestly entreated her to name the day that was to make him the happiest of men; and though such a solicitation must be waved for the present, the lady felt no inclination to trifle with his happiness. The stupidity with which he was favoured by nature, must guard his courtship from any charm that could make a woman wish for its continuance; and Miss Lucas, who accepted him solely from the pure and disinterested desire of an establishment, cared not how soon that establishment were gained.

Sir William and Lady Lucas were speedily applied to for their consent; and it was bestowed with a most joyful alacrity. Mr. Collins's present circumstances made it a most eligible match for their daughter, to whom they could give little fortune; and his prospects of future wealth were exceedingly fair. Lady Lucas began directly to calculate with more interest than the matter had ever excited before, how many years longer Mr. Bennet was likely to live; and Sir William gave it as his decided opinion, that whenever Mr. Collins should be in possession of the Longbourn estate, it would be highly expedient that both he and his wife should make their appearance at St. James's.[1] The whole family in short were properly overjoyed on the occasion. The younger girls formed hopes of *coming out*[2] a year or two sooner than they might otherwise have done; and the boys were relieved from their apprehension of Charlotte's dying an old maid. Charlotte herself was tolerably composed. She had gained her point, and had time to consider of it. Her reflections were in general satisfactory. Mr. Collins to be sure was neither sensible nor agreeable; his society was irksome, and his attachment to her must be imaginary. But still he would be her husband. – Without thinking highly either of men or of matrimony, marriage had always been her object; it was the only honourable provision for well-educated young women of small fortune, and however uncertain of giving happiness, must be their pleasantest preservative from want. This preservative she had now obtained; and at the age of twenty-seven, without having ever been handsome, she felt all the good luck of it. The least agreeable circumstance in the business, was the surprise it must occasion to Elizabeth Bennet, whose friendship she valued beyond that of any other person. Elizabeth would wonder, and probably would blame her; and though her resolution was not to be shaken, her feelings must be hurt by such disapprobation. She resolved to give her the information herself, and therefore charged Mr. Collins when he returned to Longbourn to dinner, to drop no hint of what had passed before any of the family. A promise of secrecy was of course very dutifully given, but it could not be kept without difficulty; for the curiosity excited by his long absence, burst forth in such very direct questions on his return, as required some ingenuity to evade, and he was at the same time exercising great self-denial, for he was longing to publish his prosperous love.

As he was to begin his journey too early on the morrow to see any of the family, the ceremony of leave-taking was performed when the ladies moved for the night; and Mrs. Bennet with great politeness and cordiality said how happy they should be to see him at Longbourn again, whenever his other engagements might allow him to visit them.

'My dear Madam,' he replied, 'this invitation is particularly gratifying, because it is what I have been hoping to receive; and you may be very certain that I shall avail myself of it as soon as possible.'

They were all astonished; and Mr. Bennet, who could by no means wish for so speedy a return, immediately said,

'But is there not danger of Lady Catherine's disapprobation here, my good sir? – You had better neglect your relations, than run the risk of offending your patroness.'

'My dear sir,' replied Mr. Collins, 'I am particularly obliged to you for this friendly caution, and you may depend upon my not taking so material a step without her ladyship's concurrence.'

---

1   That is, at court.
2   A young girl's official entry into adult society, and thus the marriage market.

'You cannot be too much on your guard. Risk any thing rather than her displeasure; and if you find it likely to be raised by your coming to us again, which I
should think exceedingly probable, stay quietly at home, and be satisfied that *we*
shall take no offence.'

'Believe me, my dear sir, my gratitude is warmly excited by such affectionate
attention; and depend upon it, you will speedily receive from me a letter of
thanks for this, as well as for every other mark of your regard during my stay in
Hertfordshire. As for my fair cousins, though my absence may not be long enough
to render it necessary, I shall now take the liberty of wishing them health and
happiness, not excepting my cousin Elizabeth.'

With proper civilities the ladies then withdrew; all of them equally surprised to
find that he meditated a quick return. Mrs. Bennet wished to understand by it that
he thought of paying his addresses to one of her younger girls, and Mary might
have been prevailed on to accept him. She rated his abilities much higher than any
of the others; there was a solidity in his reflections which often struck her, and
though by no means so clever as herself, she thought that if encouraged to read
and improve himself by such an example as her's, he might become a very agreeable companion. But on the following morning, every hope of this kind was done
away. Miss Lucas called soon after breakfast, and in a private conference with
Elizabeth related the event of the day before.

The possibility of Mr. Collins's fancying himself in love with her friend had
once occurred to Elizabeth within the last day or two; but that Charlotte could
encourage him, seemed almost as far from possibility as that she could encourage
him herself, and her astonishment was consequently so great as to overcome at
first the bounds of decorum, and she could not help crying out,

'Engaged to Mr. Collins! my dear Charlotte, – impossible!'

The steady countenance which Miss Lucas had commanded in telling her story,
gave way to a momentary confusion here on receiving so direct a reproach;
though, as it was no more than she expected, she soon regained her composure,
and calmly replied,

'Why should you be surprised, my dear Eliza? – Do you think it incredible that
Mr. Collins should be able to procure any woman's good opinion, because he was
not so happy as to succeed with you?'

But Elizabeth had now recollected herself, and making a strong effort for
it, was able to assure her with tolerable firmness that the prospect of their
relationship was highly grateful to her, and that she wished her all imaginable
happiness.

'I see what you are feeling,' replied Charlotte, – 'you must be surprised, very
much surprised, – so lately as Mr. Collins was wishing to marry you. But when
you have had time to think it all over, I hope you will be satisfied with what I have
done. I am not romantic you know. I never was. I ask only a comfortable home;
and considering Mr. Collins's character, connections, and situation in life, I am
convinced that my chance of happiness with him is as fair, as most people can
boast on entering the marriage state.'

Elizabeth quietly answered 'Undoubtedly;' – and after an awkward pause,
they returned to the rest of the family. Charlotte did not stay much longer, and
Elizabeth was then left to reflect on what she had heard. It was a long time before
she became at all reconciled to the idea of so unsuitable a match. The strangeness

of Mr. Collins's making two offers of marriage within three days, was nothing in comparison of his being now accepted. She had always felt that Charlotte's opinion of matrimony was not exactly like her own, but she could not have supposed it possible that when called into action, she would have sacrificed every better feeling to worldly advantage. Charlotte the wife of Mr. Collins, was a most humiliating picture! – And to the pang of a friend disgracing herself and sunk in her esteem, was added the distressing conviction that it was impossible for that friend to be tolerably happy in the lot she had chosen.

Volume II, Chapter Eight

In this scene, Elizabeth and Darcy are at Rosings, and Elizabeth plays the piano while chatting to Darcy of, among other things, their first meeting at the Meryton ball, for her opinion of him continues to centre on this event. On one level the conversation concerns Elizabeth's musical performance, but on another Elizabeth is explaining her dislike of Darcy, and Darcy is expressing his admiration for her, though neither of course is fully aware of what the other intends. What is more, as is so often the case in Austen, a third party is involved in the conversation. Darcy's cousin Colonel Fitzwilliam is audience and potential suitor to Elizabeth, and his presence creates additional tensions and ironies as Darcy makes what Babb describes as 'his final, almost desperate attempt before the first proposal to come to terms with [Elizabeth]' (see Modern Criticism, p. 79).

When coffee was over, Colonel Fitzwilliam reminded Elizabeth of having promised to play to him; and she sat down directly to the instrument. He drew a chair near her. Lady Catherine listened to half a song, and then talked, as before, to her other nephew; till the latter walked away from her, and moving with his usual deliberation towards the piano forte, stationed himself so as to command a full view of the fair performer's countenance. Elizabeth saw what he was doing, and at the first convenient pause, turned to him with an arch smile, and said,

'You mean to frighten me, Mr. Darcy, by coming in all this state to hear me? But I will not be alarmed though your sister *does* play so well. There is a stubbornness about me that never can bear to be frightened at the will of others. My courage always rises with every attempt to intimidate me.'

'I shall not say that you are mistaken,' he replied, 'because you could not really believe me to entertain any design of alarming you; and I have had the pleasure of your acquaintance long enough to know, that you find great enjoyment in occasionally professing opinions which in fact are not your own.'

Elizabeth laughed heartily at this picture of herself, and said to Colonel Fitzwilliam, 'Your cousin will give you a very pretty notion of me, and teach you not to believe a word I say. I am particularly unlucky in meeting with a person so well able to expose my real character, in a part of the world where I had hoped to pass myself off with some degree of credit. Indeed, Mr. Darcy, it is very ungenerous in you to mention all that you knew to my disadvantage in Hertfordshire – and, give me leave to say, very impolitic too – for it is provoking me to retaliate, and such things may come out, as will shock your relations to hear.'

'I am not afraid of you,' said he, smilingly.

'Pray let me hear what you have to accuse him of,' cried Colonel Fitzwilliam. 'I should like to know how he behaves among strangers.'

'You shall hear then – but prepare yourself for something very dreadful. The first time of my ever seeing him in Hertfordshire, you must know, was at a ball – and at this ball, what do you think he did? He danced only four dances! I am sorry to pain you – but so it was. He danced only four dances, though gentlemen were scarce; and, to my certain knowledge, more than one young lady was sitting down in want of a partner. Mr. Darcy, you cannot deny the fact.'

'I had not at that time the honour of knowing any lady in the assembly beyond my own party.'

'True; and nobody can ever be introduced in a ball room. Well, Colonel Fitzwilliam, what do I play next? My fingers wait your orders.'

'Perhaps,' said Darcy, 'I should have judged better, had I sought an introduction, but I am ill qualified to recommend myself to strangers.'

'Shall we ask your cousin the reason of this?' said Elizabeth, still addressing Colonel Fitzwilliam. 'Shall we ask him why a man of sense and education, and who has lived in the world, is ill qualified to recommend himself to strangers?'

'I can answer your question,' said Fitzwilliam, 'without applying to him. It is because he will not give himself the trouble.'

'I certainly have not the talent which some people possess,' said Darcy, 'of conversing easily with those I have never seen before. I cannot catch their tone of conversation, or appear interested in their concerns, as I often see done.'

'My fingers,' said Elizabeth, 'do not move over this instrument in the masterly manner which I see so many women's do. They have not the same force or rapidity, and do not produce the same expression. But then I have always supposed it to be my own fault – because I would not take the trouble of practising. It is not that I do not believe *my* fingers as capable as any other woman's of superior execution.'

Darcy smiled and said, 'You are perfectly right. You have employed your time much better. No one admitted to the privilege of hearing you, can think any thing wanting. We neither of us perform to strangers.'

Volume II, Chapter Eleven

In this chapter, Darcy makes his first disastrous proposal to Elizabeth and, for the second time in the novel, Elizabeth summarily rejects a suitor confident of success. The exchange between the two is direct and increasingly heated, and while it polarizes them, they both seem to be in the right: in Schorer's provocative formulation, 'is Elizabeth not perfectly correct? [. . .] But is Darcy any less correct?' (see Modern Criticism, p. 78). Elizabeth rejects Darcy because of his treatment of her sister Jane and her favourite Wickham but, as Bloom observes, 'the real objection to Darcy is his taking her for granted and the hopeless inferiority that a marriage with him would entail. All the power is in his hands, and his only attachment to her appears to be an uncontrollable attraction without the support of either the conventional standards or a reverence for her virtue' (see Modern Criticism, **p. 92**). But at the same time Darcy's reluctance is understandable, especially given his own social standing and the determined vulgarity of Mrs. Bennet and Lydia. In Firth's view, Darcy is saying to Elizabeth, "'I know that my family will be angry, that people will frown on us and that our social positions are very different [. . .] Nevertheless, having thought it all through, I find that my love for you is so overwhelming that these objections are rendered insignificant." And, from that point of view, it's a terribly romantic proposal' (see The Novel in Performance, **p. 103**). In *The History of Sexuality*, Michel Foucault describes two competing systems of marriage: the *'deployment of alliance'* and a newer apparatus created 'particularly from the eighteenth century onward', the *'deployment of sexuality'*.[1] When Darcy proposes to Elizabeth, he is torn between the two systems, between what he owes his family and his rank (the *'deployment of alliance'*) and what he owes his own passions and preferences (the *'deployment of sexuality'*). In this scene the two systems dramatically collide: Darcy declares his preference for Elizabeth, but not without impressing upon her how fully his preference dishonours his alliance. As with Collins, Elizabeth refuses him, though in this instance the costs – social, financial, and emotional – are far higher. In Figure 9 (see **p. 134**), Darcy declares his love for Elizabeth. He stands looking down at her and she turns rather awkwardly to face him, for he has positioned himself, not in front of her chair but to its side. His arms are open and gesturing toward her but she draws back, clutching the arm of her chair with one hand and her needlework with the other. Darcy is imposing and Elizabeth is unprepared, but the imbalance is soon righted, for she is not about to take his insulting proposal sitting down.

When they were gone, Elizabeth, as if intending to exasperate herself as much as possible against Mr. Darcy, chose for her employment the examination of all the letters which Jane had written to her since her being in Kent. They contained no actual complaint, nor was there any revival of past occurrences, or any communication of present suffering. But in all, and in almost every line of each, there was a want of that cheerfulness which had been used to characterize her style, and which, proceeding from the serenity of a mind at ease with itself, and kindly disposed towards every one, had been scarcely ever clouded. Elizabeth noticed every sentence conveying the idea of uneasiness, with an attention which it had hardly received on the first perusal. Mr. Darcy's shameful boast of what misery he had been able to inflict, gave her a keener sense of her sister's sufferings. It was some consolation to think that his visit to Rosings was to end on the day after the next, and a still greater, that in less than a fortnight she should herself be with Jane

---

1   Michel Foucault, *The History of Sexuality, Volume 1*, trans. Robert Hurley (New York: Random House, 1978), p. 106.

"You must allow me to tell you how ardently I admire and love you."

Figure 9 'You must allow me to tell you how ardently I admire and love you': Charles Brock's 1895 illustration from *Pride and Prejudice*.

again, and enabled to contribute to the recovery of her spirits, by all that affection could do.

She could not think of Darcy's leaving Kent, without remembering that his cousin was to go with him; but Colonel Fitzwilliam had made it clear that he had no intentions at all, and agreeable as he was, she did not mean to be unhappy about him.

While settling this point, she was suddenly roused by the sound of the door bell, and her spirits were a little fluttered by the idea of its being Colonel Fitzwilliam himself, who had once before called late in the evening, and might now come to enquire particularly after her. But this idea was soon banished, and her spirits were very differently affected, when, to her utter amazement, she saw Mr. Darcy walk into the room. In an hurried manner he immediately began an enquiry after her health, imputing his visit to a wish of hearing that she were better. She answered him with cold civility. He sat down for a few moments, and then getting up walked about the room. Elizabeth was surprised, but said not a word. After a silence of several minutes he came towards her in an agitated manner, and thus began,

'In vain have I struggled. It will not do. My feelings will not be repressed. You must allow me to tell you how ardently I admire and love you.'

Elizabeth's astonishment was beyond expression. She stared, coloured, doubted, and was silent. This he considered sufficient encouragement, and the avowal of all that he felt and had long felt for her, immediately followed. He spoke well, but there were feelings besides those of the heart to be detailed, and he was not more eloquent on the subject of tenderness than of pride. His sense of her inferiority – of its being a degradation – of the family obstacles which judgment had always opposed to inclination, were dwelt on with a warmth which seemed due to the consequence he was wounding, but was very unlikely to recommend his suit.

In spite of her deeply-rooted dislike, she could not be insensible to the compliment of such a man's affection, and though her intentions did not vary for an instant, she was at first sorry for the pain he was to receive; till, roused to resentment by his subsequent language, she lost all compassion in anger. She tried, however, to compose herself to answer him with patience, when he should have done. He concluded with representing to her the strength of that attachment which, in spite of all his endeavours, he had found impossible to conquer; and with expressing his hope that it would now be rewarded by her acceptance of his hand. As he said this, she could easily see that he had no doubt of a favourable answer. He *spoke* of apprehension and anxiety, but his countenance expressed real security. Such a circumstance could only exasperate farther, and when he ceased, the colour rose into her cheeks, and she said,

'In such cases as this, it is, I believe, the established mode to express a sense of obligation for the sentiments avowed, however unequally they may be returned. It is natural that obligation should be felt, and if I could *feel* gratitude, I would now thank you. But I cannot – I have never desired your good opinion, and you have certainly bestowed it most unwillingly. I am sorry to have occasioned pain to any one. It has been most unconsciously done, however, and I hope will be of short duration. The feelings which, you tell me, have long prevented the acknowledgment of your regard, can have little difficulty in overcoming it after this explanation.'

Mr. Darcy, who was leaning against the mantle-piece with his eyes fixed on her face, seemed to catch her words with no less resentment than surprise. His complexion became pale with anger, and the disturbance of his mind was visible in every feature. He was struggling for the appearance of composure, and would not open his lips, till he believed himself to have attained it. The pause was to Elizabeth's feelings dreadful. At length, in a voice of forced calmness, he said,

'And this is all the reply which I am to have the honour of expecting! I might, perhaps, wish to be informed why, with so little *endeavour* at civility, I am thus rejected. But it is of small importance.'

'I might as well enquire,' replied she, 'why with so evident a design of offending and insulting me, you chose to tell me that you liked me against your will, against your reason, and even against your character? Was not this some excuse for incivility, if I *was* uncivil? But I have other provocations. You know I have. Had not my own feelings decided against you, had they been indifferent, or had they even been favourable, do you think that any consideration would tempt me to accept the man, who has been the means of ruining, perhaps for ever, the happiness of a most beloved sister?'

As she pronounced these words, Mr. Darcy changed colour; but the emotion was short, and he listened without attempting to interrupt her while she continued.

'I have every reason in the world to think ill of you. No motive can excuse the unjust and ungenerous part you acted *there*. You dare not, you cannot deny that you have been the principal, if not the only means of dividing them from each other, of exposing one to the censure of the world for caprice and instability, the other to its derision for disappointed hopes, and involving them both in misery of the acutest kind.'

She paused, and saw with no slight indignation that he was listening with an air which proved him wholly unmoved by any feeling of remorse. He even looked at her with a smile of affected incredulity.

'Can you deny that you have done it?' she repeated.

With assumed tranquillity he then replied, 'I have no wish of denying that I did every thing in my power to separate my friend from your sister, or that I rejoice in my success. Towards *him* I have been kinder than towards myself.'

Elizabeth disdained the appearance of noticing this civil reflection, but its meaning did not escape, nor was it likely to conciliate her.

'But it is not merely this affair,' she continued, 'on which my dislike is founded. Long before it had taken place, my opinion of you was decided. Your character was unfolded in the recital which I received many months ago from Mr. Wickham. On this subject, what can you have to say? In what imaginary act of friendship can you here defend yourself? or under what misrepresentation, can you here impose upon others?'

'You take an eager interest in that gentleman's concerns,' said Darcy in a less tranquil tone, and with a heightened colour.

'Who that knows what his misfortunes have been, can help feeling an interest in him?'

'His misfortunes!' repeated Darcy contemptuously; 'yes, his misfortunes have been great indeed.'

'And of your infliction,' cried Elizabeth with energy. 'You have reduced him to his present state of poverty, comparative poverty. You have withheld the advantages, which you must know to have been designed for him. You have deprived the best years of his life, of that independence which was no less his due than his desert. You have done all this! and yet you can treat the mention of his misfortunes with contempt and ridicule.'

'And this,' cried Darcy, as he walked with quick steps across the room, 'is your opinion of me! This is the estimation in which you hold me! I thank you for explaining it so fully. My faults, according to this calculation, are heavy indeed! But perhaps,' added he, stopping in his walk, and turning towards her, 'these offences might have been overlooked, had not your pride been hurt by my honest confession of the scruples that had long prevented my forming any serious design. These bitter accusations might have been suppressed, had I with greater policy concealed my struggles, and flattered you into the belief of my being impelled by unqualified, unalloyed inclination; by reason, by reflection, by every thing. But disguise of every sort is my abhorrence. Nor am I ashamed of the feelings I related. They were natural and just. Could you expect me to rejoice in the inferiority of your connections? To congratulate myself on the hope of relations, whose condition in life is so decidedly beneath my own?'

Elizabeth felt herself growing more angry every moment; yet she tried to the utmost to speak with composure when she said,

'You are mistaken, Mr. Darcy, if you suppose that the mode of your declaration affected me in any other way, than as it spared me the concern which I might have felt in refusing you, had you behaved in a more gentleman-like manner.'

She saw him start at this, but he said nothing, and she continued,

'You could not have made me the offer of your hand in any possible way that would have tempted me to accept it.'

Again his astonishment was obvious; and he looked at her with an expression of mingled incredulity and mortification. She went on.

'From the very beginning, from the first moment I may almost say, of my acquaintance with you, your manners impressing me with the fullest belief of your arrogance, your conceit, and your selfish disdain of the feelings of others, were such as to form that ground-work of disapprobation, on which succeeding events have built so immoveable a dislike; and I had not known you a month before I felt that you were the last man in the world whom I could ever be prevailed on to marry.'

'You have said quite enough, madam. I perfectly comprehend your feelings, and have now only to be ashamed of what my own have been. Forgive me for having taken up so much of your time, and accept my best wishes for your health and happiness.'

And with these words he hastily left the room, and Elizabeth heard him the next moment open the front door and quit the house.

The tumult of her mind was now painfully great. She knew not how to support herself, and from actual weakness sat down and cried for half an hour. Her astonishment, as she reflected on what had passed, was increased by every review of it. That she should receive an offer of marriage from Mr. Darcy! that he should have been in love with her for so many months! so much in love as to wish to marry her in spite of all the objections which had made him prevent his friend's marrying her sister, and which must appear at least with equal force in his own case, was almost incredible! it was gratifying to have inspired unconsciously so strong an affection. But his pride, his abominable pride, his shameless avowal of what he had done with respect to Jane, his unpardonable assurance in acknowledging, though he could not justify it, and the unfeeling manner in which he had mentioned Mr. Wickham, his cruelty towards whom he had not attempted to deny, soon overcame the pity which the consideration of his attachment had for a moment excited.

She continued in very agitating reflections till the sound of Lady Catherine's carriage made her feel how unequal she was to encounter Charlotte's observation, and hurried her away to her room.

Volume II, Chapter Twelve

In this chapter, Darcy writes to Elizabeth to explain his behaviour toward Jane and Wickham. Regarding Jane he is essentially unrepentant, but Wickham appears in a very different light after Darcy describes his dealings with him. The letter is full of private information, but Darcy trusts in Elizabeth's confidence. He assures her that he will not be renewing his offer, yet the letter demonstrates how quickly he is willing to drop his habitual reserve to gain her good opinion, and how thoroughly the challenge of her is transforming him.

Elizabeth awoke the next morning to the same thoughts and meditations which had at length closed her eyes. She could not yet recover from the surprise of what had happened; it was impossible to think of any thing else, and totally indisposed for employment, she resolved soon after breakfast to indulge herself in air and exercise. She was proceeding directly to her favourite walk, when the recollection of Mr. Darcy's sometimes coming there stopped her, and instead of entering the park, she turned up the lane, which led her farther from the turnpike road. The park paling was still the boundary on one side, and she soon passed one of the gates into the ground.

After walking two or three times along that part of the lane, she was tempted, by the pleasantness of the morning, to stop at the gates and look into the park. The five weeks which she had now passed in Kent, had made a great difference in the country, and every day was adding to the verdure of the early trees. She was on the point of continuing her walk, when she caught a glimpse of a gentleman within the sort of grove which edged the park; he was moving that way; and fearful of its being Mr. Darcy, she was directly retreating. But the person who advanced, was now near enough to see her, and stepping forward with eagerness, pronounced her name. She had turned away, but on hearing herself called, though in a voice which proved it to be Mr. Darcy, she moved again towards the gate. He had by that time reached it also, and holding out a letter, which she instinctively took, said with a look of haughty composure, 'I have been walking in the grove some time in the hope of meeting you. Will you do me the honour of reading that letter?' – And then, with a slight bow, turned again into the plantation, and was soon out of sight.

With no expectation of pleasure, but with the strongest curiosity, Elizabeth opened the letter, and to her still increasing wonder, perceived an envelope containing two sheets of letter paper, written quite through, in a very close hand. – The envelope itself was likewise full.[1] – Pursuing her way along the lane, she then began it. It was dated from Rosings, at eight o'clock in the morning, and was as follows: –

'Be not alarmed, Madam, on receiving this letter, by the apprehension of its containing any repetition of those sentiments, or renewal of those offers, which were last night so disgusting to you. I write without any intention of paining you, or humbling myself, by dwelling on wishes, which, for the happiness of both, cannot be too soon forgotten; and the effort which the formation, and the perusal of this letter must occasion, should have been spared, had not my character required it to be written and read. You must, therefore, pardon the freedom with which I demand your attention; your feelings, I know, will bestow it unwillingly, but I demand it of your justice.

'Two offences of a very different nature, and by no means of equal magnitude, you last night laid to my charge. The first mentioned was, that, regardless of the sentiments of either, I had detached Mr. Bingley from your sister, – and the other, that I had, in defiance of various claims, in defiance of honour and humanity, ruined the immediate prosperity, and blasted the prospects of Mr. Wickham. – Wilfully and wantonly to have thrown off the companion of my youth, the acknowledged favourite of my father, a young man who had scarcely any other dependence than on our patronage, and who had been brought up to expect its exertion, would be a depravity, to which the separation of two young persons, whose affection could be the growth of only a few weeks, could bear no comparison. – But from the severity of that blame which was last night so liberally bestowed, respecting each circumstance, I shall hope to be in future secured, when the following account of my actions and their motives has been read. – If, in the explanation of them which is due to myself, I am under the necessity of relating feelings which may be offensive to your's, I can only say that I am sorry. – The necessity must be obeyed – and farther apology would be absurd. – I had not been long in Hertfordshire, before I saw, in common with others, that Bingley preferred your eldest sister, to any other young woman in the country. – But it was not till the evening of the dance at Netherfield that I had any apprehension of his feeling a serious attachment. – I had often seen him in love before. – At that ball, while I had the honour of dancing with you, I was first made acquainted, by Sir William Lucas's accidental information, that Bingley's attentions to your sister had given rise to a general expectation of their marriage. He spoke of it as a certain event, of which the time alone could be undecided. From that moment I observed my friend's behaviour attentively; and I could then perceive that his partiality for Miss Bennet was beyond what I had ever witnessed in him. Your sister I also watched. – Her look and manners were open, cheerful and engaging as ever, but without any symptom of peculiar regard, and I remained convinced from the evening's scrutiny, that though she received his attentions with pleasure, she did not invite them by any participation of sentiment. – If *you* have not been mistaken

---

1   Darcy has enclosed two sheets of paper within a third sheet, and written on all three.

here, *I* must have been in an error. Your superior knowledge of your sister must make the latter probable. – If it be so, if I have been misled by such error, to inflict pain on her, your resentment has not been unreasonable. But I shall not scruple to assert, that the serenity of your sister's countenance and air was such, as might have given the most acute observer, a conviction that, however amiable her temper, her heart was not likely to be easily touched. – That I was desirous of believing her indifferent is certain, – but I will venture to say that my investigations and decisions are not usually influenced by my hopes or fears. – I did not believe her to be indifferent because I wished it; – I believed it on impartial conviction, as truly as I wished it in reason. – My objections to the marriage were not merely those, which I last night acknowledged to have required the utmost force of passion to put aside, in my own case; the want of connection could not be so great an evil to my friend as to me. – But there were other causes of repugnance; – causes which, though still existing, and existing to an equal degree in both instances, I had myself endeavoured to forget, because they were not immediately before me. – These causes must be stated, though briefly. – The situation of your mother's family, though objectionable, was nothing in comparison of that total want of propriety so frequently, so almost uniformly betrayed by herself, by your three younger sisters, and occasionally even by your father. – Pardon me. – It pains me to offend you. But amidst your concern for the defects of your nearest relations, and your displeasure at this representation of them, let it give you consolation to consider that, to have conducted yourselves so as to avoid any share of the like censure, is praise no less generally bestowed on you and your eldest sister, than it is honourable to the sense and disposition of both. – I will only say farther, that from what passed that evening, my opinion of all parties was confirmed, and every inducement heightened, which could have led me before, to preserve my friend from what I esteemed a most unhappy connection. – He left Netherfield for London, on the day following, as you, I am certain, remember, with the design of soon returning. – The part which I acted, is now to be explained. – His sisters' uneasiness had been equally excited with my own; our coincidence of feeling was soon discovered; and, alike sensible that no time was to be lost in detaching their brother, we shortly resolved on joining him directly in London. – We accordingly went – and there I readily engaged in the office of pointing out to my friend, the certain evils of such a choice. – I described, and enforced them earnestly. – But, however this remonstrance might have staggered or delayed his determination, I do not suppose that it would ultimately have prevented the marriage, had it not been seconded by the assurance which I hesitated not in giving, of your sister's indifference. He had before believed her to return his affection with sincere, if not with equal regard. – But Bingley has great natural modesty, with a stronger dependence on my judgment than on his own. – To convince him, therefore, that he had deceived himself, was no very difficult point. To persuade him against returning into Hertfordshire, when that conviction had been given, was scarcely the work of a moment. – I cannot blame myself for having done this much. There is but one part of my conduct in the whole affair, on which I do not reflect with satisfaction; it is that I condescended to adopt the measures of art so far as to conceal from him your sister's being in town. I knew it myself, as it was known to Miss Bingley, but her brother is even yet ignorant of it. – That they might have met without ill consequence, is perhaps probable; – but his regard did not appear to me enough extinguished for him to see her without some danger. – Perhaps this concealment, this disguise, was beneath me. – It is done, however, and it was done for the best. – On this subject I have nothing more to say, no other apology to offer. If I have wounded your sister's feelings, it was unknowingly done; and though the motives which governed me may to you very naturally appear insufficient, I have not yet learnt to condemn them. – With respect to that other, more weighty accusation, of having injured Mr. Wickham, I can only refute it by laying before you the whole of his connection with my family. Of what he has *particularly* accused me I am ignorant; but of the truth of what I shall relate, I can summon more than one witness of undoubted veracity. Mr. Wickham is the son of a very respectable man, who had for many years the management of all the Pemberley estates; and whose good conduct in the discharge of his trust, naturally inclined my father to be of service to him, and on George Wickham, who was his god-son, his kindness was therefore liberally bestowed. My father supported him at school, and afterwards at Cambridge; – most important assistance, as his own father, always poor from the extravagance of his wife, would have been unable to give him a gentleman's education. My father was not only fond of this young man's society, whose manners were always engaging; he had also the highest opinion of him, and hoping the church would be his profession, intended to provide for him in it. As for myself, it is many, many years since I first began to think of him in a very different manner. The vicious propensities – the want of principle which he was careful to guard from the knowledge of his best friend, could not escape the observation of a young man of nearly the same age with himself, and who had opportunities of seeing him in unguarded moments, which Mr. Darcy could not have. Here again I shall give you pain – to what degree you only can tell. But whatever may be the sentiments which Mr. Wickham has created, a suspicion of their nature shall not prevent me from unfolding his real character. It adds even another motive. My excellent father died about five years ago; and his attachment to Mr. Wickham was to the last so steady, that in his will he particularly recommended it to me, to promote his advancement in the best manner that his profession might allow, and if he took orders, desired that a valuable family living might be his as soon as it became vacant. There was also a legacy of one thousand pounds. His own father did not long survive mine, and within half a year from these events, Mr. Wickham wrote to inform me that, having finally resolved against taking orders, he hoped I should not think it unreasonable for him to expect some more immediate pecuniary advantage, in lieu of the preferment, by which he could not be benefited. He had some intention, he added, of studying the law, and I must be aware that the interest of one thousand pounds would be a very insufficient support therein. I rather wished, than believed him to be sincere; but at any rate, was perfectly ready to accede to his proposal. I knew that Mr. Wickham ought not to be a clergyman. The business was therefore soon settled. He resigned all claim to assistance in the church, were it possible that he could ever be in a situation to receive it, and accepted in return three thousand pounds. All connection between us seemed now dissolved. I thought too ill of him, to invite him to Pemberley, or admit his society in town. In town I believe he chiefly lived, but his studying the law was a mere pretence, and being now free from all restraint, his life was a life of idleness and dissipation. For about three years I heard little of him; but on the decease of the incumbent of the living which had been designed for him, he applied to me again by letter for the presentation. His circumstances, he assured me, and I had no difficulty in believing it, were exceedingly bad. He had found the law a most unprofitable study, and was now absolutely resolved on being ordained, if I would present him to the living in question – of which he trusted there could be little doubt, as he was well assured that I had no other person to provide for, and I could not have forgotten my revered father's intentions. You will hardly blame me for refusing to comply with this entreaty, or for resisting every repetition of it. His resentment was in proportion to the distress of his circumstances – and he was doubtless as violent in his abuse of me to others, as in his reproaches to myself. After this period, every appearance of acquaintance was dropt. How he lived I know not. But last summer he was again most painfully obtruded on my notice. I must now mention a circumstance which I would wish to forget myself, and which no obligation less than the present should induce me to unfold to any human being. Having said thus much, I feel no doubt of your secrecy. My sister, who is more than ten years my junior, was left to the guardianship of my mother's nephew, Colonel Fitzwilliam, and myself. About a year ago, she was taken from school, and an establishment formed for her in London; and last summer she went with the lady who presided over it, to Ramsgate;[2] and thither also went Mr. Wickham, undoubtedly by design; for there proved to have been a prior acquaintance between him and Mrs. Younge, in whose character we were most unhappily deceived; and by her connivance and aid, he so far recommended himself to Georgiana, whose affectionate heart retained a strong impression of his kindness to her as a child, that she was persuaded to believe herself in love, and to consent to an elopement. She was then but fifteen, which must be her excuse; and after stating her imprudence, I am happy to add, that I owed the knowledge of it to herself. I joined them unexpectedly a day or two before the intended elopement, and then Georgiana, unable to support the idea of grieving and offending a brother whom she almost looked up to as a father, acknowledged the whole to me. You may imagine what I felt and how I acted. Regard for my sister's credit and feelings prevented any public exposure, but I wrote to Mr. Wickham, who left the place immediately, and Mrs. Younge was of course removed from her charge. Mr. Wickham's chief object was unquestionably my sister's fortune, which is thirty thousand pounds; but I cannot help supposing that the hope of revenging himself on me, was a strong inducement. His revenge would have been complete indeed. This, madam, is a faithful narrative of every event in which we have been concerned together; and if you do not absolutely reject it as false, you will, I hope, acquit me henceforth of cruelty towards Mr. Wickham. I know not in what manner, under what form of falsehood he has imposed on you; but his success is not perhaps to be wondered at, ignorant as you previously were of every thing concerning either. Detection could not be in your power, and suspicion certainly not in your inclination. You may possibly wonder why all this was not told you last night. But I was not then master enough of myself to know what could or ought not to be revealed. For the truth of every thing here related, I can appeal more particularly to the testimony of Colonel Fitzwilliam, who from our near relationship and constant intimacy,

---

2   A popular seaside resort on the east coast of Kent.

and still more as one of the executors of my father's will, has been unavoidably acquainted with every particular of these transactions. If your abhorrence of *me* should make *my* assertions valueless, you cannot be prevented by the same cause from confiding in my cousin; and that there may be the possibility of consulting him, I shall endeavour to find some opportunity of putting this letter in your hands in the course of the morning. I will only add, God bless you.

'FITZWILLIAM DARCY.'

Volume II, Chapter Thirteen

In this chapter Elizabeth has an epiphany, a moment of revelation or discovery. She recognizes that both Wickham and Darcy are not what they had seemed, and that she has prided herself on her own perspicacity and yet made serious errors in judgement. Austen thought Elizabeth 'as delightful a creature as ever appeared in print', and we may well agree (see Contemporary Documents, p. 41). But, like Darcy, she too must divest herself of pride and prejudice. 'I meant to be uncommonly clever in taking so decided a dislike to him, without any reason', Elizabeth later confesses to Jane.[1] Writes Tanner: 'There is much in our literature as well as our experience to suggest that the person who never comes to the point of saying, "I never knew myself", will indeed remain for ever cut off from any self-knowledge [. . .] If we don't know ourselves, we don't know our world'.[2] After this scene, Elizabeth has a more accurate perception of both herself and her world.

She perfectly remembered every thing that had passed in conversation between Wickham and herself, in their first evening at Mr. Philips's. Many of his expressions were still fresh in her memory. She was *now* struck with the impropriety of such communications to a stranger, and wondered it had escaped her before. She saw the indelicacy of putting himself forward as he had done, and the inconsistency of his professions with his conduct. She remembered that he had boasted of having no fear of seeing Mr. Darcy – that Mr. Darcy might leave the country, but that *he* should stand his ground; yet he had avoided the Netherfield ball the very next week. She remembered also, that till the Netherfield family had quitted the country, he had told his story to no one but herself; but that after their removal, it had been every where discussed; that he had then no reserves, no scruples in sinking Mr. Darcy's character, though he had assured her that respect for the father would always prevent his exposing the son.

How differently did every thing now appear in which he was concerned! His attentions to Miss King were now the consequence of views solely and hatefully mercenary; and the mediocrity of her fortune proved no longer the moderation of his wishes, but his eagerness to grasp at any thing. His behaviour to herself could

---

1   Jane Austen, *Pride and Prejudice*, ed. R. W. Chapman (Oxford: Clarendon Press, 1923), Volume II, Chapter 17, p. 225.
2   Tony Tanner, *Jane Austen* (Cambridge, Mass.: Harvard University Press, 1986), p. 113.

now have had no tolerable motive; he had either been deceived with regard to her fortune, or had been gratifying his vanity by encouraging the preference which she believed she had most incautiously shewn. Every lingering struggle in his favour grew fainter and fainter; and in farther justification of Mr. Darcy, she could not but allow that Mr. Bingley, when questioned by Jane, had long ago asserted his blamelessness in the affair; that proud and repulsive as were his manners, she had never, in the whole course of their acquaintance, an acquaintance which had latterly brought them much together, and given her a sort of intimacy with his ways, seen any thing that betrayed him to be unprincipled or unjust – any thing that spoke him of irreligious or immoral habits. That among his own connections he was esteemed and valued – that even Wickham had allowed him merit as a brother, and that she had often heard him speak so affectionately of his sister as to prove him capable of *some* amiable feeling. That had his actions been what Wickham represented them, so gross a violation of every thing right could hardly have been concealed from the world; and that friendship between a person capable of it, and such an amiable man as Mr. Bingley, was incomprehensible.

She grew absolutely ashamed of herself. – Of neither Darcy nor Wickham could she think, without feeling that she had been blind, partial, prejudiced, absurd.

'How despicably have I acted!' she cried. – 'I, who have prided myself on my discernment! – I, who have valued myself on my abilities! who have often disdained the generous candour of my sister, and gratified my vanity, in useless or blameable distrust. – How humiliating is this discovery! – Yet, how just a humiliation! – Had I been in love, I could not have been more wretchedly blind. But vanity, not love, has been my folly. – Pleased with the preference of one, and offended by the neglect of the other, on the very beginning of our acquaintance, I have courted prepossession and ignorance, and driven reason away, where either were concerned. Till this moment, I never knew myself.'

From herself to Jane – from Jane to Bingley, her thoughts were in a line which soon brought to her recollection that Mr. Darcy's explanation *there* had appeared very insufficient; and she read it again. Widely different was the effect of a second perusal. – How could she deny that credit to his assertions, in one instance, which she had been obliged to give in the other? – He declared himself to have been totally unsuspicious of her sister's attachment; – and she could not help remembering what Charlotte's opinion had always been. – Neither could she deny the justice of his description of Jane. – She felt that Jane's feelings, though fervent, were little displayed, and that there was a constant complacency[3] in her air and manner, not often united with great sensibility.

When she came to that part of the letter in which her family were mentioned, in terms of such mortifying, yet merited reproach, her sense of shame was severe. The justice of the charge struck her too forcibly for denial, and the circumstances to which he particularly alluded, as having passed at the Netherfield ball, and as confirming all his first disapprobation, could not have made a stronger impression

---

3   'Contented acquiescence or consent' (*Oxford English Dictionary*). Bloom seems to have this passage in mind when he discusses how 'Elizabeth has herself criticized Jane for not expressing her attraction to Bingley more openly' (see Modern Criticism, **p. 91**). Austen uses a different meaning of 'complacency' earlier in the novel (see Key Passages, **p. 118**).

on his mind than on hers. The compliment to herself and her sister, was not unfelt. It soothed, but it could not console her for the contempt which had been thus self-attracted by the rest of her family; – and as she considered that Jane's disappointment had in fact been the work of her nearest relations, and reflected how materially the credit of both must be hurt by such impropriety of conduct, she felt depressed beyond any thing she had ever known before.

Volume III, Chapter One

In this passage, Elizabeth and her aunt and uncle Gardiner unexpectedly encounter Darcy at his Pemberley estate. It is an eye-opening experience for Elizabeth. Walter Scott believes that she does not realize she has 'done a foolish thing' in rejecting Darcy 'until she accidentally visits a very handsome seat and grounds belonging to her admirer'.[1] But George Saintsbury has 'not the slightest doubt that she would have married Darcy just as willingly without Pemberley as with it'.[2] Certainly, as Butler stresses, 'Darcy's grounds teach Elizabeth that his taste is "neither formal, nor falsely adorned", and thus refute her preconceived notion of his pomposity. The good opinion of his housekeeper and tenants is precisely the objective proof of character that she neglected to look for in the case of Wickham. And of course the existence of Pemberley hints at a future life of active social involvement for both Darcy and Elizabeth'.[3] Darcy speaks to her with civility, and treats her aunt and uncle with courtesy and respect, though they are in trade and live at an unfashionable London address. His priggishness is gone, and though she dare not believe that she is the reason for the change, Elizabeth finds herself warming to him at the same time that he shows himself capable of judging people based on merit rather than rank. The visit to Pemberley reveals to Elizabeth that Darcy is a man of integrity and taste, and the gap between the two begins to close. Figure 10 (see **p. 146**) is taken from the 1995 BBC film of *Pride and Prejudice*. In the novel Elizabeth meets Darcy when he suddenly comes 'forward from the road' that leads behind Pemberley. But in the film Darcy (Colin Firth) jumps in a lake and then emerges dripping wet to encounter Elizabeth (Jennifer Ehle). Bonnetted and with arms behind her back, she looks up at him with trepidation, curiosity, and perhaps even hope. Darcy, very informally dressed, with riding crop in one hand and silk top hat clenched in the other, is vulnerable and uneasy. As in Figure 8 (see **p. 115**) from the Meryton ball, his eyes are cast down, not in condescension as they were then, but in an attitude that seems both distracted and expectant. The magnificent structure of Pemberley looms up in the background, a reminder to Elizabeth both of his sound principles and of the possibility that she has misjudged him.

1   Walter Scott, '*Emma*' in *Quarterly Review*, 14 (March 1816), p. 194.
2   George Saintsbury, 'On *Pride and Prejudice*' in Jane Austen, *Pride and Prejudice*, ed. George Saintsbury (London: George Allen, 1894), p. xxiii.
3   Marilyn Butler, *Jane Austen and the War of Ideas* (Oxford: Clarendon Press, 1975), p. 215.

Figure 10 Jennifer Ehle as Elizabeth Bennet and Colin Firth as Mr. Darcy in the 1995 BBC version of *Pride and Prejudice.*

There was certainly at this moment, in Elizabeth's mind, a more gentle sensa-
tion towards the original, than she had ever felt in the height of their acquaintance. The commendation bestowed on him by Mrs. Reynolds was of no trifling
nature. What praise is more valuable than the praise of an intelligent servant? As a
brother, a landlord, a master, she considered how many people's happiness were
in his guardianship! – How much of pleasure or pain it was in his power to
bestow! – How much of good or evil must be done by him! Every idea that had
been brought forward by the housekeeper was favourable to his character, and as
she stood before the canvas, on which he was represented, and fixed his eyes upon
herself, she thought of his regard with a deeper sentiment of gratitude[4] than it had
ever raised before; she remembered its warmth, and softened its impropriety of
expression.

When all of the house that was open to general inspection had been seen, they
returned down stairs, and taking leave of the housekeeper, were consigned over to
the gardener, who met them at the hall door.

As they walked across the lawn towards the river, Elizabeth turned back to look
again; her uncle and aunt stopped also, and while the former was conjecturing as
to the date of the building, the owner of it himself suddenly came forward from
the road, which led behind it to the stables.

They were within twenty yards of each other, and so abrupt was his appearance, that it was impossible to avoid his sight. Their eyes instantly met, and the
cheeks of each were overspread with the deepest blush. He absolutely started, and
for a moment seemed immoveable from surprise; but shortly recovering himself,
advanced towards the party, and spoke to Elizabeth, if not in terms of perfect
composure, at least of perfect civility.

She had instinctively turned away; but, stopping on his approach, received his
compliments with an embarrassment impossible to be overcome. Had his first
appearance, or his resemblance to the picture they had just been examining, been
insufficient to assure the other two that they now saw Mr. Darcy, the gardener's
expression of surprise, on beholding his master, must immediately have told it.
They stood a little aloof while he was talking to their niece, who, astonished and
confused, scarcely dared lift her eyes to his face, and knew not what answer she
returned to his civil enquiries after her family. Amazed at the alteration in his
manner since they last parted, every sentence that he uttered was increasing her
embarrassment; and every idea of the impropriety of her being found there, recur-
ring to her mind, the few minutes in which they continued together, were some of
the most uncomfortable of her life. Nor did he seem much more at ease; when he
spoke, his accent had none of its usual sedateness; and he repeated his enquiries as
to the time of her having left Longbourn, and of her stay in Derbyshire, so often,
and in so hurried a way, as plainly spoke the distraction of his thoughts.

At length, every idea seemed to fail him; and, after standing a few moments
without saying a word, he suddenly recollected himself, and took leave.

The others then joined her, and expressed their admiration of his figure; but
Elizabeth heard not a word, and, wholly engrossed by her own feelings, followed

---

4   Compare John Gregory, *A Father's Legacy to His Daughters*: 'What is commonly called love
    among you, is rather gratitude, and a partiality to the man who prefers you to the rest of your sex'
    (see Contemporary Documents, p. 30).

them in silence. She was overpowered by shame and vexation. Her coming there was the most unfortunate, the most ill-judged thing in the world! How strange must it appear to him! In what a disgraceful light might it not strike so vain a man! It might seem as if she had purposely thrown herself in his way again! Oh! why did she come? or, why did he thus come a day before he was expected? Had they been only ten minutes sooner, they should have been beyond the reach of his discrimination, for it was plain that he was that moment arrived, that moment alighted from his horse or his carriage. She blushed again and again over the perverseness of the meeting. And his behaviour, so strikingly altered, – what could it mean? That he should even speak to her was amazing! – but to speak with such civility, to enquire after her family! Never in her life had she seen his manners so little dignified, never had he spoken with such gentleness as on this unexpected meeting. What a contrast did it offer to his last address in Rosing's Park, when he put his letter into her hand! She knew not what to think, nor how to account for it.

They had now entered a beautiful walk by the side of the water, and every step was bringing forward a nobler fall of ground, or a finer reach of the woods to which they were approaching; but it was some time before Elizabeth was sensible of any of it; and, though she answered mechanically to the repeated appeals of her uncle and aunt, and seemed to direct her eyes to such objects as they pointed out, she distinguished no part of the scene. Her thoughts were all fixed on that one spot of Pemberley House, whichever it might be, where Mr. Darcy then was. She longed to know what at that moment was passing in his mind; in what manner he thought of her, and whether, in defiance of every thing, she was still dear to him. Perhaps he had been civil, only because he felt himself at ease; yet there had been *that* in his voice, which was not like ease. Whether he had felt more of pain or of pleasure in seeing her, she could not tell, but he certainly had not seen her with composure.

At length, however, the remarks of her companions on her absence of mind roused her, and she felt the necessity of appearing more like herself.

They entered the woods, and bidding adieu to the river for a while, ascended some of the higher grounds; whence, in spots where the opening of the trees gave the eye power to wander, were many charming views of the valley, the opposite hills, with the long range of woods overspreading many, and occasionally part of the stream. Mr. Gardiner expressed a wish of going round the whole Park, but feared it might be beyond a walk. With a triumphant smile, they were told, that it was ten miles round. It settled the matter; and they pursued the accustomed circuit; which brought them again, after some time, in a descent among hanging woods, to the edge of the water, in one of its narrowest parts. They crossed it by a simple bridge, in character with the general air of the scene; it was a spot less adorned than any they had yet visited; and the valley, here contracted into a glen, allowed room only for the stream, and a narrow walk amidst the rough cop-pice-wood which bordered it. Elizabeth longed to explore its windings; but when they had crossed the bridge, and perceived their distance from the house, Mrs. Gardiner, who was not a great walker, could go no farther, and thought only of returning to the carriage as quickly as possible. Her niece was, therefore, obliged to submit, and they took their way towards the house on the opposite side of the river, in the nearest direction; but their progress was slow, for Mr. Gardiner, though seldom able to indulge the taste, was very fond of fishing, and was so much engaged in watching the occasional appearance of some trout in the water, and talking to the man about them, that he advanced but little. Whilst wandering on in this slow manner, they were again surprised, and Elizabeth's astonishment was quite equal to what it had been at first, by the sight of Mr. Darcy approaching them, and at no great distance. The walk being here less sheltered than on the other side, allowed them to see him before they met. Elizabeth, however astonished, was at least more prepared for an interview than before, and resolved to appear and to speak with calmness, if he really intended to meet them. For a few moments, indeed, she felt that he would probably strike into some other path. This idea lasted while a turning in the walk concealed him from their view; the turning past, he was immediately before them. With a glance she saw, that he had lost none of his recent civility; and, to imitate his politeness, she began, as they met, to admire the beauty of the place; but she had not got beyond the words 'delightful,' and 'charming,' when some unlucky recollections obtruded, and she fancied that praise of Pemberley from her, might be mischievously construed. Her colour changed, and she said no more.

Mrs. Gardiner was standing a little behind; and on her pausing, he asked her, if she would do him the honour of introducing him to her friends. This was a stroke of civility for which she was quite unprepared; and she could hardly suppress a smile, at his being now seeking the acquaintance of some of those very people, against whom his pride had revolted, in his offer to herself. 'What will be his surprise,' thought she, 'when he knows who they are! He takes them now for people of fashion.'

The introduction, however, was immediately made; and as she named their relationship to herself, she stole a sly look at him, to see how he bore it; and was not without the expectation of his decamping as fast as he could from such disgraceful companions. That he was *surprised* by the connexion was evident; he sustained it however with fortitude, and so far from going away, turned back with them, and entered into conversation with Mr. Gardiner. Elizabeth could not but be pleased, could not but triumph. It was consoling, that he should know she had some relations for whom there was no need to blush. She listened most attentively to all that passed between them, and gloried in every expression, every sentence of her uncle, which marked his intelligence, his taste, or his good manners.

The conversation soon turned upon fishing, and she heard Mr. Darcy invite him, with the greatest civility, to fish there as often as he chose, while he continued in the neighbourhood, offering at the same time to supply him with fishing tackle, and pointing out those parts of the stream where there was usually most sport. Mrs. Gardiner, who was walking arm in arm with Elizabeth, gave her a look expressive of her wonder. Elizabeth said nothing, but it gratified her exceedingly; the compliment must be all for herself. Her astonishment, however, was extreme; and continually was she repeating, 'Why is he so altered? From what can it proceed? It cannot be for *me*, it cannot be for *my* sake that his manners are thus softened. My reproofs at Hunsford could not work such a change as this. It is impossible that he should still love me.'

Volume III, Chapter Fourteen

In this scene, Lady Catherine de Bourgh confronts Elizabeth over her relationship with Darcy. Elizabeth's discovery that it was Darcy who tracked down Lydia after her foolish elopement with Wickham, and then generously ensured that the couple were married and respectably established, has convinced her both of his integrity and of how much she needs him. To Lady Catherine, however, such a need is grotesquely presumptuous and a shameless attempt at social climbing, for her conception of the aristocracy is clearly aligned with Edmund Burke's in his *Appeal from the New to the Old Whigs* (see Contemporary Documents, **pp. 35–6**). She knows of Lydia's 'infamous elopement', and harangues Elizabeth with the kind of snobbery that Elizabeth originally thought belonged to Darcy. But whilst Lady Catherine is a devoted member of an *ancien regime*, Darcy has shown himself to belong to the *noblesse oblige*. Lady Catherine is equally as inane as Mrs. Bennet, but while she abuses her high station and cannot distinguish between principle and caprice, Mrs. Bennet has at least as extenuating circumstances her pressing desire to ensure that her daughters avoid both penury and spinsterhood. 'Lady Catherine looked upon Elizabeth as so much white trash', declared Somerset Maugham, but Elizabeth did not take such abuse lightly (see Novelists on *Pride and Prejudice*, **p. 67**). '*Pride and Prejudice*', as Lionel Trilling remarked crisply, 'is militantly anti-snob'.[1] William Dean Howells agrees: 'It is impossible [. . .] not to feel that her triumph over Lady de Burgh is something more than personal: it is a protest, it is an insurrection' (see Novelists on *Pride and Prejudice*, **p. 65**). In Figure 11 (see **p. 151**), Lady Catherine holds Elizabeth's wrist in her left hand and hectors her with her right. Elizabeth, however, is unbowed. As Douglas Murray remarks, Elizabeth is 'the triumphant and independent gazer [. . .] who throughout the novel is symbolically associated with the eye [. . .] It is this central core of resistance which allows Elizabeth to withstand the powerful gaze of Lady Catherine – or, as the cliché puts it, to look her in the eye' (see Modern Criticism, **p. 95**).

One morning, about a week after Bingley's engagement with Jane had been formed, as he and the females of the family were sitting together in the dining room, their attention was suddenly drawn to the window, by the sound of a carriage; and they perceived a chaise and four driving up the lawn. It was too early in the morning for visitors, and besides, the equipage did not answer to that of any of their neighbours. The horses were post;[2] and neither the carriage, nor the livery of the servant who preceded it, were familiar to them. As it was certain, however, that somebody was coming, Bingley instantly prevailed on Miss Bennet to avoid the confinement of such an intrusion, and walk away with him into the shrubbery. They both set off, and the conjectures of the remaining three

---

1   Lionel Trilling, 'A Portrait of Western Man' in *The Listener*, 49 (11 June 1953), p. 970.
2   That is, they had been hired at post-stations to take Lady Catherine's carriage on by stages.

Pickering. pinxt.   *Greatbatch, sculpt.*

This is not to be borne. Miss Bennet,
I insist on being satisfied. Has he, has
my nephew, made you an offer of marriage?

Figure 11 '**This is not to be borne. Miss Bennet, I insist on being satisfied. Has he, has my nephew, made you an offer of marriage?' The frontispiece from the 1833 Bentley's Standard Novels edition of** *Pride and Prejudice.*

continued, though with little satisfaction, till the door was thrown open, and their visitor entered. It was lady Catherine de Bourgh.

They were of course all intending to be surprised; but their astonishment was beyond their expectation; and on the part of Mrs. Bennet and Kitty, though she was perfectly unknown to them, even inferior to what Elizabeth felt.

She entered the room with an air more than usually ungracious, made no other reply to Elizabeth's salutation, than a slight inclination of the head, and sat down without saying a word. Elizabeth had mentioned her name to her mother, on her ladyship's entrance, though no request of introduction had been made.

Mrs. Bennet all amazement, though flattered by having a guest of such high importance, received her with the utmost politeness. After sitting for a moment in silence, she said very stiffly to Elizabeth,

'I hope you are well, Miss Bennet. That lady I suppose is your mother.'

Elizabeth replied very concisely that she was.

'And *that* I suppose is one of your sisters.'

'Yes, madam,' said Mrs. Bennet, delighted to speak to a lady Catherine. 'She is my youngest girl but one. My youngest of all, is lately married, and my eldest is some-where about the grounds, walking with a young man, who I believe will soon become a part of the family.'

'You have a very small park here,' returned lady Catherine after a short silence.

'It is nothing in comparison of Rosings, my lady, I dare say; but I assure you it is much larger than Sir William Lucas's.'

'This must be a most inconvenient sitting room for the evening, in summer; the windows are full west.'

Mrs. Bennet assured her that they never sat there after dinner; and then added,

'May I take the liberty of asking your ladyship whether you left Mr. and Mrs. Collins well.'

'Yes, very well. I saw them the night before last.'

Elizabeth now expected that she would produce a letter for her from Charlotte, as it seemed the only probable motive for her calling. But no letter appeared, and she was completely puzzled.

Mrs. Bennet, with great civility, begged her ladyship to take some refreshment; but Lady Catherine very resolutely, and not very politely, declined eating any thing; and then rising up, said to Elizabeth,

'Miss Bennet, there seemed to be a prettyish kind of a little wilderness on one side of your lawn. I should be glad to take a turn in it, if you will favour me with your company.'

'Go, my dear,' cried her mother, 'and shew her ladyship about the different walks. I think she will be pleased with the hermitage.'

Elizabeth obeyed, and running into her own room for her parasol, attended her noble guest down stairs. As they passed through the hall, Lady Catherine opened the doors into the dining-parlour and drawing-room, and pronouncing them, after a short survey, to be decent looking rooms, walked on.

Her carriage remained at the door, and Elizabeth saw that her waiting-woman was in it. They proceeded in silence along the gravel walk that led to the copse; Elizabeth was determined to make no effort for conversation with a woman, who was now more than usually insolent and disagreeable.

'How could I ever think her like her nephew?' said she, as she looked in her face.

As soon as they entered the copse, Lady Catherine began in the following manner: –

'You can be at no loss, Miss Bennet, to understand the reason of my journey hither. Your own heart, your own conscience, must tell you why I come.'

Elizabeth looked with unaffected astonishment.

'Indeed, you are mistaken, Madam. I have not been at all able to account for the honour of seeing you here.'

'Miss Bennet,' replied her ladyship, in an angry tone, 'you ought to know, that I am not to be trifled with. But however insincere *you* may choose to be, you shall not find *me* so. My character has ever been celebrated for its sincerity and frankness, and in a cause of such moment as this, I shall certainly not depart from it. A report of a most alarming nature, reached me two days ago. I was told, that not only your sister was on the point of being most advantageously married, but that *you*, that Miss Elizabeth Bennet, would, in all likelihood, be soon afterwards united to my nephew, my own nephew, Mr. Darcy. Though I *know* it must be a scandalous falsehood; though I would not injure him so much as to suppose the truth of it possible, I instantly resolved on setting off for this place, that I might make my sentiments known to you.'

'If you believed it impossible to be true,' said Elizabeth, colouring with astonishment and disdain, 'I wonder you took the trouble of coming so far. What could your ladyship propose by it?'

'At once to insist upon having such a report universally contradicted.'

'Your coming to Longbourn, to see me and my family,' said Elizabeth, coolly, 'will be rather a confirmation of it; if, indeed, such a report is in existence.'

'If! do you then pretend to be ignorant of it? Has it not been industriously circulated by yourselves? Do you not know that such a report is spread abroad?'

'I never heard that it was.'

'And can you likewise declare, that there is no *foundation* for it?'

'I do not pretend to possess equal frankness with your ladyship. *You* may ask questions, which *I* shall not choose to answer.'

'This is not to be borne. Miss Bennet, I insist on being satisfied. Has he, has my nephew, made you an offer of marriage?'

'Your ladyship has declared it to be impossible.'

'It ought to be so; it must be so, while he retains the use of his reason. But *your* arts and allurements may, in a moment of infatuation, have made him forget what he owes to himself and to all his family. You may have drawn him in.'

'If I have, I shall be the last person to confess it.'

'Miss Bennet, do you know who I am? I have not been accustomed to such language as this. I am almost the nearest relation he has in the world, and am entitled to know all his dearest concerns.'

'But you are not entitled to know *mine*; nor will such behaviour as this, ever induce me to be explicit.'

'Let me be rightly understood. This match, to which you have the presumption to aspire, can never take place. No, never. Mr. Darcy is engaged to *my daughter*. Now what have you to say?'

'Only this; that if he is so, you can have no reason to suppose he will make an offer to me.'

Lady Catherine hesitated for a moment, and then replied,

'The engagement between them is of a peculiar kind. From their infancy, they have been intended for each other.[3] It was the favourite wish of *his* mother, as well as of her's. While in their cradles, we planned the union: and now, at the moment

---

3   As Collins's proposal to Elizabeth suggests, the marriage of cousins was not unusual in English landed families.

when the wishes of both sisters would be accomplished, in their marriage, to be prevented by a young woman of inferior birth, of no importance in the world, and wholly unallied to the family! Do you pay no regard to the wishes of his friends? To his tacit engagement with Miss De Bourgh? Are you lost to every feeling of propriety and delicacy? Have you not heard me say, that from his earliest hours he was destined for his cousin?'

'Yes, and I had heard it before. But what is that to me? If there is no other objection to my marrying your nephew, I shall certainly not be kept from it, by knowing that his mother and aunt wished him to marry Miss De Bourgh. You both did as much as you could, in planning the marriage. Its completion depended on others. If Mr. Darcy is neither by honour nor inclination confined to his cousin, why is not he to make another choice? And if I am that choice, why may not I accept him?'

'Because honour, decorum, prudence, nay, interest, forbid it. Yes, Miss Bennet, interest; for do not expect to be noticed by his family or friends, if you wilfully act against the inclinations of all. You will be censured, slighted, and despised, by every one connected with him. Your affiance will be a disgrace; your name will never even be mentioned by any of us.'

'These are heavy misfortunes,' replied Elizabeth. 'But the wife of Mr. Darcy must have such extraordinary sources of happiness necessarily attached to her situation, that she could, upon the whole, have no cause to repine.'

'Obstinate, headstrong girl! I am ashamed of you! Is this your gratitude for my attentions to you last spring? Is nothing due to me on that score?

'Let us sit down. You are to understand, Miss Bennet, that I came here with the determined resolution of carrying my purpose; nor will I be dissuaded from it. I have not been used to submit to any person's whims. I have not been in the habit of brooking disappointment.'

'*That* will make your ladyship's situation at present more pitiable; but it will have no effect on *me*.'

'I will not be interrupted. Hear me in silence. My daughter and my nephew are formed for each other. They are descended on the maternal side, from the same noble line; and, on the father's, from respectable, honourable, and ancient, though untitled families. Their fortune on both sides is splendid. They are destined for each other by the voice of every member of their respective houses; and what is to divide them? The upstart pretensions of a young woman without family, connections, or fortune. Is this to be endured! But it must not, shall not be. If you were sensible of your own good, you would not wish to quit the sphere, in which you have been brought up.'

'In marrying your nephew, I should not consider myself as quitting that sphere. He is a gentleman; I am a gentleman's daughter; so far we are equal.'

'True. You *are* a gentleman's daughter. But who was your mother? Who are your uncles and aunts? Do not imagine me ignorant of their condition.'

'Whatever my connections may be,' said Elizabeth, 'if your nephew does not object to them, they can be nothing to *you*.'

'Tell me once for all, are you engaged to him?'

Though Elizabeth would not, for the mere purpose of obliging Lady Catherine, have answered this question; she could not but say, after a moment's deliberation,

'I am not.'

Lady Catherine seemed pleased.

'And will you promise me, never to enter into such an engagement?'

'I will make no promise of the kind.'

'Miss Bennet I am shocked and astonished. I expected to find a more reasonable young woman. But do not deceive yourself into a belief that I will ever recede. I shall not go away, till you have given me the assurance I require.'

'And I certainly *never* shall give it. I am not to be intimidated into anything so wholly unreasonable. Your ladyship wants Mr. Darcy to marry your daughter; but would my giving you the wished-for promise, make *their* marriage at all more probable? Supposing him to be attached to me, would *my* refusing to accept his hand, make him wish to bestow it on his cousin? Allow me to say, Lady Catherine, that the arguments with which you have supported this extraordinary application, have been as frivolous as the application was ill-judged. You have widely mistaken my character, if you think I can be worked on by such persuasions as these. How far your nephew might approve of your interference in *his* affairs, I cannot tell; but you have certainly no right to concern yourself in mine. I must beg, therefore, to be importuned no farther on the subject.'

'Not so hasty, if you please. I have by no means done. To all the objections I have already urged, I have still another to add. I am no stranger to the particulars of your youngest sister's infamous elopement. I know it all; that the young man's marrying her, was a patched-up business, at the expence of your father and uncles. And is *such* a girl to be my nephew's sister? Is *her* husband, is the son of his late father's steward, to be his brother? Heaven and earth! – of what are you thinking? Are the shades of Pemberley to be thus polluted?'

'You can *now* have nothing farther to say,' she resentfully answered. 'You have insulted me, in every possible method. I must beg to return to the house.'

And she rose as she spoke. Lady Catherine rose also, and they turned back. Her ladyship was highly incensed.

'You have no regard, then, for the honour and credit of my nephew! Unfeeling, selfish girl! Do you not consider that a connection with you, must disgrace him in the eyes of everybody?'

'Lady Catherine, I have nothing farther to say. You know my sentiments.'

'You are then resolved to have him?'

'I have said no such thing. I am only resolved to act in that manner, which will, in my own opinion, constitute my happiness, without reference to *you*, or to any person so wholly unconnected with me.'

'It is well. You refuse, then, to oblige me. You refuse to obey the claims of duty, honour, and gratitude. You are determined to ruin him in the opinion of all his friends, and make him the contempt of the world.'

'Neither duty, nor honour, nor gratitude,' replied Elizabeth, 'have any possible claim on me, in the present instance. No principle of either, would be violated by my marriage with Mr. Darcy. And with regard to the resentment of his family, or the indignation of the world, if the former *were* excited by his marrying me, it would not give me one moment's concern – and the world in general would have too much sense to join in the scorn.'

'And this is your real opinion! This is your final resolve! Very well. I shall now know how to act. Do not imagine, Miss Bennet, that your ambition will ever be gratified. I came to try you. I hoped to find you reasonable; but depend upon it I will carry my point.'

In this manner Lady Catherine talked on, till they were at the door of the carriage, when turning hastily round, she added,

'I take no leave of you, Miss Bennet. I send no compliments to your mother. You deserve no such attention. I am most seriously displeased.'

Elizabeth made no answer; and without attempting to persuade her ladyship to return into the house, walked quietly into it herself.

Volume III, Chapter Sixteen

In this scene, Elizabeth and Darcy walk alone together and discuss the course of their relationship. The jousting, resentment, and misdirection that characterized their early conversations is over. Each has been humbled, yet neither has been diminished, and they now speak to one another frankly and as equals. Chesterton observed that 'When Darcy, in finally confessing his faults, says, "I have been a selfish being all my life, in practice *though not in theory*," he gets nearer to a complete confession of the intelligent male than ever was even hinted by the Byronic lapses of the Brontës' heroes or the elaborate exculpations of George Eliot's' (see Novelists on *Pride and Prejudice*, **p. 66**).

Darcy mentioned his letter.[1] 'Did it,' said he, 'did it *soon* make you think better of me? Did you, on reading it, give any credit to its contents?'

She explained what its effect on her had been, and how gradually all her former prejudices had been removed.

'I knew,' said he, 'that what I wrote must give you pain, but it was necessary. I hope you have destroyed the letter. There was one part especially, the opening of it, which I should dread your having the power of reading again. I can remember some expressions which might justly make you hate me.'

'The letter shall certainly be burnt, if you believe it essential to the preservation of my regard; but, though we have both reason to think my opinions not entirely unalterable, they are not, I hope, quite so easily changed as that implies.'

'When I wrote that letter,' replied Darcy, 'I believed myself perfectly calm and cool, but I am since convinced that it was written in a dreadful bitterness of spirit.'

'The letter, perhaps, began in bitterness, but it did not end so. The adieu is charity itself. But think no more of the letter. The feelings of the person who wrote, and the person who received it, are now so widely different from what they were then, that every unpleasant circumstance attending it, ought to be forgotten. You must learn some of my philosophy. Think only of the past as its remembrance gives you pleasure.'

'I cannot give you credit for any philosophy of the kind. *Your* retrospections must be so totally void of reproach, that the contentment arising from them, is not

---

1   See Key Passages, pp. 138–43.

of philosophy, but what is much better, of ignorance. But with *me*, it is not so. Painful recollections will intrude, which cannot, which ought not to be repelled. I have been a selfish being all my life, in practice, though not in principle. As a child I was taught what was *right*, but I was not taught to correct my temper. I was given good principles, but left to follow them in pride and conceit. Unfortunately an only son (for many years an only *child*) I was spoilt by my parents, who though good themselves (my father particularly, all that was benevolent and amiable,) allowed, encouraged, almost taught me to be selfish and overbearing, to care for none beyond my own family circle, to think meanly of all the rest of the world, to *wish* at least to think meanly of their sense and worth compared with my own. Such I was, from eight to eight and twenty; and such I might still have been but for you, dearest, loveliest Elizabeth! What do I not owe you! You taught me a lesson, hard indeed at first, but most advantageous. By you, I was properly humbled. I came to you without a doubt of my reception. You shewed me how insufficient were all my pretensions to please a woman worthy of being pleased.'

'Had you then persuaded yourself that I should?'

'Indeed I had. What will you think of my vanity? I believed you to be wishing, expecting my addresses.'

'My manners must have been in fault, but not intentionally I assure you. I never meant to deceive you, but my spirits might often lead me wrong. How you must have hated me after *that* evening?'

'Hate you! I was angry perhaps at first, but my anger soon began to take a proper direction.'

'I am almost afraid of asking what you thought of me; when we met at Pemberley.[2] You blamed me for coming?'

'No indeed; I felt nothing but surprise.'

'Your surprise could not be greater than *mine* in being noticed by you. My conscience told me that I deserved no extraordinary politeness, and I confess that I did not expect to receive *more* than my due.'

'My object *then*,' replied Darcy, 'was to shew you, by every civility in my power, that I was not so mean as to resent the past; and I hoped to obtain your forgiveness, to lessen your ill opinion, by letting you see that your reproofs had been attended to. How soon any other wishes introduced themselves I can hardly tell, but I believe in about half an hour after I had seen you.'

Volume III, Chapter Eighteen

In this scene, Elizabeth asks Darcy to explain how he fell in love with her, and offers her own insights into what has brought them together. She promises to continue to tease him as he takes steps to inform his family of his decision to marry her. In *Sermons to Young Women*, James Fordyce argues that 'men who understand the science of domestic happiness, know that its very first principle is ease' (see Contemporary Documents, **p. 29**). But Darcy is 'disgusted with the women who were always speaking, and looking, and thinking for [his] approbation alone', and has more wisely chosen 'liveliness of [...] mind'. Elizabeth realizes that he has 'yet to learn to be laught at, and it was rather too early to begin'.[1] But certainly she will begin, and he will no doubt have to learn, for as both have grown during their courtship, so Austen suggests that they will continue to educate and enjoy one another during their life together. Elizabeth's conviction has been confirmed: 'It was an union that must have been to the advantage of both'.[2]

Elizabeth's spirits soon rising to playfulness again, she wanted Mr. Darcy to account for his having ever fallen in love with her. 'How could you begin?' said she. 'I can comprehend your going on charmingly, when you had once made a beginning; but what could set you off in the first place?'

'I cannot fix on the hour, or the spot, or the look, or the words, which laid the foundation. It is too long ago. I was in the middle before I knew that I *had* begun.'

'My beauty you had early withstood, and as for my manners – my behaviour to *you* was at least always bordering on the uncivil, and I never spoke to you without rather wishing to give you pain than not. Now be sincere; did you admire me for my impertinence?'

'For the liveliness of your mind, I did.'

'You may as well call it impertinence at once. It was very little less. The fact is, that you were sick of civility, of deference, of officious attention. You were disgusted with the women who were always speaking and looking, and thinking for *your* approbation alone. I roused, and interested you, because I was so unlike *them*. Had you not been really amiable you would have hated me for it; but in spite of the pains you took to disguise yourself, your feelings were always noble and just; and in your heart, you thoroughly despised the persons who so assiduously courted you. There – I have saved you the trouble of accounting for it; and really, all things considered, I begin to think it perfectly reasonable. To be sure, you knew no actual good of me – but nobody thinks of *that* when they fall in love.'

'Was there no good in your affectionate behaviour to Jane, while she was ill at Netherfield?'

'Dearest Jane! who could have done less for her? But make a virtue of it by all means. My good qualities are under your protection, and you are to exaggerate them as much as possible; and, in return, it belongs to me to find occasions for teasing and quarrelling with you as often as may be; and I shall begin directly by asking you what made you so unwilling to come to the point at last. What made you so shy of me, when you first called, and afterwards dined here? Why, especially, when you called, did you look as if you did not care about me?'

'Because you were grave and silent, and gave me no encouragement.'

'But I was embarrassed.'

'And so was I.'

---

1   Jane Austen, *Pride and Prejudice*, ed. R. W. Chapman (Oxford: Clarendon Press, 1923), Volume III, Chapter 16, p. 371.

2   Ibid., Volume III, Chapter 8, p. 312.

'You might have talked to me more when you came to dinner.'

'A man who had felt less, might.'

'How unlucky that you should have a reasonable answer to give, and that I should be so reasonable as to admit it! But I wonder how long you *would* have gone on, if you had been left to yourself. I wonder when you *would* have spoken, if I had not asked you! My resolution of thanking you for your kindness to Lydia had certainly great effect. *Too much*, I am afraid; for what becomes of the moral, if our comfort springs from a breach of promise? for I ought not to have mentioned the subject. This will never do.'

'You need not distress yourself. The moral will be perfectly fair. Lady Catherine's unjustifiable endeavours to separate us were the means of removing all my doubts.[3] I am not indebted for my present happiness to your eager desire of expressing your gratitude. I was not in a humour to wait for any opening of your's. My aunt's intelligence had given me hope, and I was determined at once to know every thing.'

'Lady Catherine has been of infinite use, which ought to make her happy, for she loves to be of use. But tell me, what did you come down to Netherfield for? Was it merely to ride to Longbourn and be embarrassed? or had you intended any more serious consequence?'

'My real purpose was to see *you*, and to judge, if I could, whether I might ever hope to make you love me. My avowed one, or what I avowed to myself, was to see whether your sister were still partial to Bingley, and if she were, to make the confession to him which I have since made.'

'Shall you ever have courage to announce to Lady Catherine, what is to befall her?'

'I am more likely to want time than courage, Elizabeth. But it ought to be done, and if you will give me a sheet of paper, it shall be done directly.'

4

Further Reading

Further Reading

All the books and essays referenced in the Contexts, Interpretations, and Key Passages sections are recommended for further reading. The list that follows makes no attempt to be comprehensive, but is designed to guide readers in studying and researching *Pride and Prejudice*.

Recommended Editions

Standard edition
Chapman, R. W. (ed.), *Pride and Prejudice* (Oxford: Clarendon Press, 1923).

This edition is Volume Two in the standard edition of Austen's works. It contains the most frequently cited text of *Pride and Prejudice*, a series of useful illustrations, an 'index of characters', and much else. Cross-references to *Pride and Prejudice* in this sourcebook are keyed to this edition.

Paperback editions
Gray, Donald (ed.), *Pride and Prejudice*, third edition (New York: Norton, 2001).

Gray supplements the text of the novel with a section on 'Backgrounds and Sources', as well as nineteen critical essays that concern topics ranging from morality and irony to class and money.

Irvine, Robert P. (ed.), *Pride and Prejudice* (Peterborough, ON: Broadview, 2002).

Irvine includes a good bibliography divided into sections such as 'Literary Antecedents' and 'Gender and Politics', as well as eight appendixes that cover topics such as 'Domestic Tourism' and 'The Militia Regiments on the South Coast of England in 1793–95'.

Jones, Vivien (ed.), *Pride and Prejudice*, (London: Penguin, 1996).

Jones's introduction situates the romance of Elizabeth and Darcy amid the key political and social anxieties of the day.

Kingsley, James and Bradbook, Frank W. (eds) *Pride and Prejudice*, Introduction by Isobel Armstrong (Oxford: Oxford University Press, 1990).

Armstrong explores how *Pride and Prejudice* 'is marked, even scarred, by history', and how Austen both endorses and questions the 'assuaging and energizing dreamwork' of the novel's comedy.

Companions and Encyclopedias

Copeland, Edward and McMaster, Juliet (eds), *The Cambridge Companion to Jane Austen* (Cambridge: Cambridge University Press, 1997).
    The companion contains a solid discussion of *Pride and Prejudice* by Rachel Brownstein, and other chapters which relate the novel to key issues such as 'Class', 'Money', 'Religion and Politics'.

Grey, J. David., *The Jane Austen Handbook* (London: The Athlone Press, 1986); in America, *The Jane Austen Companion* (New York: Macmillan, 1986).
    The volume collects over sixty brief but penetrating essays that explore a fascinating variety of subjects related to *Pride and Prejudice*, including dancing, games, food and drink, topography, architecture, manners, and the military.

Lambdin, Laura Cooner and Lambdin, Robert Thomas (eds), *A Companion to Jane Austen Studies* (Westport, Conn.: Greenwood Press, 2002).
    The volume features Johanna Smith's examination of wit and subversion in *Pride and Prejudice*, and Elizabeth Langland's very useful summary of criticism on *Pride and Prejudice* from 1813 to the present.

Pinion, F. R., *A Jane Austen Companion: A Critical Survey and Reference Book* (London: Macmillan, 1973).
    Pinion includes a concise and engaging analysis of *Pride and Prejudice*, a 'glossary of words of unusual or outmoded meaning', and nearly two dozen illustrations that repeatedly illuminate Austen's world and characters.

Poplawki, Paul, *A Jane Austen Encyclopedia* (Westport, Conn.: Greenwood Press, 1998).
    This encyclopedia features a detailed section on 'Chronological Contexts', over a dozen helpful illustrations, separate entries for *Pride and Prejudice* and all its major and minor characters, and an extensive bibliography.

Books and Edited Collections

Bloom, Harold (ed.), *Modern Critical Interpretations: Jane Austen's Pride and Prejudice* (New York: Chelsea House, 1987).
    This accessible selection features nine essays on *Pride and Prejudice*, and covers topics extending from authority, propriety, and love to amicability, intelligence and pedagogy.

Folsom, Marcia McClintock (ed.), *Approaches to Teaching Austen's Pride and Prejudice* (New York: Modern Language Association of America, 1993).
    This compilation was designed to help professors teach the novel, but it also serves as a useful guide for students. It includes sections on 'Social History', 'Language', and 'Structure and Theme'.

Littlewood, Ian (ed.), *Jane Austen: Critical Assessments*, 4 vols (Mountfield, East Sussex: Helm Information, 1998).

Littlewood's edition is an extensive and extremely useful collection of material related to Austen. Volume I contains a detailed survey of nineteenth-century responses to *Pride and Prejudice*, and Volume III features thirteen twentieth-century essays on the novel.

Moler, Kenneth L., *Pride and Prejudice: A Study in Artistic Economy* (Boston: Twayne, 1989).

An introduction that runs to just over one hundred pages, and surveys the novel's historical context and critical reception before turning to its central themes, motifs, 'verbal styles', and literary allusions.

Rubinstein, Elliot (ed.), *Twentieth-Century Interpretations of Pride and Prejudice: A Collection of Critical Essays* (Englewood Cliffs, NJ: Prentice-Hall, 1969).

This book brings together a representative and readable selection of the best criticism on *Pride and Prejudice* that appeared from the 1930s through the 1960s.

Teachman, Debra (ed.), *Pride and Prejudice: A Student Casebook to Issues, Sources, and Historical Documents*.

This edition is a collection of mainly eighteenth-century legal, political, and moral writing that illuminate a series of key issues in *Pride and Prejudice*, including inheritance, marriage, and education.

Chapters and Essays

Allen, Dennis W., 'No Love for Lydia: The Fate of Desire in *Pride and Prejudice*' in *Texas Studies in Literature and Language*, 27.4 (1985), pp. 425–43.

Allen declares that Austen represses and displaces desire in *Pride and Prejudice* in order to render it compatible with social order. It is not that she does not understand desire, but that she recognizes its anarchic potential all too well.

Brown, Julia Prewitt, 'Necessary Conjunctions: *Pride and Prejudice*' in *Jane Austen's Novels: Social Change and Literary Form* (Cambridge, Mass.: Harvard University Press, 1979), pp. 65–79.

Brown contends that *Pride and Prejudice* is centrally concerned with the rituals and taboos of mating, which exist to protect the act of marriage, and extend the moral ethos of one generation to the next. 'In a sense, one must raise one's children well so that they will raise their children well'.

Bush, Douglas, 'Mrs. Bennet and the Dark Gods: The Truth about Jane Austen' in *Sewanee Review*, 64 (1956), pp. 591–6.

Bush explores the mythic archetypes that underlie *Pride and Prejudice*, from Bingley as Dionysus and Darcy as Hercules to Mr. Bennet as Pentheus and Mrs. Bennet as Venus.

Kelly, Gary, 'The Art of Reading in *Pride and Prejudice*' in *English Studies in Canada*, 10.2 (1984), pp. 156–71.

Kelly argues that Elizabeth's process of learning to read the norms and conventions that shape her self and her world mirrors the reader's process of learning the norms and conventions that shape the novel itself. 'To read *Pride and Prejudice* well is to learn how to read better; that is why we go on re-reading it'.

McMaster, Juliet, 'Talking about Talk in *Pride and Prejudice*' in *Jane Austen's Business: Her World and Her Profession*, eds Juliet McMaster and Bruce Stovel (London: Macmillan, 1996), pp. 81–94.

For McMaster, the 'highly formal and formidably verbal cultural' of *Pride and Prejudice* means that some characters use language as a vehicle for communication and incisive criticism while others abuse it in the service of pomposity and nonsense.

Monaghan, David, 'Pride and Prejudice' in *Jane Austen: Structure and Social Vision* (London: Macmillan, 1980), pp. 64–92.

Monaghan suggestively identifies *Pride and Prejudice* as controlled by social ritual: 'dancing for the problems of courtship, the visit for the broadening of social horizons, and marriage for the resolution of conflicts'.

Biographies

Cecil, David, *A Portrait of Jane Austen* (London: Constable, 1978).

This is an astute, if conservative-minded, introduction which finds that '*Pride and Prejudice* brings us closer to Jane Austen the individual woman than do any other of her novels'. The book is lavishly illustrated.

Fergus, Jan, *Jane Austen* (London: Macmillan, 1991).

This is a more probing and exciting study than Cecil's, similar in length (roughly 200 pages), but feminist in orientation, and concerned with Austen as a professional writer.

Honan, Park, *Jane Austen: Her Life* (New York: St. Martin's Press, 1987).

This is still the best full-length biography, a sympathetic and thoroughly researched account which situates Austen within her revolutionary times, and argues that the 'deepest subject' of *Pride and Prejudice* is 'happiness'.

Bibliographies

The following bibliographies provide very useful starting points for any research on *Pride and Prejudice*.

Chapman, R. W., *Jane Austen: A Critical Bibliography* (Oxford: Clarendon Press, 1953).

Gilson, David, *A Bibliography of Jane Austen* (Oxford: Clarendon Press, 1982).

Gilson, David, *A Bibliography of Jane Austen: New Introduction and Corrections by the Author* (Winchester: St. Paul's Bibliographies, 1997).

Roth, Barry, *An Annotated Bibliography of Jane Austen Studies, 1973–1983* (Charlottesville: University of Virginia Press, 1985).

Roth, Barry, *An Annotated Bibliography of Jane Austen Studies, 1984–1994* (Athens: Ohio University Press, 1996).

Roth, Barry, and Weinsheimer, Joel, *An Annotated Bibliography of Jane Austen Studies, 1952–1972* (Charlottesville: University of Virginia Press, 1973).

Stafford, Fiona, 'Jane Austen' in *Literature of the Romantic Period: A Bibliographical Guide*, ed. Michael O'Neill (Oxford: Clarendon Press, 1998), pp. 246–68.

INDEX